Total Quality Management in Education

Second Edition

Marmar Mukhopadhyay

SAGE Publications

New Delhi • Thousand Oaks • London

First published in 2005 by

SAGE Publications India Pvt Ltd
B1/I1 Mohan Cooperative Industrial Area
Mathura Road, New Delhi 110 044, India
www.sagepub.in

SAGE Publications Inc
2455 Teller Road
Thousand Oaks, California 91320, USA

SAGE Publications Ltd
1 Oliver's Yard
55 City Road
London EC1Y 1SP, United Kingdom

SAGE Publications Asia-Pacific Pte Ltd
33 Pekin Street
#02-01 Far East Square
Singapore 048763

Published by Tejeshwar Singh for SAGE Publications India Pvt Ltd, phototypeset in 10.5/12.5 CharterBT by Siva Math Setters, Chennai and printed at Chaman Enterprises, New Delhi.

Eleventh Printing 2012

Library of Congress Cataloging-in-Publication Data

Mukhopadhyay, Marmar.
  Total quality management in education / Marmar Mukhopadhyay.—2nd ed.
      p. cm.
  Includes bibliographical references and index.
  1. Total quality management in education. 2. School management and organization. I. Title.

LB2806.M75   2005   2005008607

ISBN: 10: 0-7619-3368-9 (PB)   10: 81-7829-511-3 (India-PB)
            13: 978-0-7619-3368-7 (PB)   13: 978-81-7829-511-4 (India-PB)

SAGE Production Team: Mudita Chauhan-Mubayi, Ashok R. Chandran, Neeru Handa and Santosh Rawat

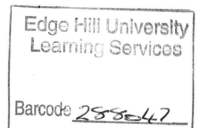

Offered at
The Lotus Feet of

Swami Satchidananda Giri

Our Gurudev

Contents

List of Tables

List of Figures

List of Boxes

Foreword

Management of quality at different stages and levels of education is a daunting task, not only in India but also the world over. In recent years, total quality management (TQM) has emerged as a viable alternative to achieve this goal. Judicious application of TQM to the contemporary scenario of education is no doubt urgently needed. But it also requires adaptation and fine-tuning to the Indian situation to make the technique of TQM optimally effective. I am happy to observe that Prof. Marmar Mukhopadhyay has eminently succeeded in reaching this particular objective, both at the conceptual and operational levels. His research and reflection are presented in this book with commendable clarity and conciseness for the benefit of educators and educational managers.

If one takes a close look at India's present education system, especially the school sector, one finds that with the globalization on one hand and growing national ambition on the other, this sector is going through a phase of fast metamorphosis. While struggling to universalize elementary education by 2010 without compromising on quality, the eyes of Indian educators are wide open to the needs of near universalization of secondary education in the coming decades. Choices, in the face of stiff international competitiveness, are limited; expansion of secondary education must be comprehensively reinforced with quality. The crusade will soon be for quality secondary education for all. From this angle, this book, *Total Quality Management in Education*, is indeed a timely contribution.

Unlike industrial products, quality in education cannot be defined by product specifications. Humans are complex body–mind–spirit organisms, not just knowledge and skill configurations. Human configurations combine values, attitudes, and a host of other affective attributes. Thus, quality education implies comprehensively developing individuals to their full potential, unfolding the 'perfection already in man' (and woman). The challenge of management of quality in education is realizing optimally that perfection already resident in individuals, not only among students but also among teachers, non-teaching staff, and principals. The importance is on the quality of life in institutions where a student is shaped and teachers and others spend the primes of their lives. Continuous quest for quality, both in education and in life, has thus become a vital goal to work on in the beginning of the new century and millennium.

TQM has emerged as a major technique in improving and sustaining quality in education. Derived from industrial applications, TQM has been extensively and intensively adapted and experimented within education all over the world. The major spurt of activities in TQM in education occurred in the 1990s. Rich conceptual and research literature appeared in several journals of education and educational management; online searches indicate an ever-growing stock on TQM in education on the Internet. Such worldwide development bears testimony to the fact that TQM is a promising movement that has not only begun but also taken off. This book has, as its backbone, the skilful review and perceptive assimilation of this vast professional literature on TQM in education.

Very often, professional literature in India is overwhelmed by western literature and wisdom. However, it needs to be adapted to the local cultures and ethos as indicated above. The texts need to be informed by western literature but anchored in the educational ethos and culture of our own society. It is heartening to note that there is a sincere effort evident in this book to anchor TQM to Indian culture and educational scenario by citing Indian experiences and cases and quoting from ancient Indian literature in Sanskrit.

To my knowledge, this is the first comprehensive book on TQM in education in India. Prof. Mukhopadhyay deserves our congratulations and gratitude for making such a pioneering effort in this vital field. I wish this valuable work all success in stimulating a movement on quality management in education.

Hamburg, Germany

Ravindra H. Dave

Former Director, UNESCO Institute of Education

Preface to the Second Edition

The response of the readers to the first edition of the book has been rather overwhelming, much beyond my expectations. When I authored the book in 2000–01, little did I realize that there is so much craving for quality in education and that educational managers are searching for a methodology for management of quality. The book was rendered in several Indian languages. Looking at the demand and continuing relevance of the theme, I decided to come up with this revised second edition.

Ever since the book's publication, I have undertaken several academic and professional exercises on total quality management (TQM) in education at various levels of education. In a project sponsored by the Ministry of Human Resource Development, Government of India, about 500 District Institutes of Education and Training were involved in a two-year-long project based on this book. Over 7,000 secondary and senior secondary schools in Gujarat have been involved in a quality management movement based on the book's Gujarati version. I have conducted a large number of training programmes and workshops and held discussions involving over 2,000 educational managers/principals of colleges and secondary and senior secondary schools on this theme. Such discussions, workshops, and experimental projects offered me new learning in the application of TQM in education in the Indian setting.

All these experiences, and my other related major research work in the intervening period on leadership for institution building in education, has substantially influenced the process of revision of this edition. It is not only up-to-date but also enriched with experience and new understanding that has offered a new tilt towards institution building through TQM.

I thank Prof. K.P. Pandey, former Vice-Chancellor of Kashi Vidyapeeth, for continuous encouragement and constructive criticism towards the book's improvement. Dr Madhu Parhar extended her helping hands in reviewing the entire manuscript of the new edition and gave meaningful suggestions. I thank her sincerely. I am indeed thankful to Mr Tejeshwar Singh, Managing Director of Sage Publications, for undertaking the publication of this edition.

NIEPA, New Delhi
18 April 2005

Marmar Mukhopadhyay

Preface to the First Edition

With the phenomenal expansion of education at all levels, the management of quality poses a major challenge. Globalization has added a new dimension; for, it is not just the globalization of economy, but also the globalization of socio-cultural institutions including education. The challenge has narrowed down to global standards.

The NIEPA has indicated its professional resilience as an institution to new developments and challenges in education. Several of my colleagues have conducted research on quality in education. These researches have not only assessed quality in education, but also shed light on what constitutes quality in education, namely indicators of quality. Continuing in NIEPA's tradition, my efforts are in search of a paradigm for management of quality.

Total quality management (TQM) is a well-tested strategy for the management of quality in education. It has been extensively experimented within both school and higher education. It has been successfully experimented within micro-operations (classroom instruction, staff selection), macro-systems (universities) and mega-systems (districts). TQM is human-intensive compared to other cost-intensive approaches; hence it suits Indian education eminently.

In this book, I have tried to adapt the philosophy and concept of TQM in the Indian educational ethos and conditions, on the basis of my experience of over three-and-a-half decades in education at different levels. Lest it be misconstrued that quality in education is an exclusively western concept, I have referred to ancient Indian texts in Sanskrit to indicate that ancient Indian education meant excellence.

I must mention that this book is one of the multiplicity of efforts in TQM in education. Two other efforts are field research in TQM in education, and training of heads of institutions, educational administrators, and research professionals in TQM in education.

Prof. B.P. Khandelwal, Director of NIEPA, has been very encouraging and supportive of my efforts in persuading quality improvement in education through TQM. I have also benefited from his comments on the manuscript. I am grateful to him for his support. I thank Prof. Ravindra H. Dave, an eminent educationist and former Director of the UNESCO Institute of Education, Hamburg, for writing the foreword.

I thank Dr Madhu Parhar for reviewing and offering critical comments on the subject at different stages of the book's development. I also acknowledge with thanks the assistance rendered by Ms Sriparna Bhattacharya in the final stage of manuscript preparation. I thank Mr P. N. Tyagi for helping me in drawing some of the figures.

The NIEPA library is very special; its very proactive culture provides significant support to such serious works. Ms Nirmal Malhotra, Senior Librarian, and her team deserve special words of appreciation for their academic support.

I thank Dr D.N. Khosla for the meticulous copy-editing of the manuscript. I am equally thankful to Mr Soumen Panja for the page-setting and Mr Sabyasachi Panja for the cover design. Mr M.M. Ajwani and Mr Amit Singhal did an excellent job of the manuscript's technical review. I thank both of them.

NIEPA, New Delhi
5 January 2001

Marmar Mukhopadhyay

Quality in Education

1

Introduction

Quality has been the goal of an eternal quest through the corridors of human history. It has been the driving force for all human endeavour. Quality is the inspiration for transcendence from the mundane to the higher realms of life. It is the source of craving behind the unfolding human civilization through ages immemorial. Yet, it has successfully eluded the dragnet of definitions proving the inadequacy of human intelligence. Quality stares at you. You recognize it. But you cannot define it. Any length of description of the anatomical details of a fragrant and beautiful flower—its petals, colour, shape, size, fragrance, softness, all put together—falls short of conveying its beauty fully. It is perceived and recognized. It is best left to the admirer to perceive and appreciate. For, quality lies in the perception of the consumer. What is 'great' for one may not be good enough for another!

Concept of quality

A wide range of efforts has been made to articulate the concepts of quality, from the mundane down-to-earth functionalist definition to the metaphysical concept of an endless journey similar to the human cravings for communion with the divine through millions of births, and 'quality' as the third of the 'Aristotelian category'.

According to the Oxford English Dictionary, the notion of quality includes all the attributes of a thing, except those of relation and quantity. The British Standards Institution (BSI) (1991) defines quality in functional terms as the totality of features and characteristics of a product or service that bear upon its ability to satisfy the stated or implied needs. Navaratnam (1997) makes it specific by defining quality in terms of functional utility of a product. Oakland (1988), after detailed analysis, concluded and defined quality as 'the degree of fitness for purpose and function'. Sallis (1996) cited the examples of the overhead projector and ballpoint pens and exhorted in the name of quality, 'they must do what they claim to do, and do what their customers expect of them'. Quality is thus a positive and dynamic idea achievable by design with meaningful investment; and not a negative idea of absence of defect (Crawford and Shutler, 1999). Since quality is a dynamic and positive idea, it has endless possibilities of evolution and unfolding, making it an endless journey with a deliberate purpose and design and not necessarily a destination (Shejwalkar, 1999). Hence, exact definitions of quality are not particularly helpful when actual 'consequences flow from different meanings' attached to quality (Sallis, 1996). The quality journey is characterized by a customer-focused approach to continuous improvement of processes, products and services through an interdependent system of planning, implementing, evaluating and decision-making (Navaratnam, 1997).

Then, there are different levels of difficulty in defining quality. The easiest is defining the quality of lifestyle and consumer products. Defining the quality of service is more complicated. This inadequacy in defining quality has been the precise problem of management of quality in the service sector. The issue gets far more complicated and nearly impossible as we move on to defining the quality of humans, as it is shaped in education.

For example, there are several attributes of a gel-based pen that determine the quality: functionality, durability, flow, shape, size, aesthetics or finish, design, colour, uniqueness, cost, and so on. There can be wide divergence of views on each of these attributes. A shape that is 'fantastic' for one may be 'awful' for another. When someone prefers durability, other may prefer a fancy shape and colour, and so on. Yet, the indicators of quality are definable. But how does one fix the quality parameters of, say, service in a hospital, a restaurant, a government office or railways/airlines reservation? The parameters can be punctuality or timeliness, cost, civility or courteousness, speed, accuracy, etc. Once again, there can be wide divergence in the perceptions of quality. For example, there are customers who prefer a slow but courteous booking clerk whereas others care a hoot for the polite, preferring time savers and the accurate. Hence, in the service sector too, the client's perception is the final index of quality.

Quality has both absolute and relative connotations, absolute at least in popular parlance. Sallis (1996) deftly dealt with the concepts of absolute and relative quality and customer-defined quality. For example, at one stage, people used to say that Sheaffer in the world of pens, and Rolls Royce in the world of cars, were the 'last word'. This implied absolute quality. The implications of absolute quality products are the expensiveness, uniqueness and prestigiousness that set the owners apart from others who cannot afford them. In the language of modern advertising, it is not owning but possessing. Similarly, the unique features of designer items are that they are expensive but 'only one of their kind'; no one else has them. Pfeffer and Coote (1991; quoted in Sallis, 1996) state this of absolute quality: most of us admire it, many of us want it, few of us can have it.

Quality is relative since there can be several shades. Relative quality becomes evident when similar products and/or services provided by several organizations are compared at a given time and place. The relativity of quality becomes evident when products or services of the same organization are compared over time, for instance, the railway reservation process before and after computerization. In total quality management (TQM), the catchphrase is 'be the best and stay there'. While being the 'best' is apparently an absolute concept, being the best among the better ones provides the relativism. Further, 'staying there' makes it all the more relative because other better ones are approaching the standard of the best and hence the best has to continuously move further. The BSI defined relative quality as 'fit for the purpose'. There are 30two implications: functionality of the product and meeting the minimum basic standards. Sallis (1996) defined quality products thus: They must do what they claim to do, and do what their customers expect of them. He cited the examples of an overhead projector and ballpoint pens.

When we compare the quality of a consumer product like Colgate, Pepsodent or Close-Up with other toothpastes, we are essentially referring to relative quality. The other relativism is over time. Stating that with computerization, railway reservation has become much easier, is an indication of relative quality of the same service by the same organization over time. Similar is the case when people nostalgically recollect how good their school was when they were students.

Thus, relativism in quality raises two parameters: measuring up to the specification and meeting the customer needs. In India, companies proudly display the ISI mark on their products as a sales strategy. The ISI mark is, indeed, indicative of product specification; the mark is available to those products that satisfy the specifications. The second parameter is customer satisfaction and requirement. Despite the ISI mark, the customer may not be satisfied. A product, say glycerine, from two different companies, both with the ISI mark enjoys different customer reaction and preference. Thus, product specification is actually the minimum necessary condition for quality, but not the sufficient condition. The sufficient condition is customer satisfaction and beyond.

Quality assurances, such as the ISI mark, BS 5750 and ISO 9001 guarantee the minimum assured quality. Such product specification, however, is not the sufficient condition since it is supplier-defined quality. As already stated, it is customer satisfaction that needs to be assured. Although more than one brand of a product may have the ISI mark and fulfil the supplier-determined quality, customers may still prefer one product over another, perhaps because he or she gets a 'buy two, get one free' deal. In a way, this is going beyond customer satisfaction. Relativism in quality, then, is also linked to the economic class of the buyer. In the affluent society, perceived quality is better determined by prestigiousness; a satisfied customer will always be prepared to pay for his or her choice. Similar trends can be found in the service sector as well. Many organizations prefer, as their security service, former armymen agencies over others although hiring charges of such agencies are costlier.

Thus, quality can be any of the following:

1. Perceptual (as perceived by the consumer)
2. Both process and product (product carries manifest quality; process provides intrinsic support)
3. Exceptional (something special; in operational terms, you have scale or steps of its achievement and a cut-off point)

4. Perfection (or consistent; in other words, it identifies a specification to be met absolutely)
5. Fitness for purpose (satisfying specified intentions)
6. Value for money (self-explanatory)
7. Transformative (captured by the terms like 'qualitative change' or 'continuous improvement' (Harvey and Green, 1993))
8. Relative, not absolute

Quality in education

Defining quality in education is a massive challenge since it deals with the most sensitive creation on earth—the human beings. Industrial products are finished goods—take them or leave them. Nothing can be done once they are finished. Service is here and now. You can look for better quality only next time. Education has no such finished product, nor even the graduates. They are on the way 'to be'. Education only charges the human propensities to evolve and unfold it till the last breath, a process that covers the human journey from 'womb to tomb'. Human beings continue to learn, and evolve, 'to be'. Education facilitates this very evolution of the individual. No wonder then that the concept of quality in education has attracted scholarly attention in India as well as in the west.

Quality in education: The western viewpoint

Education is goal-oriented. Accordingly, quality of education has been seen with reference to the following goals:

- Excellence in education (Peters and Waterman, 1982)
- Value addition in education (Feigenbaum, 1983)
- Fitness of educational outcome and experience for use (Juran and Gryna, 1988)
- Conformance of education output to planned goals, specifications and requirements (Crosby, 1979; Gilmore, 1974)
- Defect avoidance in education process (Crosby, 1979)
- Meeting or exceeding customers' expectations of education (Parasuraman et al., 1985)

For Seymour (1992), meeting or exceeding customer needs, continuous improvement, leadership, human resource development in the system, fear reduction, recognition and reward, teamwork, measurement and systematic problem solving are the quality principles in higher education. Seymour's emphasis is on processes rather than products.

The International Commission on Education for the 21st century called for holistic development of individuals, thus optimizing physical, mental, intellectual and spiritual potentialities. Quality education must be supported by the four pillars of learning: learning to know, learning to do, learning to be and learning to live together (UNESCO, 1996). Holt (2000) argues, 'I shall suppose that education is concerned with the development of minds of the pupils; schools produce educated persons who, by virtue of their schooling, make their way in society to their own and society's benefit. . . . How are these benefits to be construed? Is our aim to be in the pursuit of happiness? The creation of wealth through capitalism? The religious life, made manifest? Our concept of quality is dependent upon what we choose.'

There are wide variations in social goals too. American priority on human rights and personal freedom in the 1960s has changed to success in global economy in the 1990s; Britain's current emphasis is on what the students 'know and can do' rather than on numinous goals (Holt, 2000). A Japanese white paper on education in the 1980s changed the focus to invention rather than adaptation of technology. The Indian social goal is also changing: from a literate society in the 1960s to a knowledge society (indeed a knowledge superpower) in the 2000s. Emphasis is also shifting from the previous value-neutral education to a value-oriented one.

Empirical research in education raises several quality-related issues. The most prominent contention is that the effectiveness is the indicator of quality. School effectiveness is an objective referenced mechanism of school assessment. It, more or less, surfaced with the landmark work of Coleman and others, in 1966, in the USA. Later on, a similar study was conducted in the UK. Subsequently, such research spread all over the world. *The International Handbook of School Effectiveness* by Teddlie and Reynolds (2000) provides a comprehensive critical document on the subject. Certain authors have also indicated their reservation that school effectiveness fails to accommodate the moral component of education (Reid, 1997). The measures of effectiveness centre around a few tangible criteria whereas there are several intangible elements in the quality in education. For example, the percentage of students who graduate from high school and the percentage of students getting letter-grades is the most popular indicator of school effectiveness. This offers a limited opportunity to use school effectiveness as a comprehensive indicator of quality.

The second major debate has been around 'accountability'. Schools that impose and fulfil the benchmarks, and relentlessly work towards the achievement of targets and results are accountable; hence they have quality. There is often a risk in the benchmark-based concept of quality. Even if the curriculum and instructional processes are weak and conventional, a school may achieve targets since they are in tune with the school tests and the public examination. Hence, despite accountability, a school may not offer quality in education (Winch, 1996). In a decentralized school-based management, a school can design broad-based curriculum and offer a wide range of learning and assessment opportunities with freedom and opportunity to innovate enhancing pupil engagement; thus, it can offer quality (Holt, 2000). Abu-Duhou (1999) concluded, on the basis of a comprehensive review of experiences and outcomes of school-based management, that there is very little evidence that school-based management leads to quality in education.

The prescribed curriculum, weightages to subjects, timetables, specification of teacher qualification, prescribed organizational rules, student admission criteria, etc., can be labelled as the supplier specifications of quality in education. Yet, parents choose one school or college over another. We know several instances when some parents are scrambling to get their children admitted in one particular school for good quality education, some others withdraw their children from the same school for dissatisfaction with its quality of education. Parents, as customers, define the quality of education differentially.

Quality in education: The Indian perspective

Indian educational history dates back over 5000 years. Indian scriptures professed education as an emancipating and liberating force, a process that manifests 'perfection' already existent in man. Metaphysically then, quality education is concerned with the nature and destination of human beings.

The nature of human beings is related to their origin. Inter-faith research contends that human beings are divine. For, they are made in the image of God (Mukhopadhyay, 2003). The Biblical story of how the original man and woman—Adam and Eve—were created out of God's will and consciousness is similar to the Hindu view that Lord Brahma, the Creator of this universe, wished, 'Ekoham bahushyama' (I am One, let me be many). Just as God materialized Adam and Eve out of cosmic energy, Adam and Eve too were divinely capable of creating their following without using their bodies. Once they sinned—ate the fruit of the forbidden tree—they lost that divine power. Even then, 'child is through you from God' (Kahlil Gibran, *The Prophet*). Thus, every human being is an incarnation of God; indeed, a constituent of the Total Consciousness. Swami Vivekananda argued: Unless each one is part of the whole and in continuous communication, how else can one transfer the thought to another? Now, the attributes of God are perfection and completeness (*purnattwa*[1]): 'That (the Absolute Self) is full. This (the world we experience through our mind and senses) is full. If This fullness is taken away from That fullness, what remains is full' (From *Ishopanishad*, English rendering by Swami Jyotirmayananda). Sri Aurobindo's philosophy, particularly the concepts of superman and supramental, contributes to a similar understanding of human nature.

While for western theorists, evolution is primarily biological, the Indian viewpoint includes evolution of the mind and consciousness with the body as the host. This evolutionary theory also promises a rise to the cosmic or supra-cortical consciousness (Mukhopadhyaya, 1987; Jitatmananda, 1991). Inspiration for another structural framework can be derived from the *Kathopanishad* and *Charak Samhita*. Human beings live in a multi-plane configuration consisting of physical, mental, intellectual and spiritual planes.

---

[1] *Om Purnamadah, Purnamidam, Purnat Purnamudachyate
Purnasya Purnamadaya Purnamevavashisyate. (Ishopanishad)*

In depicting the structural nature of human beings, particularly from the angle of education, the role of sense organs has been highlighted both by western and Indian thinkers. Indian scriptures mention six such senses (eyes, ears, nose, tongue, skin and mind) and five action organs (hands for activity, legs for locomotion, mouth for speech and organs needed for excretion and procreation). Swami Vivekananda (1999), in *Raja Yoga*, mentioned that the sense organs are active only when charged by the mind. Metaphorically, an electric bulb by itself does not emit light; it glows only after receiving the power when the switch is put on.

Another element in the structural thesis of the human being is the interrelationship between senses, mind, intelligence, body and the self or soul. The *Kathopanishad* describes the relationship beautifully in The Parable of the Chariot:

Know the self as the Lord of the Chariot and the body as verily the chariot, know intellect as the charioteer and the mind as verily the reins. The senses, they say, are the horses; the object of the sense the paths (they range over); (the self) associated with the body, the senses and the mind—wise men declare is the enjoyer.

(English rendering by Radhakrishnan, 1998)

Education is training of the senses (horses) to be receptive and sensitive, of the mind to control the senses, of intelligence to be discriminative to give right direction and of the body to be able to host the self, part of the Total Consciousness. *Triguna* or three qualities—*Tamas* (idle or inert, narrow), *Rajas* (active, dominating, adventurous) and *Sattwa* (enlightened, quiet)—are said to be the constituents of human nature. Quality education facilitates the movement from *tamasic* to the *rajasik* to the *sattwic* stages, and beyond to the *trigunatita* (attribute of the omniscient and omnipresent).

The *Chhandyogya Upanishad* called upon quality in all actions. In the *Gita*, Lord Krishna told Arjuna, '*Yogaha karmasu kaushalam*', or that quality at work itself is *sadhana* or the way to unite with God. In the *Kathopanishad*, Nachiketa asks for the highest form of learning—the theory of soul—from Yamaraj. To test his keenness to learn, Yamaraj offers Nachiketa all the wealth and beauties in the world. Nachiketa remains unmoved. Yamaraj offers him then the highest knowledge, and also prays that only such students should come to him. Early Indian universities such as Takshashila in the Brahmanic period and Nalanda in the Buddhist period were known only for excellence (Das, 1986). The purpose of education has accordingly been defined.

One important landmark of quality is the goal of education. Do we know what kind of products—members of the society—we need? If we define them as engineers or clerks, we are defining only one, though significant, skill set: technical and economic. The same individual will grow to be a father or a mother, a husband or a wife, a brother or a sister, a neighbour and a member of social and political systems. He or she is born with potentialities. The quality in education has to take into consideration the individual goals in the larger context of social goals. Indeed, goals that are worthwhile. For Swami Vivekananda, education is the manifestation of perfection already in man. This goal conforms with the contention of the goal of 'learning to be' and not 'become' (UNESCO, 1996).

Since human beings are made in the image of God and are children of the eternity, their final destination is the state of bliss and joy. Human evolution moves from the physical self (*annamoy kosha*) to the state of bliss (*anadamoy kosha*) through life (*pranamoy*), mind (*manamoy*) and knowledge (*vigyanaamoy koshas*). The purpose of education is to move from the lowest to the highest level of human evolution.

As would be evident, the western view of quality education is functional: what a graduate 'can do'. The Indian view of quality education transcends functionalism and reaches the metaphysical level: what a graduate 'can be'. The ultimate destination is the perfection hidden in human beings. Accordingly, the search for contents and processes of education is formulated.

The goals of education determine its contents and processes. The content or knowledge, *vidya*, has been classified into *paravidya* and *aparavidya*. *Paravidya* is the direct knowledge through experience and perception (often extra-sensory) achieved through *sadhana*. *Aparavidya* is the indirect or *paroksha gyan* achieved through secondary sources, often through the sensory mechanism. What we learn in schools and colleges is classified as *aparavidya* or *paroksha gyan*. Further, *paroksha gyan* has been termed as *vigyan* and *pratyaksha gyan* as *gyan* in the *Gyan-Vigyan Yoga* in the *Gita*. Besides these broad classifications, ancient Indian education has a large variety of course offerings (Das, 1986).

A more interesting depiction of the Indian concept of education is in its processes. Shikshaballi, in the *Taittiriya Upanishad*, says this of education: 'the teacher is the prior form; the pupil is the later form, knowledge is their junction; instruction is the connection'[2] (Radhakrishnan, 1998). Importantly, it does not accept the conventional view of transfer of knowledge from teacher to student as education. Instruction is the connection and knowledge is the junction. This view gets further strengthened in the *Upanishad* invoking God to bless both the Guru and the disciple to learn together, and asking that one does not become jealous of the other.[3] It emphasizes the importance of continuity of learning, which was also reflected in Tagore's writings about the teacher: 'a candle that does not continue to burn itself, cannot light another'. This fundamental principle that resembles today's constructivist paradigm contained in a multi-channel learning systems leads to instructional designs and strategies. In one of the approaches, Indian scriptures recommended a four-stage learning process for quality: listening, studying, teaching and applying. The four-stage learning indicates first that any one source is not enough. Also, it offers taxonomy of learning; as one moves from listening to application, indeed one moves from lower to higher levels of cognition. The multi-channel learning paradigm was also professed in the *Hastana Satak* of the great epic *Mahabharata*: 'A quarter of the

---

[2] *Acarya purva-rupam, antevasy uttara-rupam, vidya sandhi,*
Pravachanas samdhanam, ity adhividyam (Taittiriya Upanishad, I.4.1).
[3] *Saha nababatu, saha nau bhunaktu saha birya karababahai*
Tejaswinavadhitamavastu ma vidwisabahai.

learning accrues each from the *teacher, self study* and talent, *interaction with* peers, and rest with time *through experience*.' (Emphasis added).[4]

Quality in education has also been depicted in terms of its impact. *Sa vidya ya vimuktaye* (that which liberates human beings from narrow bondages is quality education). Another indicator of quality of education, according to Indian scriptures, is the modesty of the learner/scholar (*vidya dadati vinayam*)—quality education makes a scholar modest or 'he/she knows what she does not know compared to fools who do not know what they know'. The third impact of education is the ability to discriminate between *paravidya* and *aparavidya* (or *avidya*). Indian society attaches significant value to such qualities; hence quality education is also depicted by its impact on the individual.

There are several educational institutions and chains of institutions inspired by this Vedantic philosophy of education. These include the DAV institutions, Ramakrishna Mission institutions, Viswabharati at Shantiniketan, Chinmaya Mission Schools, Bharatiya Vidya Bhavan institutions and educational institutions at Sri Aurobindo Ashram or Yogoda Satsanga Ashram. The necessity for a philosophical underpinning for quality in education is equally shared by other religions in India. Christianity provides a sound philosophical basis for education through Christian missionary schools. The Sikh philosophy guides the Guru Harkrishan Public Schools and schools run by *gurudwaras*. *Madrassas* and *maktabs* provide education based on the philosophy of Islam.

Quality education warrants strong philosophical underpinnings, depicting the kind of human beings to be developed through schooling. All these schools are not only high-quality in conventional terms but are qualitatively different from other institutions because of their philosophies. The major emphasis is on value-centric education since the human being is a value configuration, rather than a robot-like knowledge configuration. Education is the most powerful means of modification of human behaviour. Human behaviour is depicted by a series of choices or preferences in methods of earning money (through ethical or unscrupulous means), being truthful or acting according to convenience, being selfish or sharing resources with others among other preferences within a larger behavioural choice matrix. Values guide such personal choices. I recollect an incident narrated to me by one of my seniors. When one of his classmates got a doctoral degree, my senior ran home and told his semi-literate mother about his friend's great achievement. His mother replied coolly, 'Yes, he has become a "doctorate" but not a good human being.' Missing human values like cooperation, sharing of responsibilities, care for others, sympathy for weaker ones, etc., were uppermost in her mind. The International Commission wrote, 'Wherever it met, the Commission heard the hope expressed that formal education, and secondary education in particular, could play a larger part in helping develop the *qualities of character* (emphasis added by author) that would enable young people to anticipate and adapt to major changes' (UNESCO, 1996).

---

[4] *Acaryat padamadatte*
Padam sishya swa-medhaya
Padamekam swa brahmachirivvi,
Padam kala kramena hi.

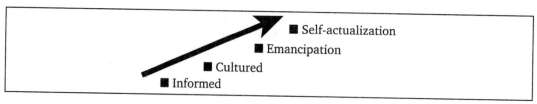

Figure 1.1   Taxonomy of educatedness

Quality education focuses on the identification of the propensities of each individual and nurturing such propensities for the holistic development of individuals. Mirambika, a school set up by the Aurobindo Ashram, is an outstanding example; every student creates his or her own curriculum. The school that nurtures and helps each child to optimize his/her potential, instead of converting all students into uniform industrial products, is the one that offers quality in education.

Further, each school has a personality of its own and differs from the other. Looking at every school as a product of an industrial line function is fraught with risk. For offering quality education, each school must optimize on its own potential. Every school has certain manifest qualities and rich latent potentialities. The total quality is the function of manifest quality and optimization of potential quality.

Let us now see it in applied form. I have worked on a concept, which I call 'educatedness'. This is the quality attribute of the product of education. As shown in Figure 1.1, individuals can be placed on a taxonomy of educatedness (Mukhopadhyay, 1999).

Informed: The lowest in the hierarchy is being informed—either through formal or informal educational processes. Information is bits of facts, figures, concepts, etc. These bits are not necessarily interrelated. Knowledge is in the organized form where information is woven into a meaningful pattern, a configuration. Hence, the first purpose of education is informing and processing information into organized knowledge. But this is only the first stage.

Cultured: The second level is the level of being cultured. Culture represents an integrated personality that is well rounded, emits warmth and follows human values. It is manifested in the way an individual treats himself or herself, other human beings, animals, plants, places, objects and the like. It is the totality of the person. For example, a well-dressed person who unhesitatingly litters a railway platform or airport with cigarette butts may be qualified but not necessarily cultured. Acharya Vinoba Bhave's concept of *prakriti* (nature), *vikriti* (deformity or distortion) and *sanskriti* (culture) represents this concept very well. The purpose of education is to culture the individual—develop the *sanskriti.*

Emancipation: One level ahead of culture is emancipation where individuals rise above the known artificial boundaries of religion, caste, creed, gender and linguistic or geographic belongingness. A person can be proud of his or her mother tongue and heritage while respecting and appreciating the national heritage and diversity of India. One can simultaneously be a proud Indian and a member of the international community.

This is basically achieving freedom from the strangleholds of ignorance, intolerance, etc. The purpose of education is to liberate—*sa vidya ya vimuktaye.*

Self-actualization: The last and final attribute of educatedness is self-actualization where the emphasis is on achieving the best of the potential already within the individual. The emphasis is on holistic development—Vivekananda's concept of 'perfection already in man' is also an indicator towards the same direction. Self-actualization implies achieving the best in all four planes of life.

Thus, quality in education can be indicated by the educatedness of the products of education. Being informed at whatever level of excellence is not enough. It is, at best, the first step in being educated.

Quality lies in meeting the expectations of the customers. But quality of education is more than meeting the expectations of the customers. In the context of distance education, Henderikx (1992) contended that quality can be defined as the intrinsic validity of the product of education with regard to fulfilling its academic mission. Further, a technological definition of quality involves matching the technical quality of the product with the technological requirements through quality assurance during the production process, e.g., course development needs monitored by effective project management and supported by educational technologists to make a product suited for a flexible learning system.

Quality management issues

There are several major issues in quality management. These issues are related both to the concept of quality and techniques of quality management. Indeed, it is the concept that determines adequacy and effectiveness of quality management tools and techniques. Quality management has been defined as a 'set of concepts, strategies, tools and beliefs, etc., which are aimed at improving the quality of products and services reducing the waste and saving costs' (Navaratnam and O'Connor, 1993).

Evolution of quality management

Quality control was probably the first technique to arrive on the scene in early 1930s, as far as quality management is concerned. The term 'total quality control' was originally coined by Feigenbaum (1983). 'Quality control in its broadest sense, refers to a spectrum of managerial methods for attempting to maintain the quality of manufactured articles at a desired level' (*International Encyclopedia of the Social Sciences,* 1979). The basic agenda of quality control is the detection and elimination of products that do not match the product specification. Quality control takes place after the event (Fidler, 1996). It has been defined as 'the procedure of establishing acceptable standards with defined limits of variation in quality of material, size, weight, finish or other characteristics for goods or services, and maintaining these standards' (Johannsen, 1968). Quality control can thus also mean avoiding too high a quality as well as too low a quality—in other words, sticking to the predefined quality (Johannsen, 1986). As a typical process of quality control in industrial production, sampled products are picked up from the conveyor belt and subjected to scrutiny as per the product definition. This obviously implies scrap and waste, and increase in production cost.

Quality control also takes the active support of statistical quality control techniques. 'Statistical quality control can refer to all those methods that use statistical principles and techniques for the control of quality. In this broad sense, statistical quality control might be regarded as embracing in principle all the statistical methodology for quality control' (*International Encyclopedia of the Social Sciences*, 1979).

The alternative form of ensuring quality is quality assurance (Tovey, 1994). This involves designing systems to deliver quality before the event (Fidler, 1996). Quality assurance is a later development in quality management. As the title suggests, its emphasis is on assurance, rather than on detection and elimination of products that do not match the product definition. Quality assurance is a strategy of prevention of production of wasteful defective pieces. Oakland (1988) identified five stages or attributes of quality assurance mechanism:

1. Dealing with quality planning
2. Providing quality advice and expertise
3. Training of personnel
4. Providing inward goods, process and finished products' appraisal methodology
5. Analysing customer's complaints, warranty claims and product liability cases

Thus, 'a quality assurance system, based on the fact that all functions share responsibility of quality, provides an effective method of acquiring and maintaining desired quality standards' (Oakland, 1988). BS 5750 contains a particular set of quality assurance procedures.

A significant emphasis in quality assurance is on the quality of the product design—an advance prototyping of the product. Equal emphasis has been laid on the quality of translating the design into a product conforming to the original design. The product is the outcome of the interaction of inputs and processes. The quality assurance mechanism ensures the right quality of raw material and equipment (inputs) and also rigorous process quality so that product quality is ensured. The specifications of raw material, equipment and process go a long way in assuring quality. This has been defined as a mechanism for ensuring 'zero-defect' and 'right first time, right every time' product.

TQM is an extension of the quality assurance approach. The emphasis is not only on managing quality at the input and process points but in developing a 'quality culture' among all employees. The thrill in TQM lies in thrilling the customer. Once pleased, customers then talk to their friends; and hence the reputation of the product, and of the company, rises. Consequently, the product market goes on expanding. Being a dynamic concept, TQM also accommodates the concept of changing customer needs and wants;

hence TQM anticipates and changes the products to meet the changing customer needs. Unlike quality control and quality assurance, TQM is dynamic; it does not accept any definition of quality as final. Its effort is to define new heights in quality and achieve them. The next chapter deals with the concept of TQM in detail.

Sallis (1996) depicts the evolution of quality management from inspection to quality control (for detection) to quality assurance (for prevention) to TQM (for continuous improvement). Dale and Plunkett (1990) reviewed quality control, quality assurance and TQM, preceded by quality inspection in a hierarchic model of quality management (Table 1.1).

The evolution of quality management techniques has given rise to Six Sigma, a quantitative concept derived from the distribution of population in the normal probability curve. There are two different schools of thought: one contends that Six Sigma is a natural development from TQM. Another group believes that it is an alternative methodology since TQM has not succeeded as it is claimed to have. Six Sigma has been implemented and tried out in the industry particularly for consumer products. There is not enough evidence to prove that this new technique has been used in education or other service sectors.

Table 1.1   Hierarchy of quality management

Quality management approaches	Activities
Total quality management	Involves suppliers and customers Aims for continuous improvement Concerns products and processes Responsibility with all workers Delivered through teamwork
Quality assurance	Use of statistical process control Emphasis on prevention External accreditation Delegated involvement Audit of quality schemes Cause-and-effect analysis
Quality control	Concerned with product testing Responsibility with supervisors Limited quality criteria Some self-inspection Paper-based system
Inspection	Post-production review Reworking Rejection Control of workforce Limited to physical products

Source: Dale and Plunkett (1990).

Quality management

The issue of quality management can be examined for industrial, service as well as the education sector. Let us take the example of an industrial product, from its design to production and marketing stages (Figure 1.2).

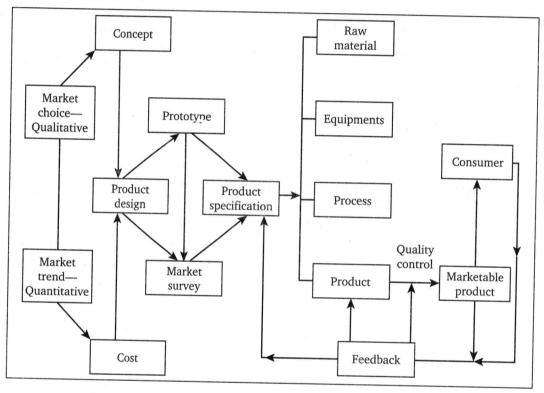

Figure 1.2   Quality management in industry

Evidently, quality choice and quantitative demands are the driving forces in quality management of industrial products. The 'concept' (a typical expression of designers)—the creative or artistic impression of the product—jointly with cost consideration, goes as an input into the product design. The product design leads to the development of prototypes of the product itself; in fact, the first consumer, namely the wholesaler approves the product prototype before it is put to production. The product design specifies the type and the grades of the raw material, the equipment to be used, the process (e.g., at what temperature for how long) and of course, the product. The product thus produced is subjected to sample quality checks before being put into the market for the consumer. The quality management vis-à-vis industrial product depicts the seminal importance of quality of design and quality of conformation to the design (Oakland, 1988).

This brief description of the industrial product with built-in quality management allows us to take three possible strands from where the issue can be examined: quality control, quality assurance and total quality.

Service sector

The second strand is to look at quality concepts in the service sector. As mentioned earlier, this is more difficult than dealing with quality issues vis-à-vis industrial products. First, unlike consumer products, it is difficult to precisely define the quality specifications in service sector. For example, when you commission an agency for cleaning your institutional premises, you cannot precisely define what quantity of dust (left) is acceptable. Several authors have dealt with this issue earlier. The major problems pointed out are as follows:

- Unlike industrial products, service providers are in direct contact with the user; obviously, perception of quality of service gets influenced by the inter-personal relationship skills of the provider and the consumer. For example, the account holder prefers a bank employee in the teller counter with courteous treatment to customers to another who may be faster and more accurate but irritable. There is a further rider to this. Although service providers are in direct contact with customers, they are down-the-line junior employees, not the ones that design and manage service quality.
- Appreciation of service is directly related to the timing. The hospital that provides quick service to an accident victim is always considered better in quality than another which is slow in offering the service despite the hospital being more clean and expensive.
- Defective consumer products can be repaired, mended or sold on 'sale' at a cheaper price. Service cannot be repaired or recycled because it is 'here and now', it is already provided. It cannot go back in time though it can ensure better service in future. In fact, that is the most serious problem—in poor quality health service, for example, the damage is done. Once done, health cannot be restored.
- Finally, service being a relatively abstract concept, it is difficult to put forward what an agency actually offers. Often the sales personnel bring examples and evidences from the past. Schools and other service providers depend upon indirect arguments and evidences to impress upon the customer the quality of their service. For example, unable to present what a service company actually offers, the promotional material mentions how many institutions have hired their services, and so on. Let me share an incident. During my first visit to the US, I took some photographs and gave the film for developing to a store. On the specified date, I went to collect the photographs. Unusual though in the US, my film was not yet processed. I was given another date. I went on that day and was given the photographs. I offered the due charges, but they were politely refused with an apology since the date was missed by the store. In this event, for example, what does the store say to market itself—that it serves free if it fails to provide on date.

- There is wide divergence in the way customers perceive and describe the quality of the same service. Thus, the quality of service is determined by the way the customer perceives rather than the way in which it is provided. The consumer becomes the supreme judge of quality.

Thus, there are five clear quality indicators in service:

1. Inter-personal relationship
2. Timing and punctuality
3. Best here and now
4. Indirect evidence of quality
5. Consumer perception

Conclusion

Quality has thus been defined in a host of ways—in terms of absolute and relative quality and consumer perception. Some have contended that the defining quality is not particularly helpful; it is futile. Yet every one searches for of it. The perception and assessment of quality differs from that of lifestyle products, organizational quality and service quality. An effort has been made to bring in the generic debate around the concept and methods of assessment of quality. This, I hope, will help in looking at the issue of quality of education from a sound conceptual platform.

The quality of education is determined by the kind of humans it produces. In education, where shaping of the person takes place, quality is a more holistic concept. Drawing from the taxonomy of educatedness, inputs and processes that ensure development of culturedness, emancipation and self-actualization of all aspects of human potential indicate quality education. Quality in education cannot be restricted to the supplier specification and even apparent customer satisfaction in terms of employability. There is the inner world in human life; quality in education includes processes that nurture the seeds of inner development.

The fundamental problem in dealing with quality at the conceptual level is the wide gap between the functional and metaphysical definition of a human being. The quality management methodology developed so far has been tried and tested for the functional goals. Deliberately designed and empirically tested means for managing quality for holistic development of human beings is a new challenge, though this was a common practice in the *Ashramik* institutions in ancient India.

TQM: Educational Applications

2

Introduction

The credit for developing a comprehensive philosophy and strategy for total quality management (TQM) goes to Deming and Juran. TQM was originally developed by Deming on the basis of his experience before and during World War II. As a philosophy, Deming's TQM was largely experimented with tremendous success in post-war economic reconstruction of Japan resulting in massive trade imbalance now between the USA and Japan (Crawford and Shutler, 1999). Deming's book, *Out of the Crisis*, published in 1986 is a landmark. Other outstanding contributors to this philosophy are Juran (1988, 1989), Crosby (1979, 1984) and Ishikawa (1983, 1985). As TQM became popular, several authors contributed to its philosophy. They contributed confirmations and reinforcements of certain principles, though not without contradictions on certain issues. Tuttle (1994) traced four stages of the development of TQM:

1. Awareness and early experiments
2. Blind following characterized by frenzied activity
3. Negative scepticism arising out of failures of over-enthusiasm in Stage 2
4. Stage of maturity with continuing momentum but well-informed adoption of activities

Whereas many countries are in the fourth stage, we in India are just beginning to realize the potential and are at the early stage of experimentation with TQM in education. Let us briefly review the basic tenets of TQM. There is a debate about the originality of TQM since terminology, including 'total quality control', has been around. The most authentic source of the concept or principles of TQM is the literature on the cardinal principles of TQM, propounded by the three original gurus: Deming (Box 2.1), Juran (Box 2.2) and Crosby (Box 2.3).

A critical examination of the cardinal principles of TQM as enunciated by Deming, Crosby and Juran indicates a marked shift in emphasis in quality management from product to people. The strongest emphasis is on human resource development (HRD) and capacity building—not only technical capacity, but also managerial and participative

---

Box 2.1 DEMING'S 14 PRINCIPLES OF TQM

1 Create constancy of purpose for improving the product and service, with the aim of becoming competitive and staying in business, and providing jobs.
2 Adopt a new philosophy.
3 Cease dependence on mass inspection to achieve quality.
4 Terminate the awarding of business on the basis of price.
5 Improve constantly and forever the system of production and service, to improve quality and productivity, and thus to constantly decrease cost.
6 Institute training on the job.
7 Institute leadership.
8 Drive out fear so that every one may work effectively for the company.
9 Break down the barriers between departments.
10 Eliminate slogans, exhortations and targets asking for new levels of productivity without providing the workforce with the methods to do the job better.
11 Eliminate work standards that prescribe numerical quotas.
12 Remove the barriers that rob people of their rights to pride of workmanship.
13 Institute a vigorous programme of education and self-improvement.
14 Put everyone in the company to work to accomplish the transformation.

Box 2.2 JURAN'S 10 STEPS FOR TQM

1 Create awareness for the need and opportunity for improvement.
2 Set explicit goals for improvement.
3 Create an organizational structure to drive the improvement process.
4 Provide appropriate training.
5 Adopt a project approach to problem solving.
6 Identify and report progress.
7 Recognize and reinforce success.
8 Communicate results.
9 Keep records of change.
10 Build an annual improvement cycle into all processes of the company.

---

capacity leading to empowerment. TQM calls for a shift from quantitative to qualitative terms of reference for quality improvement. Importantly, the emphasis is on constancy of purpose, quality consciousness and continuous improvement as a way of organizational life. The list unveils Deming's emphasis on the management cadre. Poor quality indicates

---

Box 2.3   Crosby's 14 steps towards TQM

1   Establish full management commitment to the quality programme.
2   Set up a quality team to drive the programme.
3   Introduce quality measurement procedures.
4   Define and apply the principle of the cost of quality.
5   Institute a quality assurance programme.
6   Introduce corrective action procedures.
7   Plan for the implementation of a zero-defect system.
8   Implement supervisor training.
9   Announce a zero-defects day to launch the process.
10 Set goals to bring about action.
11 Set up an employee-management communication system.
12 Recognize those who have actively participated.
13 Set up quality councils to sustain the process.
14 Do it all over again.

---

a failure of the management. Juran (1989) reinforced this contention of the importance of the system with his popular 85/15 theory—85 per cent of the problems that an organization faces are due to systems failure (faulty process design), while only about 10–15 per cent of the failures and problems are due to individuals. Thus, improving quality is synonymous with improving management. Crosby's (1979) contributions are the theories of 'quality is free' and 'zero-defects'. Recycling cost of wastage is more than enough for achieving quality. It is possible to produce with zero-defect.

By implication, the structures and systems of an organization have greater roles to play than individual efforts and competencies in quality management. This, however, does not undermine the roles and contributions of individuals. Instead, individuals should be used productively and not to patch up basic design flaws (Hormi and Lingren, 1995). Conceptually, TQM is a significantly fresh and dynamic idea. As Oakland (1993) puts it, the 'distinctiveness of TQM lies in two major features—a commitment to continuous improvement and involvement of all members of the organization'.

Besides the contributions of Deming, Juran and Crosby, the main features of TQM have been succinctly summarized by Saylor (1992) as follows:

> The Total Quality Management philosophy provides an overall concept that fosters continuous improvement in an organization. This philosophy stresses a systematic, integrated, consistent organization-wide perspective involving everyone and everything. It focuses primary emphasis on total satisfaction for both internal and external customers, within a management environment that seeks continuous improvement of all processes and systems. The TQM philosophy emphasizes the use of people, usually in multi-functional teams, to bring about improvement from within the organization.

In Hill and Taylor's (1991) view

> Essentially, it is concerned with organizational improvement through the identification and solution of problems by groups of employees at various levels in the structure. This problem solving is usually supported by the development of the teams and a focus on corporate goals. However, the teams primarily identify with problems of specific relevance to their own functions in order to engender a sense of involvement in organizational affairs. TQM is a holistic paradigm which recognizes that all employees can make an impact upon the quality of goods and services provided.

In an effort to redefine and/or identify attributes of TQM as a management strategy, Yudof and Busch-Vishniac (1996) have identified the following:

- Customer focus—'organizations should listen to whom they serve'
- 'Unhealthy' and 'healthy' organizations, in the context of customer focus vis-à-vis internal political processes determining the organizations goals
- Focus on systemic change—'good management means devising systems that more fully encompass the entire range of observable behaviour'
- Implementation through knowledge—linking data to systems view and decision-making
- Active involvement of all employees in the process of change

Although practising TQM requires time, the potential pay-off is large—complete organizational redesign and 'elimination of inefficient and overly complex processes'. Thus, the central focus in TQM is customer satisfaction, the indicator of quality being the customer response to a product. With this central focus , TQM sets out to develop an organizational philosophy and management strategy to achieve the philosophy. It sets an organization on a trajectory in search of new heights with a predefined set of corporate goals on a continuing basis, indicating consistency of purpose with the involvement of all, where people in teams are in continuous search for self-actualization. The organization strategically invests in capacity building and empowerment with increasing decentralization of decision-making on facts and figures through mentoring leadership roles in various areas of organizational functioning. The emphasis is on people—external and internal customers—and organizational processes.

Assessment of impact

The US General Accounting Office (1991) was among the first to study the issue of impacts. The GAO provided performance measures in four categories (Table 2.1).

Table 2.1   Performance measures for TQM

Employee-related indicators	Operating indicators	Customer satisfaction	Financial performance indicators
• Employee satisfaction • Attendance • Turnover • Safety/health • Suggestions received	• Reliability • Timeliness of delivery • Order-processing time • Errors or defects • Product lead time • Inventory turnover • Costs of quality • Cost savings	• Overall customer satisfaction • Customer complaints • Customer retention	• Market share • Sales per employee • Return on assets • Return on sales

Two sets of messages emanate from Table 2.1:

1. Areas of indicators of success of TQM—indicators related to employees, operations, customer satisfaction and financial performance
2. Indicators of success in each area

This is a useful tool, as it elaborates and lists details of the indicators. It uses direct as well as indirect indicators. For example, in the case of employee-related indicators, it uses turnover and suggestions received as indirect indicators along with employee satisfaction as direct indicators. Similarly, customer retention is an important indirect indicator where overall customer satisfaction is the direct indication of quality management. The operating indicators provide a meaningful set of process control mechanisms for quality assurance.

Ancient Indian education: Holistic (total) quality

The *gurukula* system of education was probably the best example of quality management in education. In a *gurukula* (preceptor's home or family) system, students lived with the guru in his family till the time they completed their studies. There are several implications of this internship.

*   The guru chose the student on the basis of learning potential. The test for admission was not necessarily based on intellectual quality. For example, when Satyakam approached Guru Gautam for admission, Guru Gautam asked him his *gotra* (caste). Satyakam mentioned how his mother had got him by serving many people in her youth—she did not know his *gotra*. This dangerous truthfulness was enough

indication for Guru Gautam to assess Satyakam's *gotra*—the *gotra* of truthfulness (*satya*) and enlightenment (attributes of Brahmins as per concepts of *varnashram* and not *jativeda* or *sattvik* qualities). The Guru asked Satyakam to get some *kusha* (a specific grass variety) and get ready for initiation.

- The guru decided the curriculum suited to the individual disciple's talent, interest and ability—optimization of human potential.
- Disciples saw the guru in all facets of his life; the guru's life was an open book for ethics and value modelling.
- While living in the guru's family, disciples shared the household work; thus they learned life skills in holistic living where education was not preparation for life but living itself.
- A disciple could leave the *gurugriha* (preceptor's house) only when the guru was satisfied that the disciple had completed learning; there was no grade or class and the emphasis was on mastery in learning.
- There was no discrimination among the disciples by the guru. Young Kachh was sent by the gods to be trained under Guru Sukracharya, the guru of the *danavas* (devils). Yet, Guru Sukracharya gave his full wisdom to Kachh.

What is important is the emphasis on all-round development of students, highest quality in performance, and the challenge to every disciple to achieve his/her best.

The *gurukula* tradition of holistic or total quality was successfully transferred to the early Indian universities, such as Nalanda and Takshashila. About admission in Nalanda, Hiuen Tsang says, 'If men of other quarters desire to enter ... the keeper of the gate (*Dwarapandits—scholar gatekeepers*—as they were called [emphasis added]), proposes some hard questions; many are unable to answer and retire. ... Those who fail compared with those who succeed are as seven or eight to ten' (Beal in Das, 1986). Similarly, studies in Takshashila were not only diverse but also of the highest form and quality (Das, 1986). In *Chhandogya Upanishad*, the highest form of learning—*paravidya*—has been recommended. This emphasis on quality in education was lost during the medieval and modern colonial periods.

The ancient Indian educational experience, however, was limited to the micro-institutional framework. With the ushering in of democratic values and education as a human right, the issue is of 'education for all'. The challenge is one of educating the millions with quality. TQM as an approach offers a significant opportunity for its adaptation to improve educational quality in a holistic manner. Let us examine the feasibility of adapting TQM in modern post-colonial Indian educational setting.

TQM in contemporary education

The applicability of TQM in education drew significant attention from many authors such as DeCosmo et al. (1991), Edwell (1993), Sherr and Lozier (1991) and Bonser (1992).

They pointed out that educational institutions have turned to TQM for many of the same reasons that businesses have instituted quality programmes (Kwan, 1996): the escalating number of students, lack of consistent leadership style, increasing need for accountability to the public and changing attitudes towards universities. Adaptation of TQM in education was also due to resource constraints and increasing pressures (DeCosmo et al., 1991).

Motwani and Kumar's (1997) review brings both enthusiasm as well as scepticism about TQM. Also, TQM offers an alternative management and institution building paradigm (Sherr and Lozier, 1991). TQM professes a systematic, not random, approach to operations. Its emphasis is on continuous improvement of quality. In this context, Shewhart's (1931) Plan–Do–Check–Act (PDCA) cycle offers a scientific method for continuous process improvement.

Tuttle (1994) ascribes the adaptation of TQM into two-fold external and internal forces due to a reduction of public funds. External forces are difficulties in recruiting outstanding new faculty and retaining existing faculty; competition among institutions for faculty; competition for students, both initial enrolment and retention (quality education leads to increased student referrals, hence increased enrolment); donor demand for accountability (may explicitly ask an institution to discuss its quality management process as a condition for the receipts of funds) and competition for corporate funding. Internal forces are increases in productivity in teaching; administration and support functions; shared governance; poor teacher morale due to reduced funding and effect of low faculty morale on students, including higher tuition and hostel fees.

Crawford and Shutler (1999) made an interesting and useful comparative analysis of the application of TQM in education, as proposed by Crosby and Deming. Sherr and Lozier (1991) pictured TQM as a three-dimensional model, comprising design, output and process. Further, elaborating on the TQM theory as applied to education, authors chose five focus areas: mission and customer focus, systematic approach to operation, vigorous development of human resources, long-term thinking and commitment.

Going back to the 'originals', it will be interesting to examine the implications of each of cardinal principles proposed by Deming, Juran and Crosby for education. For brevity, let us examine Deming's principles (Table 2.2).

Such educational application and implications of each one of the 14 principles proposed by Deming are also borne out by the analysis by Crawford and Shutler (1999). Similarly, Juran and Crosby propound the 85/15 and 'zero-defect product' theories, or quality at no cost. They imply that 85 per cent of the variance of quality in education can be explained by the system (structures and processes) while 15 per cent can be explained by individual skills, competence and commitment. The equivalent of 85/15 in education is Bloom's Mastery Learning, which proves that by adjusting instructional processes (modifying systems), 80 per cent of the students are capable of securing 80 per cent of the marks. In other words, it is the system that is responsible for low performance in education, not necessarily the students.

'Quality is free' a landmark idea contributed by Crosby. In reality too, quality-oriented management does not necessarily cost more money. On the contrary, quality management

Table 2.2 Deming's propositions and implications for education

Deming's propositions	Educational implications
Create constancy of purpose for improvement of the product and service, with the aim of becoming competitive and staying in business, and providing jobs.	Even if the institutions do not need to become competitive and stay in the business since it is a seller's market, institutions ought to improve on a continuing basis because of explosion of knowledge and changing styles in learning. Institutions need to develop long- and medium-term perspectives for development and move towards those.
Adopt a new philosophy.	Quality is a continuous journey. Make it part of the institutional mission. Educational implications are the adoption of a new philosophy and consequent approach for holistic development of students, for instance, building education on the four pillars of learning (UNESCO, 1996).
Cease dependence on mass inspection to achieve quality.	Replace external inspection by a continuous internal mechanism of quality assurance.
Terminate the awarding of business on the basis of price.	Opt for the best available teachers and instructional resources at affordable prices, not the lowest prices.
Improve constantly and forever the system of production and service, to improve quality and productivity, and thus to constantly decrease costs.	Constantly improve instruction, student assessment and management to improve quality and reduce costs by reducing wastage.
Institute training on the job.	Initiate institution-based on-the-job training for teachers and staff.
Institute leadership.	Enforce decentralized responsibility and authority, and mentor leadership in staff.
Drive out fear so that everyone may work effectively for the company.	Encourage teachers to innovate. Assure them security and the right to fail. Celebrate equally the success or failure of an innovative experiment.
Break down the barriers between departments.	Create structures with subject disciplines as departments and cross-departmental activities to form interdisciplinary task forces.

(Continued)

Table 2.2 *(Continued)*

Deming's propositions	Educational implications
Eliminate slogans, exhortations and targets asking for new levels of productivity without providing the workforce with the methods to do the job better.	Replace sermons and slogans for quality with on-the-job training for quality improvement in whatever one does in the institutions, thus helping them do a little better than before.
Eliminate work standards that prescribe numerical quotas.	Underplay numerical quotas of classes and student assessment. Build quality consciousness in each activity.
Remove the barriers that rob people of their rights to pride of workmanship.	Encourage and recognize innovation and uniqueness on the job. Remove roadblocks and facilitate experimentation.
Institute a vigorous programme of education and self-improvement.	Develop an institutional mechanism whereby every staff member charts out his/her own development path and method to achieve his/her goals.
Put everyone in the company to work to accomplish the transformation.	Involve every staff in visioning and setting out the mission and goals. Involve everyone in institutional diagnosis, planning and execution of improvement plans.

should lead to reduction in costs, 'although it can be achieved at higher costs through mismanagement'. The sustainability of quality management in education is directly linked to and dependent upon effective management of costs (Freeston, 1992). Education provides a beautiful illustration of this concept.

It is estimated that about 18 million students appear for the Standard 10 Board examination every year. Only about 50 per cent of them qualify; hence, about 9 million students fail every year. The estimated cost of 10-year schooling is about Rs 20,000. Even if we assume that 50 per cent of the cost is wasted (the other 50 per cent for residual learning and experience of schooling), the annual financial loss due to failure is Rs 10,000 or $225 per failed candidate, and Rs 90,000 million or $2,925 million per year for the country. If invested and used efficiently, this Rs 90,000 million can create quality enough and no one would fail in a Board examination! In a four-year-long experiment, at an additional investment of Rs 48 (about $1) per child per year, the dropout rate among 6,430 children enrolled in village primary schools was brought down from 49 per cent to 17 per cent; 1,952 children were prevented from dropping out of primary school. With an investment of Rs 48 per child per year, the saving was Rs 800 (estimated annual unit cost of primary education) per child per year (Mukhopadhyay, 1999).

Experimental application of TQM in education

There has been considerable work on testing the concept and practice of TQM in education. Hansen and Jackson (1996), in an experiment, applied TQM (they called it 'total quality improvement') in the classroom. They applied the principles of customer focus (students), team process (student involvement) and continuous improvement. The researchers concluded, 'The TQI approach changed the role of the teacher. ... With multiple objectives ... the instructor becomes a manager of resources rather than an oracle on the podium. ... The second lesson is how scarce, and hence how valuable, the time of students is. ... The scarcest resource to manage was students' time and goodwill.'

Cole (1995) concluded that the application of TQM resulted in improved processes in optimizing job definition and improving recruitment methodologies, creating better alignment between faculty needs and expectations. The University of Maryland has developed the Strategic Performance Measurement Methodology (SPMM) by identifying key result areas (Tuttle, 1994) for determining whether TQM is working in the universities or colleges. In SPMM, financial measures like value added and value lost per graduate and non-financial measures like customer satisfaction and operational indicators were developed. It would be interesting to review the thesis on comparative indicators in 'private sector indicators' and 'higher education indicators' (Table 2.3).

Table 2.3   Comparative indicators in private sector and higher education

Private sector indicator	Higher education indicator
• Customer retention • Product development • Cycle time • Unit cost • Warranty cost	• Graduated rate • Number of months needed to launch a new course • Cost per credit hours delivered • Alumni cost

Source: Tuttle (1994).

In this table, Tuttle has made one-to-one correspondence between indicators in private sector and higher education. Indeed, the rate of graduation can be nearest to customer retention as much as unit cost can be compared to cost per credit hours delivered, or cost per unit of class as well as cost per graduate. The most imaginative comparison is the warranty cost with that of alumni.

Adaptation of TQM in education

Several experiments on TQM in higher education have substantiated Deming's claim regarding the relevance and applicability of TQM in education. Yet, there are sceptics who doubt the applicability of TQM in education. Sherr and Lozier (1991) mention, 'We need to step back and ask whether our universities are doing all they might to help the country address its most important problems—leading competitiveness, poverty, inadequate public education, environmental hazards and many more.' The question has perfect resonance in all the countries and is equally pertinent to educational institutions at all levels.

By all evidence, however, TQM is applicable in education, perhaps with the adaptation of certain concepts and strategies. For example, the central issue in TQM is that of customer focus. In education, who is the customer: student or parent or employer or provider (government) or all? Society being the main provider of education, assessment of quality in education cannot be restricted to needs of the students; it must take into account the perceived needs of other constituents, namely parents, community, government and employers. Powar and Panda (1995) argued 'that an institution of high quality efficiently and effectively meets its stated purpose(s) or mission(s) developed taking into account the clients' stated as well as implied needs'.

Chaffe and Tierney (1988) identified nine areas of sensitivity that provide a broad context within which to consider application of TQM.

1. Find internal contradictions
2. Develop comparative awareness
3. Clarify the identity of the institution
4. Communicate
5. Act on multiple, changing forms
6. Treat every problem as if it has multiple solutions
7. Treat every solution as a fleeting solution
8. Look for consequences in unlikely places
9. Be aware of any solution that hurts people or undermines strong values

Applying TQM in education is a continuous search for quality at personal, group, institutional and societal levels. Kaufman and Zahn (1993) emphasized the need for mega, macro and micro perspectives. Kaufman (1992) raised some important questions vis-à-vis each of these levels.

Societal/Mega: Do you care about the success of learners after they leave your educational system and become citizens?

Organizational/Macro: Do you care about the quality—competence—of completers and leavers when they leave your educational system?

Small groups/Individual/Micro: Do you care about the specific skills, knowledge, attitudes and abilities of the learners as they move from course to course, and level to level?

Operational/Process: Do you care about the efficiency of your educational programmes, activities and methods?

Inputs/Resources: Do you care about the quality and availability of your educational resources, including human, capital, financial and learning?

Evaluation: Do you care about the worth and value of your methods, means and resources? And do you care about the extent to which you have reached your educational objectives?

The responses to these questions can significantly alter our perceptions about our own institution and lead to developing alternative pathways for quality management. TQM is an exhortation in the improvement of management of institutions. Since education in India is not market-driven, quality is not a criterion for survival. Should accountability to public money, however, be a concern, TQM offers an important opportunity for resource-starved educational institutions to improve quality without investment. The National Assessment and Accreditation Council of India, for example, has been set up by the University Grants Commission to assess all universities and colleges against certain pre-defined criteria with relative weightage. State support to the universities and colleges will now be linked to their ability to manage quality.

There are significant potentialities that TQM can offer to education. First, TQM offers a justification and a technique for the continuous search for quality and excellence. Second, it develops willingness and hence a culture for change; related to that, organizations learn to be more flexible and responsive. Third, TQM makes qualitative shifts in decision-making: first on the location of decision-making by active participants irrespective of their levels in the hierarchy of the organization rather than concentrating at the top of the hierarchy, and second on decision-making based on facts. Another contribution of TQM is the shift from external to internal performance measures (Yudof and Busch-Vishniac, 1996).

TQM and Indian institutions

TQM as a management philosophy and its associated strategies are applicable to Indian schools, colleges and universities. Navaratnam (1997) makes a forceful statement on quality on the basis of his personal experience. He was able to differentiate between the 'good' and the 'not so good' schools: 'I knew then that only well managed schools could provide quality education. ... My knowledge and experience tell me that a managed education means a quality education. My perception of quality was represented by school facilities, teachers, principal, fellow students, learning materials, teaching methods, assessment and technology as well as the surrounding economy, community and the political system. ... I also perceived that every school and its system could provide quality education, but some did and others did not.' But this indifference is fraught with great risk. For India to be globally competitive in the manufacturing and service industries, it has to depend upon the educational systems to provide appropriate manpower, now as well as in the future.

The Indian educational scenario is a curious mix of modernism and tradition; internationally comparable (international baccalaureate) quality institutions such as IBO-affiliated schools, Presidency College, St. Stephen's College, the Indian Institutes of Technology and the Indian Institutes of Management co-exist with extremely poor quality institutions. A minuscule buyer's market in an otherwise colossal seller's market; a massive network of schools and higher education institutions with less than 40 per cent (secondary education) and 7 per cent (higher education) of the relevant age groups participating in education. We need to examine relevance and adaptability of TQM in Indian schools in this context. Further, empirical studies indicate that (in 1990–91) per capita institutional costs in Kendriya Vidyalayas, state government schools and unaided schools were Rs 904.52, Rs 1,019.04 and Rs 747.63, respectively (Aggarwal, 1991). Thus, per capita cost is not necessarily related to quality. Indeed, quality education is managed education. It can be derived that a large majority of Indian schools is not offering managed education. TQM offers that alternative philosophy and strategy for the management of educational institutions.

Among parents who pay for their wards' education in private schools, there is an increasing awareness about their rights. This is indicated by the active interest and participation of parents' forums in the development of curriculum framework, litigation on enhancement of fees and school facilities, etc. Recent reports indicate a growing demand for education (*PROBE Report*, 1999). The 350 million-plus Indian middle class is prepared to 'buy' good quality education. This is indicated by the increase in private cost of education, particularly parental investment in private tuitions for coaching of their wards. The writing on the wall is clear—parents will be prepared to pay for good quality education; if the state cannot offer it, they will choose alternative means. All these developments and the reduction in fund availability lead to higher social accountability of education. The TQM concept of customer focus is a mechanism of establishing a functional accountability system in education.

Despite the customer focus, accountability cannot be developed in a day. It needs a long-term perspective and, hence, long-term planning. Further, each school has a unique personality. It must recognize that and nurture it to make it 'special', locally relevant and accountable. Developing a school on the basis of its unique personality requires vision effectively converted into missions and goals.

Ever since Independence, there has been significant emphasis on HRD in education. The effort in HRD in education was stepped up in the period following the National Policy of Education (1986), with a number of schemes at all levels for continuous upgradation of teachers, institutional heads as well as field-level educational administrators. Increasing devolution of power, coupled with training and development, is an effort at capacity building and empowerment. The effectiveness or outcome of the effort is another question.

Finally, the development of process capabilities has been emphasized by all earlier management methods related to institution building, including Management by Objectives (MBO), Organization Development (OD) and Quality Circle (QC). Thus, various elements of TQM have either been under trial in Indian institutions or have relevance and significant potential. TQM offers a systemic approach to institutional development and quality management on a continuing basis. Hence, TQM holds tremendous potential to draw out Indian educational institutions from their current crisis of quality.

Quality improvement and management in education can be achieved in more than one way. It can be capital-intensive (infrastructure- and technology-intensive) and/or human-intensive. Though many educational administrators believe that quality in education is a function of high-quality infrastructure and technology, this is not borne out by evidence. Both infrastructure and technology are instruments in the hands of humans in the system. Hence, both technology- and infrastructure-intensive approaches to quality management depend upon human quality. Within the given infrastructure and technology, human efforts can create wonders. If infrastructure and technology are necessary conditions, human quality is the sufficient condition. Further, TQM with its focus on 'clients' and 'involvement of all' is essentially a human-intensive approach to quality management. The approach is relevant, feasible and applicable to Indian educational institutions.

TQM in Indian education: In search of a meaning

The publication of the first edition of this book, *Total Quality Management in Education*, in 2001 triggered off a chain of interesting events. There was extensive consultation and experimentation on TQM in different types of educational institutions in India.[1] In many Indian universities, postgraduate and doctoral research have been initiated on TQM developed and presented in this book; some researchers are also using the tools like MIPQ (see Appendix II) and/or complete set of MIAS tools (see Appendices II, III, IV, V and VI) for assessing quality. This intensive interaction and experimentation during the last four years has provided me some important insights into institutional mindsets, receptivity and the need for adapting TQM concepts for schools, colleges and universities. This has resulted into the identification of 15 fundamental principles for TQM in education.

1. Nurture a vibrant familial ambience in the institution
2. Ensure proactive participation of all the partners in the institution: parents, students, teachers, non-teaching staff, persons and organizations interested in the institution
3. Create awareness that schooling is a holistic living experience
4. Create mechanisms for the expression of mutual concern among the partners in schooling and record that; consult students and parents about their expectations

---

[1] I involved nearly 30 professors from different universities for four weeks in two capacity-building programmes on total quality management to act as resource persons on the subject. In one of the projects sponsored by Government of India at a cost of Rs 1.5 million, principals of nearly 500 District Institutes of Education and Training (DIETs) were trained in TQM for two years, based on the first edition of this book. I conducted technical sessions on TQM education and discussed the concept presented in this book with more than 150 principals of colleges. I conducted courses and discussed TQM in education with over 200 principals of government and various networks of private schools. I also had discussions with more than 200 field-level educational administrators on TQM. Besides, I addressed large learned gatherings in higher and professional education institutions on TQM in education. There was a massive debate in the capacity-building programmes on total quality management in education based on the Gujarati version of this book involving all 7,000 schools, district resource persons, and school management.

5. Develop collective future vision and long-and short-term perspective plans
6. Develop indicators of quality and benchmarks (minimum acceptable level) for each major and minor activity in the institution
7. Define quality parameters and insist on quality in every sphere and activity
8. Review and redefine goals and targets for continuous improvement
9. Develop data and information systems on each activity and function
10. Introduce cost analysis and develop cost consciousness
11. Create mechanisms for inter-departmental and inter-subject group dialogue and planning, breaking barriers
12. Develop a staff development blueprint for each staff member and execute with care
13. Mentor leadership
14. Innovate and encourage innovation; document and discuss outcomes
15. Celebrate organizational successes and failures

The identification of these principles emerged from the need to look for alternative meanings when TQM is applied to education and in particular cultural settings. In my field explorations, consultations and reviews of conceptual literature on education and the nature of human beings, I found a viable and valid new platform to look at the issue differently, perhaps more decisively.

It would be interesting to derive the meaning, epistemologically, from the three words that constitute the epithet. I have dealt elaborately with the concepts of 'quality' and 'management'. My primary emphasis here at this stage will be to derive the inspiration out of the word 'total'.

The business of education is essentially one of human development—'drawing out the best in human beings' or 'manifestation of perfection already in man'. Interfaith research reveals the divine nature of human beings (Mukhopadhyay, 2003). Quality education is that which unveils this truth—*sa vidya ya vimuktaye*—releasing human minds from the stranglehold of the narrow concept of self that is selfish and sense-driven. As of now, the emphasis in education—in schools, colleges and universities—is on intellectual development. By implication, if at all, education optimizes only the intellectual dimensions of human beings. But that does not lead us to the 'total'. Thus, TQM in education poses a greater challenge; the challenge is of ensuring total quality education. Let us explore some kind of an analytical process to generate a meaningful framework to propose a conceptual paradigm of management.

According to Indian scriptures, human beings live in multiple planes: physical, intellectual, emotional and spiritual. This has been corroborated by scriptures from other religious traditions as well. More recently, the International Commission on Education in the 21st Century in its report submitted to the UNESCO has also recognized the need for organizing education to foster the development of human beings in all these planes of living. Accordingly, the role of education is to develop human beings to their full potential in all four planes of their lives. The implication of 'total' quality management in education then is ensuring quality management in education for the development of all the four planes of living.

Taking the issue further, TQM in education is for the development of 'total quality mind' (Chakraborty, 2002) moving from *annamoy* (the primeval living or living in physical plane) to *anandamoy kosha* (living in the state of bliss), through *pranamoy, manomay,* and *vigyanmoy koshas,* as mentioned in Chapter 1. The challenge of TQM in education is moving human beings from *annamoy* to *anandamoy koshas* through the intermediary stages. That is about the learners (clients)! Let us now extend this concept and framework on to the institutional level of education.

First, the goal of institutional education is to provide education that ensures total development of students, literally optimizing the full potential for 'manifestation of perfection already in man'. To achieve this, there has to be synchronization between the organizational culture and its goals. The institution—school, college or university—has to be perceived and respected as a dynamic living being that lives in physical, intellectual, emotional and spiritual planes. It also needs to be developed in all these four planes. Only when quality management comprehensively takes charge of the development of an institution in all its planes, will it make TQM meaningful and functional.

For an educational institution, the infrastructure, personnel, finances, rules and regulations, protocols, etc., provide the physical basis or plane of living. Quality management of all these, forms an integral part of TQM. However, just as a subset never equals the set, quality management of infrastructure is not equal to TQM. The intellectual plane of an educational institution is indicated by the curriculum, curriculum transaction or the teaching-learning processes, evaluation and intellectual discourses among the faculty and among the students and the faculty. This is another important dimension of TQM in education although this too is unequal to TQM *per se*. The mental or the emotional dimension of an educational institution is indicated by the interpersonal relationships, affiliations to the institution, concern for the employees, organizational climate and other such non-intellectual attributes. It is this dimension that provides emotional security to its employees, and is probably the most significant determinant of quality of life in an institution. Besides students, teachers and other employees, including the principal, spend a large part of their lives in the institution; to that extent, educational institutions are 'second homes'. Just as men cannot live on bread alone, intellectual and infrastructural dimensions cannot ensure quality of life in an educational institution. Quality institutions need rich emotional content. The fourth dimension is the spiritual dimension. Deriving implication from the word 'spirit', the spiritual aspect of institutional life is indicated by attributes like higher goals, innovation, experimentation, exploration of new areas and modes of working, social and community concern and service. Whenever we witness creativity, the inner health of the organization—non-partisan decisions, non-exploitation of the weak and the low, inspiration, institution above self—we experience its spiritual qualities. All that strives to reach higher levels, transcending the mundane, is spiritual. It is this component that renders quality an endless journey in search of new heights all the time.

Thus TQM, as applied to education in general and educational institutions in particular, means management of quality of infrastructure, intellectual, emotional and spiritual dimensions of institutional life. Only such comprehensive TQM of educational institution can lead to total quality education nurturing a student in all four planes of living and developing a total quality mind.

Conclusion

There are two dimensions of quality management hidden in the term 'total quality management'. One is the 'total quality' and the other is 'quality management'. This implies that quality can, and probably should, be seen in a holistic manner. A partisan or fragmented way of looking at quality in any organization is neither desirable, nor feasible, for an action in one area sets out a chain of reactions in several other areas of management of an educational institution. TQM provides an important opportunity to look at quality in a holistic fashion and also provides instrumentalities for managing quality.

The conventional concept of quality control, as applied to education, is the pass–fail mechanism. All those who pass satisfy the product specification; in industrial terms, the failures are the detected and eliminated 'products'. This mechanism of quality control is expensive and wasteful. Further, this failure is also dangerous, for it damages the self-concept of these energetic young people. The control is in specification of the raw material, equipment and processes. In other words, these are well-managed schools, hence good-quality schools (Navaratnam, 1997). The endeavour of TQM is to create a culture of management, leading to quality.

Systems Thinking and Organizational Micro-analysis 3

Introduction

Every educational institution, as contended in Chapter 2, is a 'dynamic (living) being' with a physical body, mind, intelligence and spirit of its own, giving it a uniqueness, indeed a personality. Hence, for quality management, each institution must be seen in its own uniqueness and totality. No wonder then that within the common framework of the educational systems in a country, the increasing emphasis is on institution-based management; school-based management is the accepted terminology (Abu-Duhou, 1999).

Each institution comprises several sub-components that are interrelated and interdependent: infrastructure, personnel, instructional resources, programmes, activities, etc. Action in one area often results in a chain of reactions in other areas. For total quality management (TQM), it is necessary to develop holistic thinking about the institution. This need for 'looking at an institution as a complete organism' is what I would call systems thinking. For the application of TQM, we would also need to take the anatomical view, getting into most minute details that constitute the sub-systems of an educational institution; I have called it organizational micro-analysis. Thus, what we need for TQM is an analytico-synthetic approach to the understanding of our educational institutions.

Systems approach

The origin and development of the systems approach can be traced to cybernetics, biological sciences and industrial management. Romiszowaski (1994) contends that 'the term "systems approach" grew out of general systems theory and cybernetics as a creative and heuristic approach to the understanding and improvement of probabilistic systems'. It was recognized that the complexity involved in social systems could not be controlled or manoeuvred easily as can be done in simple mechanical processes. Hence, a systems approach is characterized by careful analysis of interrelationships and interdependence of constituent units and sub-systems and 'interpretation of these interactions in terms of predicting what may happen in other parts of the system if certain changes are made in a particular part' (Neil, 1979). 'From the perspective of managing change, a system may be defined as being an organized assembly of components, which are related in such a way that the behaviour of any individual component will influence the overall status of the system.' 'All systems, physical or "soft", must have predetermined objective that the inter-related components strive to achieve' (Paton and McCalman, 2000).

In biological sciences, the human body is seen as a system, comprising several components like limbs and the main body, which further comprises various systems, like the digestive, the circulatory, the reproductive, etc. Although these are called systems, these are parts of the larger system, the human body itself. Obviously, we know through our sufferings what happens to other systems if and when, for example, our digestive system does not function well. The important issue is to recognize that like the human body, any system comprises several sub-systems, and these sub-systems are interrelated and interdependent.

Taking this further, the human being (not just the human body) as a system comprises the body, the mind and the soul. Medical research is bringing into sharp focus the mind's relationship with, and effect on, the body. Thus, the human body and mind are sub-systems of the human being.

Page and Thomas (1977) defined the systems approach to education, in *The International Dictionary of Education*, as: 'Conscious use of systems analysis and systems design techniques is an endeavour to identify and solve complex problems in learning and instructional systems. The components of the approach include the establishment of a systems boundary, the identification of all actual or possible inputs and outputs to the system and examination of their interaction.' The few important concepts that emerge out of the definition by Page and Thomas and other authors on systems approach are as follows:

Problem solving: The purpose of the systems approach is to solve complex problems. Hence, the systems approach is not about fancy intellectual gymnastics but about practical tools for problem solving. The main contention in the systems approach is to solve a problem in the context of interrelationships so that the impact—adverse or otherwise—of the action in other areas is anticipated and recognized.

Systems boundary: The digestive system is a system. It is a sub-system of the human body as a system. The human body is a sub-system of the human being as the system. This illustrates the case for defining the systems boundary so that one may restrict the analysis and action for problem solving to a meaningful limit.

Input: The word 'input' is self-explanatory. It includes all that is invested to create a product. In industrial terms, input includes raw material, infrastructure and human resources.

Process: The term 'process' implies, largely, the activities that go on to convert the input into a product or an output. Whatever a goldsmith, for example, does to convert gold into ornaments is the process.

Output: The output is the product that comes out of a system. It is the input converted through processes.

Environment: The environment is the setting in which a system works. It is an extremely important concept, particularly in social systems, for not only does a system influence the environment but also vice versa. Despite having equivalent inputs, rural schools generally perform lower than their urban counterparts; the rural environment is an important determinant of the system's efficiency.

Feedback: Set in an environment with a well-defined boundary, the input, the process and the output are in a linear sequence. Since there are causal relationships, it is believed that feedback has the potential to improve system performance in the quality and quantity of products through adjustment of inputs and processes, and sometimes by adjusting systems goals.

Systems have also been explained in terms of components (sub-systems) and their interrelationships. There are, however, no contradictions between these two approaches. The various components of a system mentioned above are represented diagrammatically in Figure 3.1.

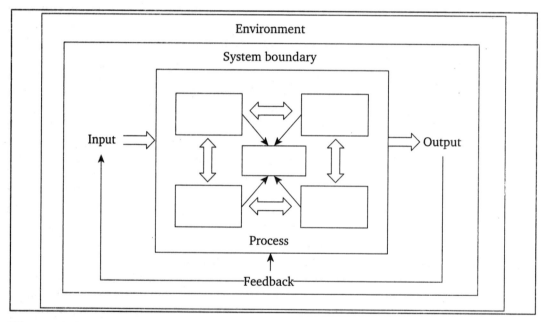

Figure 3.1　Systems approach

From this understanding of the general systems approach, we should now look at an educational institution as a system.

The educational institution as a system

An educational institution as a system has inputs such as students, infrastructure, financial resources and instructional resources. The processes are admission, instruction, evaluation, etc., while the outputs are the graduates and their behavioural, academic and physical qualities. An institution has a well-defined boundary and an environment in which it is set. Further, these components as inputs, processes and outputs are not independent of one another; they are interlinked and interdependent in a systemic framework.

Unlike in industrial systems, the inputs, processes and outputs are not cut and dried in educational institutions. The debate often is in defining the boundaries between the input and the output in an educational institution. This is primarily because the output at one stage is an input in another stage; it becomes a cyclic process. For example, management and administration as processes produce teacher satisfaction on the job (output). Satisfaction on the job acts as an input for improved instructional systems and student performance (output) (Figure 3.2).

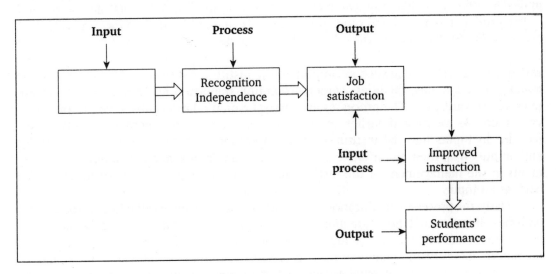

Figure 3.2   Output at one stage as input to the next

Another major complexity in applying the systems approach in education is the quantifiability and measurability of input and output. Within these limitations, let us look at what constitutes input, output as well as the process in an educational institution. As the word itself indicates, input implies such elements that are invested in an institution. Navaratnam (1997) identified students, employers, universities, parents, community and government as the customers and stakeholders of school education. Key inputs into schooling are curriculum, students, teachers, support staff, administrators, managers, facilities, classrooms and government policies. Key processes are curriculum development, accreditation, teaching, enrolment, financing or funding, administration, management, student support services, community services, commercial activities, human resource management, facility development and promotion and marketing. Similarly, key outputs are educated and trained graduates, research findings and community services.

In an industry, the raw material, which is the input, is processed to produce finished goods. Drawing this analogy for education, raw material in the form of students' cognitive, conative and affective qualities is processed through instruction, co-curricular activities, student assessment and other activities to develop the student's all-round personality. Just as industrial raw materials require machines, equipment, workshops as well as humans to be processed into a finished product, institutes also require teachers and principals as well as textbooks, laboratories, audio-visual aids, classrooms, sports facilities, etc., to process the raw material—the qualitative attributes of students—to transform them into educated and cultured humans.

From this analogy, the output of the education system is the quality of the students. This not only implies their academic achievement and excellence, but also their performance in other areas like physical, mental, emotional, intellectual, moral and spiritual.

The principal, teachers and other staff spend six to eight hours in a day and 220 days in a year for 20–25 years, in the school. Hence, the development of staff members, their career growth and their job satisfaction are also very important. Job satisfaction and career growth can also be seen as outputs of the institutional system. The inputs are the management systems, facilities, career promotion opportunities, provisions for incentives and rewards, etc. The processes are inter-personal relationships, recognition, motivation, etc. As mentioned earlier, in an educational institution, many such outputs are recycled as inputs into the institution. It is important for a principal to identify inputs and outputs with their quantitative and qualitative attributes, and also identify such elements in the management of the institution that are recycled—where an output is fed back as an input.

Similarly, the processes in educational institutions comprise instruction in classrooms, laboratories, libraries and field situations, examination, evaluation, co-curricular activities, management and administration, linkage and interface, etc. There are wide divergences in the nature, intensity and quality of these processes. Within the same school, there may be an effective mechanism of emphasizing and managing co-curricular activities, but the instructional processes may not be as well designed or implemented. There are schools with strong traditions of social service (linkage and interface) with average performance in academic activities. Just as in the case of input and output, it is necessary to identify various processes in the schools with their qualitative attributes. Further, in the case of processes, it is necessary to identify micro-processes for better management. For example, instruction in classroom, laboratory practicals, projects and field trips are micro-processes that constitute the instructional system. We will deal with this in detail later in the chapter.

Sub-systems

A system obviously comprises several sub-systems. The basic approach to systems thinking is identifying the sub-systems and understanding their interrelationships and interdependence. In fact, it is the interlinking and interdependence of sub-systems that configure a system. Hence, a sub-system can never be equal to the system. The sub-systems concept as applied to institutions has been defined and described in several ways. The various sub-systems are infrastructure, instructional systems, linkages and interfaces, management and administration, etc. In one of our exercises, we identified 10 such areas or sub-systems of an educational institution (Mukhopadhyay and Narula, 1992).

1. Vision, mission and goals
2. Academics
3. Personnel
4. Finance
5. Infrastructure
6. Linkages and interface
7. Student services
8. Rules, regulations, methods and procedures
9. Institution building
10. Managing people at work

The theme that cut across all these sub-components like the thread in a garland is the management of quality; TQM involves ensuring quality in each of these functions and moving beyond.

You would probably notice that the sub-systems vary from one another in their very nature. For example, finance and infrastructure are somewhat concrete and measurable while vision, mission and goals are abstract. Academic activities, student services, managing people at work are organizational processes. But their interdependence is obvious. For example, infrastructure and finance are mutually interdependent, as much as academic activities are dependent upon infrastructure and finance. And, vision, mission and goals guide all aspects of the institution. The interrelationship of all these sub-systems is depicted in Figure 3.3.

Institution building is the goal of TQM since it provides a management philosophy. Figure 3.3 indicates the interactive pattern of various aspects of institutional management for institution building—the ultimate goal of management. It also indicates the pivotal role of excellence in management—the qualities of a principal in managing people at work. In fact, it holds up the entire edifice of institutional management. On the top end are the vision, mission and goals that guide the path of development of an institution. Then there are 10 interrelated and interdependent components that actually constitute the institution.

Vision, mission and goals: Vision provides the direction of movement to an institution. Vision is futuristic, painting the picture of an institution as it will be in years to come.

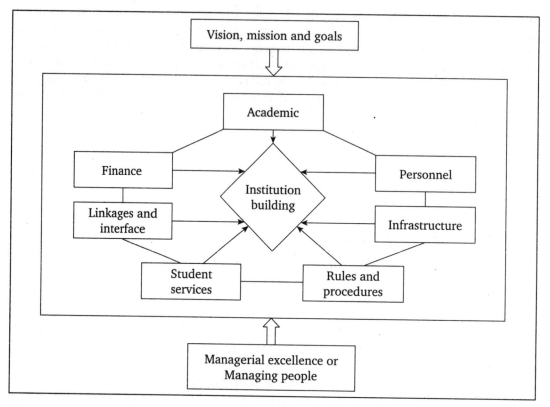

Figure 3.3   Interrelated sub-systems of an educational institution

Missions are 'unbundling of vision' into landmarks. Goals are the milestones on the way to the vision through missions.

   Academic management: Academic management is the core of an institutional process. It comprises planning and management of admission, curriculum, instruction, examination and co-curricular activities.

   Personnel management: An institution rests on the shoulders of its people. Hence, personnel management can hardly be overemphasized. Personnel management comprises personnel recruitment and induction, staff development, maintenance of personnel records, management of staff unions, conducting staff meetings, staff welfare, job allocation and management, etc.

   Financial management: There are several aspects of financial management in an educational institution. These are budgeting, resource mobilization, resource development and optimization, resource utilization, accounting and auditing, etc.

   Infrastructure management: While infrastructure is developed with resources, it is the foundation for all the activities of an educational institution. It comprises construction and extension of buildings, utilization and maintenance of infrastructure, library, laboratory, audio-visual aids, hostel, sanitation, sports and games facilities, vocational education facilities, etc. Proper planning and management ensures optimal utilization of resources to yield higher quality of schooling.

Linkages and interface: Institutions no more live in isolation. They are located in a larger environmental canvas where the institutions and the environment mutually influence each other. Further, with the new emphasis on 'client orientation' in TQM, the need for linkages and interfaces with 'clients' or beneficiaries has assumed new significance. The linkages and interface can be examined in relation to parents, old students, immediate neighbourhood and the community, local bodies like Panchayats, municipal corporations, authorities at higher levels, non-educational authorities like the public works department, transport, health, etc., educational institutions at the local, regional, national and international levels, employers, etc.

Student services: In the context of TQM, the quality of life in schools is more important, not just the performance in examination. Students are the main beneficiaries of an institution. Hence, student services hold the key to improvement of quality of life in institutions. The management of student services can be examined with respect to the creation and management of student (and parent) information systems, guidance and counselling facilities, student amenities, incentives and other facilities (scholarships, etc.), and involvement and student participation in decision-making.

Rules and procedures: Educational institutions are formal organizations, governed by certain rules and procedures that are common across institutions under one dispensation, say a university, state government or the Kendriya Vidyalaya Sangathan. Institutional management deserves understanding and dynamic interpretation of the rules, regulations, acts, statutes as well as various administrative procedures like purchase, departmental promotion, writing off, performance appraisal, grievance handling, inventory control and management, costing and cost optimization, etc.

Managerial excellence or managing people: Managerial excellence pervades all aspects of institutional management, and is based on the personal qualities of the principal as a manager and a leader. This component comprises understanding the self, communication (oral and written), leadership, group dynamics and team building, decision-making, management of motivation, time and change, etc.

Institution building: Management of an educational institution can lead to any of the three stages: organizational degeneration, maintenance of status quo or organizational development through the process of institution building. Institution building is the principal's *dharma* (religion is a poor translation). The Indian philosophy is loud and clear:

Swadharme nidhanam shreyaha, paradharmo bhayabaha.

To die performing one's duty is no ill;
But who seeks other roads shall wonder still.

(Matthew Arnold in *The Song Celestial*)

It is the religious duty of a principal to build the institution; neither maintain status quo, nor allow degeneration. What is teaching for a teacher is institution building for the principal. Institution building comprises several steps: institutional evaluation, organizational diagnosis, institutional planning and organizational development.

Each area comprises several activities or components. For TQM, it would be important to identify the most minute sub-components in each area. This, we will accomplish in organizational micro-analysis.

Organizational micro-analysis

Initially, let us examine one area: academic management. It constitutes five major components: admission, curricular planning and management, management of instruction, management of student assessment, and planning and management of co-curricular activities (Figure 3.4).

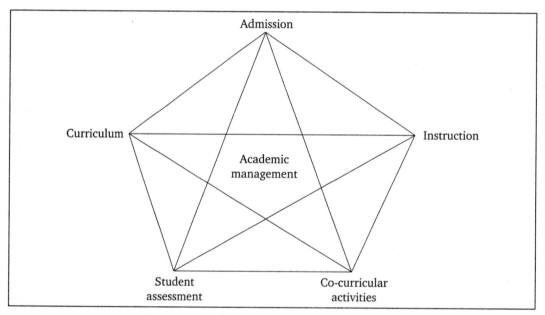

Figure 3.4   Interrelated dimensions of academic management

Figure 3.4 also illustrates the interdependence of the components. For example, instruction is dependent on curriculum, examination, admission as well as co-curricular activities. The quality of instruction is guided and informed by the quality of students admitted in a school, nature of the curriculum, expected learning outcome, etc. Similarly, depending upon the emphasis, curricular and instructional planning takes into consideration co-curricular activities and so on. Each component of academic management comprises several sub-components. This can be illustrated by further analysing the components of any one of the five areas. Let us take the case of teaching learning process or instruction, which includes the following:

- Classroom instruction
- Home assignments for students
- Project work
- Laboratory practicals
- Field visits
- Others like peer group consultation and Internet surfing

Let us go one step further and analyse classroom instruction, which may comprise a whole range of methodologies, including the following:

- Lectures
- Structured lectures (with computerized presentations)
- Cooperative learning
- Tutorials
- Video-based learning
- Workshop (design)
- Heuristic or discovery learning
- Others

The lecture, the most commonly used classroom instruction, comprises several component skills and competencies; about 21 different verbal and non-verbal skills have been identified through research on micro-teaching. The most commonly used verbal skills are as follows:

- Introduction
- Explanation
- Illustration with examples
- Using chalkboard/white board
- Asking questions
- Reinforcing student response
- Summarization

Non-verbal skills include movement in the classroom, hand and facial gestures, etc. This stage-wise analysis of different components and their sub-components and micro-components is called organizational micro-analysis. In this example, we analysed the following:

1. Academic management (in four components)
2. Of the four, analysed teaching-learning process (in six components)
3. Of the six, classroom instruction (in eight micro-components)
4. Of the eight, lectures (in seven micro-components)

This is four-stage organizational micro-analysis. A similar analysis needs to be carried out in all other areas. There are two important implications of this for TQM.

First, in order to understand and appreciate systems approach and need for holistic consideration of organizational management, it is important and necessary to identify the various micro-components that constitute the system. The greater the details of the micro-components known, the greater is the understanding of what constitutes the system and, therefore, the more sound the basis for systems approach.

Second, success in TQM is guided by management of quality of each micro-component of an organization. For example, research on micro-teaching proves that the quality of a classroom lecture can be substantially improved by improving the quality of each of the component skills identified above and its integration into the total process. Thus, organizational micro-analysis provides a sound tool for TQM.

Let us illustrate this point with a mundane event that happens every day in our homes. To prepare a curry, we need a host of things: oil/*ghee*, turmeric, chilly, mustard seeds, two or three vegetables, utensils, oven, a platform, light, ventilation, etc. While these are analytical components of the curry, the end product is synthetic. Now for quality management, we ensure the quality of each item as well as the quality of each process: size of vegetable pieces, degree of cleanliness after washing, amount of oil and temperature at which vegetables are put in, timing of putting the spices and so on. Other considerations are sequence of events, time, frequency and rigour of stirring, low versus high heat and so on. Thus, quality management in preparing a curry needs an analytical as well as a synthetic view. This is equally true if we take the organization of our drawing room or our library in the institute.

It should be evident that various dimensions (sub-components for sub-systems) of management of an educational institution are actually inseparable. A change in any one area triggers off changes in many others. Hence, it is essential that the entire institution is kept in focus for TQM. Ensuring quality in management of every sub-component will not only have summative but also productive effects in achieving TQM in an educational institution. For practitioners, it is advisable that such micro-analysis is carried out at least to the third or fourth level.

Although in systems thinking, there have been efforts in applying input–process–output models for management of educational institution, there are certain inherent difficulties. Educational institutions include human beings who are sensitive, temperamental and diverse in terms of their instinctive qualities. For example, a school or a college admits students of varying patterns of intelligence (Gardener, 1983), emotional intelligence and maturity, creativity and other attributes. Even students with the same degree of abstract or academic intelligence differ in their behavioural attributes and also in academic performance on the basis of their emotional maturity. Yet, there is indeed scope for holistic systemic thinking for TQM.

The main argument in favour of the application of a systems approach to management of educational institutions is that it can ensure that the institution is seen as a dynamic living organism and not as a static conglomeration of various tasks, people and infrastructure. The latter fragmented view is manifested in various ways, such as teachers, placed in charge of examinations, the library or student activities consider their respective areas as the most important and thus insist on priority. However, the head of an institution cannot afford to possess such a fragmented view.

Similarly, principals who are good teachers and enjoy teaching tend to devote most of their energies into teaching at the cost of other areas of institutional management. There are others who enjoy the 'authority' associated with the position and concentrate on rules and regulations and financial management; the academic management or management of interface and linkage with the outside world gets neglected. Only late in the day do they figure out lop-sided developments in the institution where hands do not cooperate with the legs, and the collective body (staff) refuses to work with the mind (the principal). Institution building, the central agenda of TQM in education, is a wholesome game. There has to be a holistic view and consideration. Further, it is important to percolate systems thinking down to the staff to facilitate understanding of the mutuality of roles, functions and interdependence of sub-systems.

Conclusion

In Chapter 2, we referred to the concept of total quality mind and the Indian emphasis on a state of bliss as the indicator of total quality. This paradigm is equally valid for institutions and organizations. Some institutions manage their bare survival with reluctant teachers and learners huddled in dingy, unclean classrooms; some others manage marginally beyond survival with some scarce enthusiasm; some are agog with activities keenly involved in the knowledge enterprise and yet others emit the fragrance of intense human relationships, concerns and love for each other and stay in the mood of celebration and joy. Knowledge in systems approach has so far been able to measure and reflect on the basics of the system constructs.

Each educational institution has a unique personality. Though there are elements common to both the structure and processes, the way these components relate to one another and create the configuration of an institution is unique. That is exactly how some institutions revel in academic achievement, some others in sports and games, and yet others in cultural activities though affiliated to the same board of secondary education, or the same university, evidently guided by the same set of rules and regulations, and even curriculum and examination. Indeed, this warrants looking at each institution as an independent being, a system. For TQM, the onus is on the principal. He/she must begin with organizational micro-analysis and contain the components in a systems framework. It requires lesser cognitive skills to conceptualize micro-components since these are more concrete. Synthesis or systems concept is relatively abstract, hence challenges higher order cognition. Nonetheless, the principal ought to look at his/her institution as a total organism, not as fragments of activities and structures, and transmit the concepts to others in the system.

Percener Focus: Involving All

4

Introduction

Customer focus has been the backbone of the philosophy of total quality management (TQM), indeed its ultimate goal. This is a relevant question since the saleability of industrial products or service packages depends upon customer satisfaction and demand. This becomes more important as one moves from monopolies to competitive markets. But who is the customer? And what are the indicators of the customer's satisfaction? How does one assess whether a customer is satisfied or not?

The answers are relatively easy in case of industrial products. Anyone and everyone who buys and/or consumes (uses) a product indicates some degree of satisfaction. Growth in sales provides a better indicator. So, consumers of products are the customers. The definition of customer can become more complicated as one moves from industry to service sector, and within that, to education. The most complex question is who is the customer in education: students, parents, employers, community, government or all? If students are customers, who or what is the product? This set of questions need to be examined.

Customer or percener

The connotation of the word 'customer' is a commercial relationship, based on the transaction of goods or services in exchange of money between two individuals or two groups. Indian education has been sensitive to such a concept. The customer is an inconvenient word in Indian education because the word labels the teacher as a supplier and the student as a consumer. This kind of teacher–student relationship is culturally alien to Indian society.

Education has been cradled in the *gurukulas*. And the Indian psyche is still attached to the concept of the teacher as a guru. Evidently, the guru is not just a teacher but much more. A teacher teaches but a guru dispels darkness.

Agyana timirandhasya gyananjana salakaya
Tat padam darshitam jena tashmoyee Sri gurabe namaha

The guru dispels the darkness of the mind caused by attachments to the senses and body consciousness. In the Indian tradition, the preceptor is to be treated as God: *acharya deva bhava*.

The word 'guru' has now entered the international vocabulary. Sallis (1996) refers to Deming, Juran and Crosby as the 'gurus' of TQM. This western use of the word does not represent the same spirit, meaning and implication as it is meant in Indian classical tradition. While the disciples treat the guru as God, the guru also prays to God that both guru and *shishya* are able to learn together and be equal to the expectations of the *shishya*:

Saha nababatu, saha nau bhunaktu saha birya karababahai
Tejaswinavadhitamavastu ma vidwisabahai

This indicates the sacred relationship between the teacher and the taught that has been the hallmark of Indian tradition. Hence, the word 'customer' connoting the 'delivery' of education in lieu of money has been largely unacceptable. Before we either accept or reject this western concept emerging out of materialistic philosophy, we need to examine the objective conditions or ground realities in Indian education, as they are today and likely to be tomorrow.

The British era brought in the new industrialized model of educational organizations, through classrooms and schools. The major changes in the new system were as follows:

- Students were enrolled with schools and colleges, no more with teachers
- Students learnt what was decided by the state, not by their teacher
- Teachers were recruited by the state; students had no choice in choosing their preceptors
- Teachers received cash salaries in exchange of classes instead of services by the students and contributions by the community
- Students paid cash fees to schools, colleges and universities(Government grants also comprise money paid by parents through indirect taxes)
- Good institutions charged more fees than the poor ones—higher price for better quality

Does this indicate that education since the British era has brought in a qualitative shift, leading to the sale of education for a price and teachers taking classes in exchange of money? Added to this is the contemporary aberration in educational systems: what proportion of teachers fulfils its commitment, taking at least the classes supposed to be taken in exchange of the salary?

Further, if we look into the parallel processes of education, a large number of students take private tuition from the very teachers that teach them in their institution. This is a direct transaction of money between teacher and students. My own village database indicates that even at the primary level, more than 88 per cent of the students take private tuition. In Delhi, and perhaps this is true of other places also, private tutors charge fees by the hour and maintain proper attendance records. There are also contract systems where a tutor contracts charges for the percentage of marks secured by the student. Private coaching classes or parallel colleges of Kerala are well-known. This scenario is almost all-pervasive though there are small islands of exceptions.

Now, is Indian education commercialized enough or market-driven enough to merit the concept of students and parents as customers and teachers and educational managers as suppliers? Is this trend likely to intensify as we move on through the new millennium and private initiatives in education become increasingly prominent? If that be so, irrespective of the discomfiture and cultural hang-ups, 'customer orientation' is a relevant concept in Indian education too. I shall not insist on the term 'customer', but the concept is extremely important for quality management.

Our search for non-commercial synonyms for 'customer' ends with words like 'client', 'end-user' and 'beneficiary'. I am not uncomfortable with any of the words that suit my readers provided it does not imply a donor–receiver relationship because teachers and educational managers are not donors; they provide education in exchange of money, either directly or indirectly. From these considerations, we may use the word 'client' or 'beneficiary' to mean the people whom other authors have termed 'customers'.

But education is a team game, a game of partnership and collaboration where every one—parents, teachers, state, and employer—has a stake in the education of the students. They cannot be placed in a hierarchy in terms of their importance. They all are partners and hence *perceners* in Secretan's (1999) conceptual framework. In the customer or percener orientation, the focus is on accountability and interdependence. The major agenda is to ensure that the customer gets what he or she pays for—value for the money (Navaratnam, 1997)—directly or indirectly, in the form of fees, opportunity costs and non-tuition private costs. And, from that angle, percener focus demands accountability— economic as well as social.

Perceners

On the basis of percener orientation in TQM, there is a paradigm shift in focus: from providers of education in the conventional system to the students in the TQM scenario. Figuratively, it amounts to reversal of the base and altitude of a triangle, inverting the pyramid (Figure 4.1).

In the conventional system, the highest importance is given to the principal and members of the Board of Governors. Their decisions percolate down to the teachers who implement; the students are on the receiving end—often passive. Students are handed down programmes decided by the managers. Simple questions like 'what do you want to

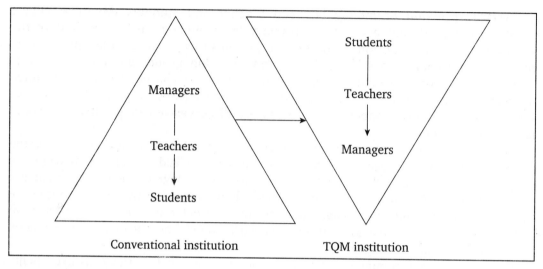

Figure 4.1   Shifting focus from managers to students

learn in physics?', answers to which can involve students and facilitate participative decision-making are absent. In the TQM culture, it is the perceners' needs and wants that determine the educational programme. In other words, educational programmes are designed by teachers and managers on the basis of the perceners' needs. This indeed is a paradigm shift in the culture of management of educational institutions. While percener focus is accepted as a major characteristic of TQM, who are the perceners? Students receive education; hence they are perceners. Parents and the government pay for the education; hence they too are perceners. On the 'queue' are employers, community, society, etc. Hence, perceners in education need to be looked at afresh.

For TQM, there are at least two kinds of perceners: external and internal (Figure 4.2). External perceners are parents, employers, immediate community and the state—government and the society at large. Internal perceners are teachers, non-academic staff, principal and educational managers. Students are internal as they are not only part and parcel of the institution but also the very core of the institution; they are also external since they are the immediate customers of the day-to-day transaction of education in the school or a college.

Among the external perceners, students and parents are central; government, community and employers are end-users of the human capital formed through education.

The aim of percener orientation in TQM is percener satisfaction. That challenges us with not only social and economic accountability but also a mutual moral accountability. We will revert back to this shortly. Before that, let us review the issue in the triangle of needs, wants and satisfaction as depicted in Figure 4.3.

We need to sort out the relationships among the three nodes of the triangle. There are several in-equations. First, customer needs may or may not be equal to wants. Second,

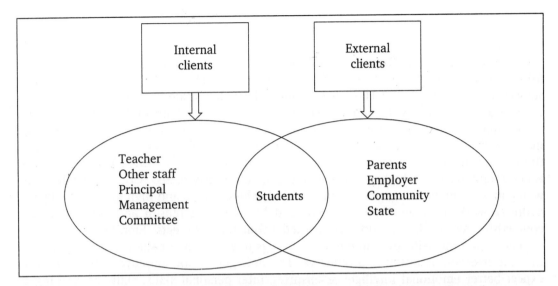

Figure 4.2   Internal and external customers and location of students

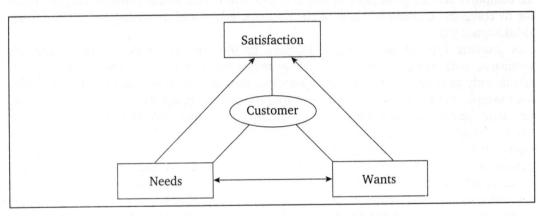

Figure 4.3   Customer's needs-wants-satisfaction triangle

the needs of different perceners of the same institution—students, parents, community members, employers—can be different. Third, percener satisfaction may not be equal to need satisfaction; it may be much more, depending upon, say, the satisfaction of wants. Hence, in education, customer or percener satisfaction is rather tricky. Drawing an analogy from Herzberg's classification, meeting percener needs is the 'hygienic' factor whereas meeting 'wants' is 'motivating'. I guess, satisfaction is beyond meeting the wants. Economic accountability is concerned with needs satisfaction (value of the money and minimum expected returns). Social accountability goes beyond and is concerned with 'wants satisfaction' (value addition). Moral accountability transcends the mundane and enters the inspired zone where education becomes a passion, beyond profession or vocation.

We need to ascertain what satisfies the students. Some relevant questions are the following: What do they want to gain out of a course? What do they want to learn of a subject or a unit or a topic? There is a popular claim that students want good marks and a certificate, not necessarily learning. There are, however, students in the same institution who demand 'actual education', not just marks. Parents, second on the queue, want high marks and certificate·but not necessarily without effort. Between the parents, I guess there is a difference in expectation between the mother and the father. The mother who is better endowed with higher emotive human qualities, associated with the female brain, wants human qualities, not merely intellectual achievements and high marks; the father, endowed with the male brain characterized by logic and reason and exposed to the competitive job market, is more concerned about job prospects. Employer satisfaction depends upon the skills that an employee brings in so that he or she is readily usable by the employer and is instantly productive. The new generation employers, however, also expect better emotional intelligence ensuring inter-personal skills, skills of working in teams, managing work stress, etc. Andrew & Yule, a multinational company, recruited all 12 computer science graduates of one batch of the Ramakrishna Mission Vidyamandira for its computer division because of their values, ethics and grooming in Indian culture (Mukhopadhyay, 2004).

A growing expectation among employers in the western world is the employee's familiarity with TQM (Tuttle, 1994). Many major Indian employers use marks and certificate only as eligibility criteria for application; they do not recruit on the basis of marks. For example, banks, the Life Insurance Corporation, the Union Public Service Commission, the state service selection boards, etc., conduct their own selection tests. Only those candidates who succeed and survive on a competitive basis are called for interviews. This is equally true of the admission process for institutes of higher education. Most universities, Indian Institutes of Technology, medical colleges and private institutions conduct their own entrance tests. Hence, the employer expectation is not the exit quality of the graduates but the entry quality of recruits in the organization. While there is no obvious one-to-one correspondence between exit quality and job-entry quality, what they look for is the nearest match or equivalence.

Government expectations also vary between the government as an employer and the government as the state machinery responsible for human resource development. As an employer, it also wants readily usable skills. As an agency responsible for deciding and implementing educational policy, its expectation is citizenship qualities that enrich community and national life. The immediate neighbourhood and community have their own expectations from a school. The teachers and students of Udang High School, a typical government-aided senior secondary school in Howrah (West Bengal) takes on itself the responsibility of fire fighting, epidemic and flood management and rehabilitation in the community. The local youth groups use school premises for staging plays and the school ground for sports and games activities. The community expects the school to belong to it. The community makes a significant contribution in the maintenance and development of the school, including its cultural life. The community expects students to be caring for the community and its interests (Mukhopadhyay, 2004).

Expectations of different categories of perceners of the same institution are different; and sometimes incongruous with one another. How does a school satisfy perceners with contradictory expectations? There are some common grounds to satisfy apparently contradictory needs. For example, high-quality instruction differentiated according to abilities, leading to mastery over learning strategies ensures both (a) good performance and high scoring as well as (b) good learning. Hence, it should satisfy students, parents and perhaps the employer too. Similarly, though students and parents expect good academic performance, they appreciate exposure and excellence in sports and games as well. In TQM jargon, we may call it providing 'beyond expectation'. It is true for human qualities as well; no parents, nor even the students despise them though they may not be prepared to pay the price for developing them.

There are changing expectations too. With the increasing number of competitive examinations for jobs and also entry into institutions of higher learning, students and their parents are realizing that good marks in the Board examination are no more an adequate or valid license to a higher education or a good job. Competencies and skills, including inter-personal skills, are necessary requirements. Children develop these social skills either by imitation or by non-deliberate emulation. There is hardly any school that offers a deliberately designed programme on social skill development. Considering social and inter-personal skills as important life skills, any effort on the part of the school to develop these skills will satisfy all categories of perceners.

There are two issues that bother us now. First, expectations are diverse and changing. Second, expectations are largely unassessed, hence unknown. For TQM, it is necessary to periodically assess the needs of different perceners. The problem of needs assessment becomes difficult with first-generation learners and their illiterate or marginally educated parents. For, their expectations are not adequately informed; and they may not have the skill or confidence to articulate their needs (Sansodhan, 1999). Customer orientation, the way it is done in the western world or can probably be done in the private fee charging institution in the Indian metropolis, may not be possible in all types of schools, colleges and universities. We need to build programmes for parents, management, community, etc., for developing and articulating expectations.

Percener education

While most rural parents think education is 'free' (school) or very cheap (college, university), they rarely realize that it is paid for through the indirect taxes they pay. Hence, education for their children is not by the courtesy of the state or the school. They have every right to ask for account and performance. This is just one instance. A large majority of the external perceners is still ill-informed about its rights and expectations. Hence, conventional percener orientation may not be as effective as it can be with perceners who are well-informed and who buy education directly from the fee-charging private institutions.

Another important alternative is to look at some of the specifications and examine whether customer expectations and satisfaction can be built around each one of them. There are certain input and process specifications, though not product specifications (Table 4.1).

Table 4.1   Input and process specifications for schools

Input	Process
• Principal/Headmaster	• Number of working days
• Qualified teacher	• Prayer meetings
• Salary	• Number of classes per day
• Teacher: pupil ratio	• Laboratory practical
• All-weather rooms	• Co-curricular activities
• Laboratories	• Study visits/Field trips
• Library	• Internal supervision
• Playground and materials	• Periodic inspection
• Audio-visual equipment and material	• Accounting and auditing

Percener education can be built around such input and process components. There are specifications for all the items listed in Table 4.1. These specifications are prescribed by the state. For example:

- It is specified that there should be 220 working days per year. Students and parents will be satisfied if a school actually works for 220 days in a year.
- For teaching in senior secondary classes, teachers should have postgraduate degrees. Should the school ensure that senior secondary classes are taught by qualified teachers, it should provide minimum satisfaction to the perceners.
- However, should the teachers teach well, be affectionate to the students and also cooperate well with the parents, percener satisfaction will be much higher.

There are two important points. First, these specifications are quality benchmarks. Second, the specifications offer only the minimum basic conditions. For example, will the students be more satisfied with a teacher who has a first-class postgraduate degree but is unconcerned about them and treats parents as unnecessary liabilities compared to another teacher with, say, a honours degree but very caring towards the students and respectful towards the parents? In education, specifications of inputs and processes are necessary conditions, but behavioural components, largely indefinable, are sufficient conditions. Thus, customer orientation and percener need assessment will need to be looked into from a whole range of behavioural expectations from the students, teachers, principals and other staff by the parents, and members of the community, etc., and vice versa. Incidentally, reputations of institutions are also built on such attributes. But these are the 'external perceners'.

Satisfaction of internal perceners is equally important in TQM. For, their satisfaction as mentioned in Chapter 3 becomes a significant input for quality management of the institution. The principal, teachers and non-teaching staff live considerable parts of their lives in schools. Their quality of life, including satisfaction, is directly related to their satisfaction on the job. Further, satisfaction of external perceners is significantly related to and dependent upon the satisfaction of their internal counterparts. A dissatisfied teacher cannot teach well; nor can he or she inculcate values in the students. Hence, understanding the needs of the internal perceners and their satisfaction is critically important in management of total quality. The needs of the staff are the following:

- Feel motivated and inspired
- Be able to work in teams
- Be satisfied on the job
- Be able to lead their respective sections or departments

TQM demands the satisfaction of such needs of the internal perceners. Leadership at the top echelon of the institution is responsible for management of motivation, staff morale, satisfaction on the job, building work teams, mentoring leadership, etc. This is another area of percener need satisfaction. There are many instances. Let me cite two instances to draw home the points.

1. During my service at Technical Teachers' Training Institute (TTTI) Bhopal, we visited a large number of polytechnics in the western region. All polytechnics in Madhya Pradesh are governed by the same set of rules and regulations. It was quite common to hear complaints about lack of facilities or mismanagement in most of the polytechnics in the state and in the region. The exception was SV Polytechnic in Indore, about which we never heard a complaint—neither in public, nor in private. The general attitude at SV was that 'in such a large establishment, there can be some problems and mismanagement; rather than being critical and upset, we try to sort them out'. Most teachers were enthusiastic and positive.

2. Jalgaon Polytechnic is one of the larger institutions in Maharashtra. In my first visit there, I found that the principal's table was spotlessly clean (no files), and he was busy calculating some examination scores. On my asking, I was told that he was doing some research on pattern and trend of performance of students in final examination. Having seen most other principals bent forward with the weight of their administration, this case appeared intriguing. I asked about his administration. He gave me a remarkable reply, and I quote, 'Well, my job is very simple. I have to manage only five people. My colleagues have a lot of work—they have lot more to manage.' On further enquiry, he clarified that he has to manage (lead) only five heads of departments including

administrative officer, but each head has large number of people and tasks to manage. Subsequently, I held detailed discussions with the heads of departments. What I learnt was that the principal worked with heads of the department at the planning stage, and encouraged them to implement their plans in their own respective styles. The principal removed roadblocks and mentored leadership among the heads of departments, and slowly but steadily brought himself to the background.

Both these cases are instances of internal percener satisfaction. It is this satisfaction that keeps an organization growing and self-renewing.

Supplier–receiver chain

There is a special relationship among the internal perceners, more prominently in the schools, in the form of a supplier–receiver loop. A Standard 7 teacher receives students from Standard 6. The quality of performance of the Standard 7 students in mathematics depends significantly upon their learning of the subject in Standard 6. Thus, the Standard 6 teacher is the supplier and the Standard 7 teacher is the receiver. The latter becomes supplier to the eighth grade teacher and so on. Performance in, say geography, among many other variables, is also dependent upon the articulation or language skills which is expected to be developed by the language teacher. It is hence necessary to recognize the interdependence among the internal perceners and their mutual accountability. We may now take a comprehensive look at the concept of percener orientation in TQM (Figure 4.4).

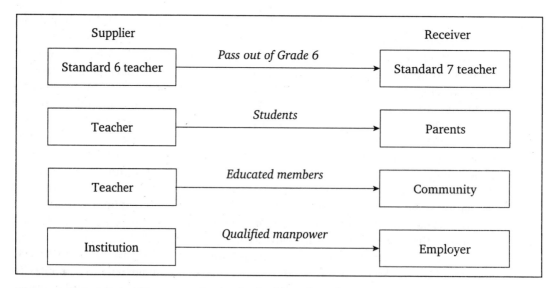

Figure 4.4   Supplier–receiver chain in schools

The fundamental issue in customer or percener focus in TQM is building education around the needs of all involved in the process of education: learner, parents, employer, community and the state. And, the needs of these perceners cannot be met without meeting the needs of the internal perceners. The challenge lies in strategic synchronization of meeting the needs of external and internal perceners. That brings us back to the conceptual shift from sectarian economic skill development to holistic human development.

The focus on perceners spells out a different philosophy and approach to quality management. First, by identifying internal and external perceners in the process of education it establishes the need for involvement of all stakeholders into the process of education of the students where students are not excluded from this framework. For, the onus of learning in the newly developing instructional sciences is on the students themselves as self-regulated learners. Second, it also builds a mechanism for activation and expression of mutual concern and interdependence; mutual concern or 'concern for others' is an important human value that education intends to inculcate among the students, teachers and all its perceners. Hence, focus on the perceners is not only sound strategy for quality management but an important moral option in institution building.

Conclusion

The purpose of education is the optimization of students' physical, mental, emotional, intellectual and moral potential. The focus on meeting the students' needs imply simultaneous development of all these aspects of their lives. It cannot be restricted to intellectual development. Hence, the primary issue in 'percener focus' is developing an educational programme that can simultaneously facilitate development in all five facets of human living. The human being, whether a 'product' of a secondary school or college or a school of engineering sciences, is never a finished product. Humans evolve every day. The focus of TQM is to ensure this process of continuous development.

In TQM, we must also emphasize on the important internal percener, namely, the teacher. Transferring Rabindranath Tagore's philosophic concept of a teacher—'A candle that does not continue to burn itself, cannot light another'—to this context, it would mean the following:

- A teacher who is not growing physically (health management to build inner strength) cannot help a student grow physically
- A teacher who is not growing mentally cannot help a student's mental development
- A teacher who is not maturing emotionally cannot help a student achieve emotional maturity

- A teacher who is not intellectually active cannot help another to grow intellectually
- A teacher who is not developing morally cannot inspire his/her students to achieve higher moral standards

TQM institutions need to develop an ethos that would ensure continuing development and evolution of teachers and a paradigm of educational programme that would ensure holistic development of the students, far beyond just the intellectual aspect.

Assessment of Institutions 5

Introduction

Quality management or institution-building initiatives must be based on a sound under-standing of the institution. Within the system's framework, the understanding must be able to map the strengths and weaknesses of an organization. Hence, as a matter of strategy, assessment of the institution is the first step in a total quality management (TQM) initiative. Besides indicating the relative strengths and weaknesses of an institution, such an assessment provides the baseline data on various aspects of the institution on which development could be built up. Thus, institutional assessment can be effectively used for organizational diagnosis and also for quality benchmarking. While Sallis (1996) deals with ISO 9000 in detail, some researchers have described the application of BS 5750 to a secondary school for assessment and quality benchmarking. There have been several other efforts at institutional assessment (DoE, 1990; Franke-Wikberg, 1990; Maassen, 1987; SCERT, 1993).

Institutional assessment and institutional evaluation are often used interchangeably. The Government of Maharashtra developed an instrument for institutional evaluation. Way back in late 1970s and early 1980s, I was involved in an elaborate exercise on institutional evaluation for polytechnic institutions. Ever since the publication of the first edition of this book, the Mukhopadhyay's Institutional Profile Questionnaire (see Appendix II) has been used literally in hundreds of educational institutions—schools, colleges, and teacher training institutions by the concerned institutions[1]—for assessment of institution and organizational diagnosis. There are several interrelated issues pertaining to institutional assessment. The major ones are as follows:

- Parameters of assessment
- Tools of assessment
- Participants in institutional assessment
- Quantitative versus qualitative analysis
- Use of assessment data

---

[1] Also, used by educational researchers for their postgraduate and doctoral dissertations.

Parameters of assessment

There is a wide divergence in opinions on what constitutes quality or what the indicators of quality of a school or college are (Cook and Semmel, 1995; Davies and Ellison, 1995; Fetler, 1989; Kevin, 1997; Moore, 1996; Navaratnam, 1997). Kevin mentioned sense of responsibility, open-mindedness, critical thinking ability, multi-language proficiency, and active interest in other cultures as the goals to serve as school quality indicators. Moore's study is on teacher quality for school quality indicators. Bryan deals with reforms to conclude that 'effective-schools research failed to produce unambiguous quality indicators'. Fetler's work, on the California School Quality Indicator System, deals with administrative mechanisms in quality management. Davies and Ellison's study is different from the studies referred above. Depending on the perceptual aspect of school quality, they identify three categories of respondents: students, teachers, and parents. The major issues identified as indicators of quality are as follows:

Students

- Quality of teaching and learning
- Satisfaction with staff
- Communications
- Standards of student behaviour
- Quality of school facility
- General factors and overall satisfaction with the school
- Extent of equal opportunities for students

Parents

- Quality of teaching and learning
- Satisfaction with staff
- Communications
- Standards of student behaviour
- Quality of school facility
- General factors and overall satisfaction with the school
- Role of governors in the school

Teachers

- Communication in the school
- Quality of working environment for the staff
- Professional environment in the school
- Quality of education supplied by the school

- Professional support offered to the teachers
- Role of the governing body
- General satisfaction with the school

Frazier (1997) advised keeping in mind several factors like identification of internal and external customers, surveying customers for valid requirements and satisfaction, scanning the environment for current and future trends, using a conceptual framework for establishing a baseline, and benchmarking for comparative analysis. Navaratnam (1997) mentioned that quality education is managed education. It would be evident that the quality indicators for a school vary from one category of respondents to another. This is largely due to client orientation vis-à-vis quality of schooling. There are yet other ways of defining parameters of institutional assessment. For example, Johnston County Schools' Total Quality in Education, cited by Frazier (1997), developed an instrument for directly assessing the status of an institution vis-à-vis the TQM paradigm.

According to Boyer (1996), there are five priorities for quality schools.

1. Building a sense of community within that institution
2. Centrality of language: the study and use of symbols
3. Curriculum with coherence
4. Creating a climate for creative learning: a place for active, not passive learning; a place where people learn to be creative, not just conform; where they learn to cooperate, as well as compete
5. Creating a climate that affirms the building of character for every student

Vanvught and Westerheijden (1993) identified meta-level coordinating body, self-evaluation undertaken within institutions, external peer review, publication of reports, and an indirect link to funding for quality assessment. Sallis (1996) presented a comparative picture of quality and ordinary institutions (Table 5.1).

Further, other scholars like Cheng and Tam (1997) proposed seven models of education quality (Table 5.2).

Such classification has certain problems. The educational quality cannot be built on either inputs or processes. Neither goal nor satisfaction can offer a comprehensive model. Ideally, these are seven components of a functional model.

The indicators of quality can be defined in terms of input, processes, and output. And, taking a cue from Davies and Ellison's study, it may vary among the perceners, implying what is a quality indicator for teachers may, or may not be, the quality indicator for parents.

One important way of identifying indicators of quality is to use systems approach and identify the components of input, processes and output. As mentioned earlier, the major problem is of the interdependence between process and product; the product at one stage becomes the input for the next (for instance, teachers' job satisfaction and teaching quality). During one of my workshops on quality management in educational institutions, the participating senior educational administrators cited the following five indicators of quality.

1. Discipline and punctuality of students and staff
2. Cleanliness and maintenance of the school campus
3. Excellence in academic achievement
4. Excellence in non-academic achievement
5. Organizational climate and satisfaction of the customers

Table 5.1 Differences between a quality institution and an ordinary institution

Quality institution	Ordinary institution
Customer-focused	Focused on internal needs
Focused on preventing problems	Focused on detecting problems
Invests in people	Is not systematic in its approach to staff development
Has a strategy for quality	Lacks a strategic quality vision
Treats complaints as an opportunity to learn	Treats complaints as nuisances
Has defined the quality characteristics for all areas of the organization	Is vague about quality standards
Has a quality policy and plan	Has no quality plan
Senior management is leading quality	Management role seen as one of control
Improvement process involves everybody	Only the management team is involved
Has a quality facilitator to lead the improvement process	No quality facilitator
People seen to create quality; creativity encouraged	Process and rules all-important
Clear about roles and responsibilities	Vague about roles and responsibilities
Clear evaluation strategies	No systematic evaluation strategy
Sees quality as a means to improve customer satisfaction	Sees quality as a means to cut costs
Plans long-term	Plans short-term
Sees quality as a part of the culture	Sees quality as another, troublesome initiative
Develops quality in line with its own strategic imperatives	Examines quality to meet the demands of external agencies
Has a distinctive mission	Has no distinctive mission
Treats colleagues as customers	Has a hierarchical culture

Source: Sallis (1996).

Table 5.2   Models of education quality in schools

Model	Conception of education quality	Conditions for model's usefulness	Indicators/Key areas for quality evaluation
Goals and specifications model	Achievement of stated school goals and conformity to given specifications	When school goals and specifications are clear, consensual, time-bound, and measurable; when resources are sufficient to achieve goals and conform to specifications	School objectives, standards, and specifications listed in the school/programme plans, e.g., academic rate, dropout rate, etc.
Resource input mode!	Achievement of needed quality resources and inputs for school	When there is a clear relationship between school inputs and outputs; when quality resources for the school are scarce	Resources procured for school functioning, e.g., quality of student intake, facilities, financial support, etc.
Process model	Smooth internal process and fruitful learning experiences	When there is a clear relationship between school process and educational outcomes	Leadership, participation, social interactions, classroom climate, learning activities, experiences, etc.
Satisfaction model	Satisfaction of all-powerful school constituencies	When the demands of the constituencies are compatible and cannot be ignored	Satisfaction of education authorities, management board, administrators, teachers, parents, students, etc.
Legitimacy model	Achievement of school's legitimate position and reputation	When the survival and demise of schools must be assessed; when the environment is very competitive and demanding	Public relations, marketing, public image, reputation, status in the community, evidence of accountability, etc.
Absence of problems model	Absence of problems and troubles in school	When there is no consensual criteria of quality but strategies for school improvement are needed	Absence of conflicts, dysfunctions, difficulties, defects, weaknesses, troubles, etc.
Organizational learning model	Adaptation to environmental changes and internal barriers; continuous improvement	When schools are new or changing; when environmental change cannot be ignored	Awareness of external needs and changes, internal process monitoring, programme evaluation, development planning, staff development, etc.

The emphases in all the five components are on the outcomes: excellence in academic and non-academic activities are tangible and overt, whereas outcome in discipline, punctuality, cleanliness, and job satisfaction are largely intangible and covert. Thus, certain dimensions are prerequisites for quality and certain others are the manifest forms of quality. From such a stance, quality is built on certain foundations, which are as important, if not more, as the known indicators of quality. Hence, the first stage is to clearly define the indicators of quality, as far as possible, in measurable terms. The quality of students, teachers, (leadership qualities of the) principal, physical infrastructure, instructional resources, and financial resources are some of the examples of inputs for quality.

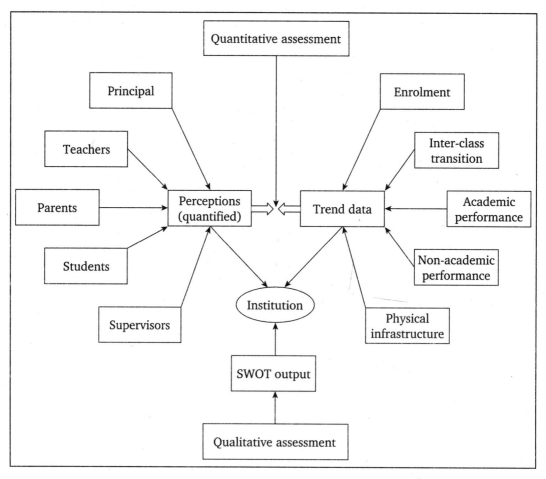

Figure 5.1   Mukhopadhyay's Institutional Assessment System

Similarly, the quality of classroom-based and out-of-classroom instruction, student assessment and examination, co-curricular activities, office management, and linkages with outside agencies are some indicators of process quality. Performance in external examination, zonal, district, state and national level sports, and other such co-curricular activities, staff morale, and satisfaction on the job, etc., are the indicators of product quality. What is really necessary is to develop and/or adopt a comprehensive institutional assessment system that covers all aspects of an institution. Further, such an assessment system should include both qualitative and quantitative methods of assessment (Figure 5.1).

Accordingly, the Mukhopadhyay's Institutional Assessment System (MIAS) was designed as the 360-degree appraisal mechanism where an educational institution is assessed by the principal and supervisors, teachers, parents and the community, and students (Figure 5.2). However, it is not necessary that all the different dimensions of the educational institution are assessed by all the four perceners of the system.

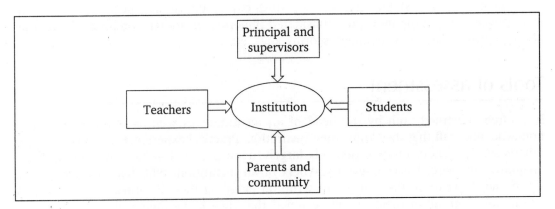

Figure 5.2   360-degree appraisal framework for an educational institution

The MIAS covers the following perceptual areas:

- Leadership of the principal
- Teacher quality: preparation, competence, commitment
- Linkage and interface: communication with the environment
- Students: academic and non-academic quality
- Co-curricular activities: non-scholastic areas
- Teaching: quality of instruction
- Office management: support services
- Relationship: corporate life in the institution
- Material resources: instructional support
- Examination: purposefulness and methodology

- Job satisfaction: staff morale
- Reputation

These are measured on rating scales developed separately for teachers, principal and supervisors, students, and parents. Similarly, the trend data covered in the MIAS is as follows:

- Class-wise enrolment with break-ups for girls and boys
- Inter-class transition rate
- Performance including excellence in academic areas
- Performance in non-academic areas
- Physical infrastructure

The trend data is for five years. Quantitative assessment is supported by qualitative assessment through a SWOT analysis. The MIAS covers almost all aspects of a school. It is, however, built on the indicators considered important in Indian condition. The MIAS also comprises tools for assessment, scoring keys, etc.

Tools of assessment

It is often construed both by the head of an institution as well as the academic and non-academic staff that they know their institution. Practical experience, however, proves otherwise. The understanding depends largely upon personal values and beliefs. In a qualitative exercise, I asked seven teachers of an institution, who had spent between seven and 20 years in the college, to write an essay on their institution in about 500 words. Although all of them initially claimed that they knew their college, they wrote different essays. They differed rather widely probably because of their perceptions, beliefs, and values.

In order to develop a more objective viewpoint of the institution, particularly for diagnosing its strengths and weaknesses, it is necessary to use a scientifically developed assessment instrument. There are several instruments developed to assess institutions. The evaluation instruments accommodate various dimensions of an institution that are identified as indicators of quality such as organizational discipline and cleanliness, performance of students in academic and non-academic areas, instructional processes, job satisfaction of the staff, reputation, work culture, etc. Whether you use a readily available instrument or design one especially for your institution, you must first specify the areas of measurement or areas of assessment and then develop assessment questions on each area.

There are several instruments for assessment of institutions. As mentioned earlier, the Government of Maharashtra's Department of Education has developed an instrument.

Johnston County Schools: Total Quality in Education (Frazier, 1997) is another such example. We will present here the instruments in the MIAS, namely,

- Teachers' questionnaire (MIPQ)
- Principal's questionnaire
- Students' questionnaire
- Parents' questionnaire
- Data and information blank

Mukhopadhyay's Institutional Profile Questionnaire (MIPQ)

The MIPQ has been widely used for generating institutional profiles. Although the MIPQ is largely used to elicit teachers' perceptions, it has also been administered to the principals and non-academic staff. The MIPQ comprises 11 areas that are considered indicators of quality.

1. Leadership
2. Teacher quality: preparation, competence, commitment
3. Linkage and interface communication with the environment
4. Students: academic and non-academic quality
5. Co-curricular activities: non-scholastic areas
6. Teaching: quality of instruction
7. Office management: support services
8. Relationship: corporate life in the institution
9. Material resources: instructional support
10. Examination: purposefulness and methodology
11. Job satisfaction: staff morale

The list indicates the inclusion of input indicators like leadership, teacher and student quality, and material resources; process indicators like leading, linkage and interface, teaching, co-curricular activities, office management, and examination; and product indicators like job satisfaction and relationships. It is implicit that these are critical success factors for quality.

This list takes basics like discipline, punctuality, and maintenance of premises for granted. The major difference in this case, however, is the emphasis on process—of leadership, teaching, co-curricular activities, examination, office management, etc. It includes the issue of quality of vital inputs like teacher quality, students, instructional resources, etc. It also includes within its ambit, intangibles like relationships, job satisfaction, linkage with the outside world, etc. The fundamental assumption is that an institution that is strong in all or most of these areas is a quality institution. Excellence in academic and non-academic activities as outputs missing from this list are presumed to be automatic products of a good institution (Deming's argument). These are, however, covered in the information blank.

The MIPQ consists of 110 items, 10 on each area of an institution mentioned above. Out of the 10, five are positively keyed and five are negatively keyed. For each respondent, for each area, the scores in positively keyed items are adjusted against the responses to the negatively keyed items. Hence, the summated score in each area can be positive or negative. Respondents are asked to respond to each and every item by checking out one of the five possible responses, namely, Very True (VT), Largely True (LT), Partly True (PT), Not Sure (NS), or False (F). For the purpose of scoring, a numerical value of 4 to 0 is attached to each category of response; the actual value depends upon the item, whether it is positively keyed or negatively keyed. In Table 5.3, an example is given on scores vis-à-vis response to a positively (+) keyed item and a negatively (−) keyed item.

Table 5.3 Sample scoring plan for positively and negatively keyed items

Items	Keyed	VT	LT	PT	NS	F
Teachers prepare before teaching (*Preparing for teaching contributes to good teaching, hence a positive feature*)	+	4	3	2	1	0
It is an isolated institution (*Isolation deprives an institution from understanding percener expectations and learning innovative practices from others, hence a negative feature*)	−	−4	−3	−2	−1	0

Respondents→ Areas↓	1	2	3	4	5	6	7	8	9	Average
Principal	8	6	5	−3	2	7	5	2	4	2.44
Teacher	10	7	9	6	11	5	7	8	6	7.67
Linkage	5	2	2	3	5	2	0	3	−2	0.67
Students	7	5	8	6	5	7	3	6	6	5.89
CCA	9	5	7	−4	−3	2	4	6	3.	3.22
Teaching	7	4	9	6	−3	6	4	−5	1	·3.00
Office	−3	−5	0	1	4	6	4	−5	−4	−0.22
Relation	8	7	9	6	8	7	6	9	11	7.89
Resources	5	8	4	4	3	−6	−4	2	6	2.44
Examination	6	9	11	5	7	5	9	3	8	0.78
Satisfaction	10	8	6	9	5	9	6	7	7	7.44

With 10 items—five positively and five negatively keyed—each area can have score ranging from a maximum of 20 ($5 \times 4 - 0 \times 5$) to minimum of –20 ($5 \times 0 - 5 \times 4$). The questionnaire, scoring key, and sample tabulation sheet are given in Appendix II. The scores in each of the 11 areas generate a profile of the institution. Organizational ethos and satisfaction are matters of perception. Let us take an instant case to illustrate what the MIPQ offers. The scores of nine teachers of a school on each area have been tabulated in the sample-scoring sheet. The average score in each area has also been worked out.

The tabulation sheet indicates several trends.

- In each area there is wide divergence in the perception of teachers, e.g., +8 to –5 on principal as leader
- There are divergences among the areas, e.g., from a maximum average score of +7.89 in relationships to –0.22 in office management
- Inconsistencies like good teachers as indicated by a score of +7.67 but not so good teaching by a score of +3.00 only
- There are apparent relationships between two or more areas, e.g., relatively high scores of 7.89 and +7.44 in relationships and satisfaction

In order to define a crude cut-off point/score to label areas as weak or strong, an institutional average score point is calculated by averaging the averages of various areas. In the instant example, 3.75 is the institutional average score. All areas with scores above 3.75 are stronger areas and all below that are weaker areas (Table 5.4 and Figure 5.3).

Table 5.4   Average scores in sub-areas of the MIPQ

Areas	Scores <3.75	Scores 3.75+
Principal as leader	2.44	
Teacher quality		7.67
Linkage	0.67	
Students quality		5.89
Co-curricular activities	3.22	
Teaching	3.00	
Office	–0.22	
Relation		7.89
Resources	2.44	
Examination	0.78	
Satisfaction		7.44

The plotted averages yield Figure 5.3, which illustrates the stronger and weaker areas of the school and also indicates their relative position among each other. The MIPQ can

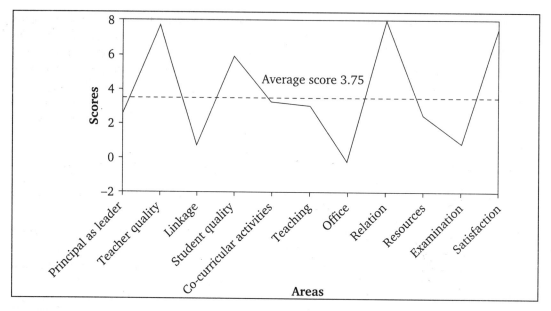

Figure 5.3 Organizational profile

be administered to teachers, non-academic staff, students, and supervisors. Each category of respondents will generate different profiles because of their differential perceptions of the various aspects of the institution.

Other questionnaires and information blank

- One questionnaire is for the principal, seeking his/her own perception in areas such as punctuality, relationship with teachers, decision-making, accessibility, his/her approach to management, etc.
- Another questionnaire is for the students, seeking their perceptions about discipline, support systems, human relations, and standards of academic and non-academic activities.
- Yet another questionnaire is for the parents, seeking their views on discipline, reputation, teachers' attitude towards students and parents, accessibility to teachers and principal, etc.
- The information blank deals with factual information and data on enrolment, transition rate, performance in academic and non-academic activities, resources and facilities (physical infrastructure, financial resources, and staff).

The scoring keys for each of the questionnaires are given in Appendices III through VI. It should be evident that the instruments have been designed to measure both facts and perceptions. Punctuality, discipline, reputation, professional support, and relationships are elements of perceptual measures. Excellence in achievement, enrolment, resources, etc., are factual and data based. Data over the last few years can be used profitably to derive the trend of development. The various areas where data-based assessment can be used meaningfully are the following:

- Enrolment in the institution
- Academic achievement: inter-grade transition rate and excellence
- Performance in co-curricular activities
- Utilization of library
- Inventory and utilization of physical infrastructure
- Inventory of audio-visual aids, and their uses

Most of the items in the questionnaire can be responded to either on a four- or a five-point scale. The scores can be summated to find the sub-total in an area. More than the quantitative aspect, however, what is important is to get the qualitative view of the situation so that the basic purpose of assessing institutional strengths and weaknesses can be achieved easily.

Although the first assessment provides the baseline survey, what is really required is the trend analysis over a few years. So, even at the first instance, the data on such items should be collected for five years. The data will indicate the trend of either growth or decay or stability in each aspect of performance of the institution.

Qualitative methods: SWOT analysis

A major qualitative method in organizational assessment and diagnosis is SWOT, Strengths, Weaknesses, Opportunities, and Threats analysis (Mukhopadhyay, 1989). This is a participative technique for organizational diagnosis whereby members collectively decide, rather identify, their strengths, weaknesses, opportunities, and threats. A SWOT analysis facilitates answering questions such as the following:

- What are the strengths that can be trusted and built upon?
- What are the weaknesses that need to be taken care of and improved?
- What are the opportunities for the institution that can be converted into strengths?
- What are the threats that need immediate attention so that they do not endanger organizational survival or growth?

There is more than one way of carrying out an organizational SWOT analysis. A relatively simple approach is to create a SWOT sheet (Figure 5.4), and ask every member to fill it in with brief one line statements against serial numbers in each quadrant.

Strengths	Weaknesses
1 2 3 4 5	1 2 3 4 5
Opportunities	Threats
1 2 3 4 5	1 2 3 4 5

Figure 5.4   Sample SWOT sheet

The compilation of the responses will indicate the convergence as well as divergence of views among institutional members. The findings of the first analysis are presented back to the respondents, primarily to indicate the convergence and differences in their perceptions. The participants are then asked to generate a common SWOT. This leads to rigorous discussion. Through discussion, respondents arrive at a consensus regarding the strengths, weaknesses, opportunities, and threats of an organization.

While there are several advantages of this participatory qualitative assessment, there are obvious limitations. For example, in collective diagnosis, very often, the articulate few dominate and overrule the silent majority who may have equal or better capability of analysing the situation. Increasingly, we tend to mix quantitative measurement with qualitative techniques. For example, teachers may first be administered the MIPQ. The individual and collated scores are presented back to the respondents. The SWOT analysis is then based on this data.

Participants in institutional assessment

The predominant hierarchical culture in educational institutions is an obstruction to participative assessment as much as participative assessment is a danger for hierarchical culture in organizations. TQM, in particular, emphasizes on involvement of all: from assessment to diagnosis to development to quality improvement. Hence, choice of respondents and participation of all or many are important prerequisites. Proper assessment depends upon the ground commonly known to the principal and staff. The case of known anmd

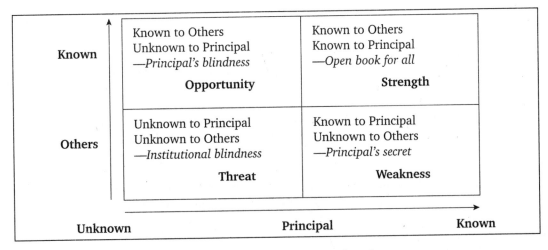

Figure 5.5 Illustrated Johari window on a school

unknown elements of an institution to the principal and others can be meaningfully plotted in the window panes of a Johari window (Figure 5.5) (Luft, 1970).

There are four window panes. Specific attributes are inscribed in each window pane. The important message in this window is institutional blindness as a major threat. Principal's secret as well as principal's blindness are equally serious weaknesses. However, principal's blindness can be converted into an opportunity if he/she is open to others' views of institutional assessment. With increased participation and sharing, the partition between known and unknown on both sides can move enlarging the 'known-known' window. There are two guiding principles in the choice of respondents:

1. Multiple category of respondents
2. Multiple respondents from the same category

Depending upon the size of the institution, the instruments can be administered to all or sampled respondents. Let us take the case of teaching staff only. Should the size of the teaching staff be under 30, it is worthwhile involving every one. Should the size of the staff be large, say over 75, a sample of about 30 can be taken. There are several ways of sampling. The two most important ones are as follows:

1. Index the names of all staff members alphabetically. Choose every third or fifth or tenth so that total number comes to about 30.
2. Categorize the staff into certain meaningful categories, such as

    - Female/Male
    - Experience, say, less than five years, six to 10 years, 10–20 years, 20 or more years
    - Age, say, less than 30 years, 30–40 years, 40–50 years, 50 years or more

- Subject specialization
- Nature of job (academic, administration, head)

Select the respondents in a manner that every group is well represented in the sample. For example, if there are 60 women and 40 men in the staff and you decide to have 30 respondents, choose 18 women and 12 men. Then take experience: choose 18 women in a fashion that they represent different cohorts of years of experience. On several areas, more than one category of respondents can respond and should do so. For example, students, teachers, and heads of the institutions as well as parents can assess the issue of discipline and quality.

The same procedure can be followed for other categories of assessors like non-academic staff, parents, employers, students, etc. The basic principle is to involve all categories of perceners who have a stake.

Administering the tools

There are just two ways: either you hand over the tools to the sampled respondents and they respond at leisure, or you call them to a place at a given time, administer the instrument then and there, and collect the response sheets. The loss of respondents when they are allowed to respond at leisure increases significantly without much improvement in the quality of the data. Since respondents will primarily express their perceptions and not facts, it is wiser to administer in a group at a pre-decided time and venue. Also, your instruction should include statements such as 'Please do not brood over any item for long; respond quickly and record the first response that comes to your mind. Do not consult one another. You may or may not write your name, but be frank about your assessment on each item.'

Quantitative versus qualitative analysis

Each questionnaire comes with a scoring key. Using the scoring key, the average score of the staff of an institution in all the component areas of an institution can be arrived at. A sample data sheet on the MIPQ, followed by a graph, has been given earlier. This provides an institutional profile that indicates relative strengths and weaknesses.

SWOT analysis statements can be tabulated under each head: strengths, weaknesses, opportunities, and threats. On one hand, the frequency of same and similar statements can be calculated; on the other hand, a detailed content analysis of statements can be carried out to assess the trend under each head. However, if the first exercise of individual SWOT analysis is presented and a discussion is steered towards consensus, this analysis may not be necessary.

In many of my experiences in organizational diagnosis, I have found it useful to use structured assessment tools like the MIPQ, quantify the data, and then go for qualitative analysis with or without SWOT sheets. A typical activity sequence of SWOT in such a case is given in Box 5.1.

Box 5.1 **SEQUENCE OF ACTIVITIES IN SWOT ANALYSIS**

1 Administer the MIPQ.
2 Score the MIPQ.
3 Tabulate and calculate average score on each area of the MIPQ.
4 Draw the profile graph.
5 Present the graph to the staff: 'Our collective view looks like this.'
6 Allow people to debate and discuss whether this is the real profile or a distorted one.
7 Try to draw the discussion towards consensus: 'OK, we may not be as weak in co-curricular activities as –6, but weak we are; should we say we are at point –4?'
8 Try to derive points of strengths, weaknesses, opportunities, (e.g., high-quality teachers), and threats (poor material resources).
9 Allow items not covered in the test to figure in the SWOT list.

The watchword is acceptability of the assessment by the majority of the staff, if not all. We must notice that till the development of the profile graph, it was quantitative. Subsequent steps are qualitative. The quantitative method provides a scientific basis to the qualitative analysis.

Use of assessment data

There are several uses of the assessment data. Three primary uses are creation of baseline, identification of areas and strategies for intervention, and development of mileposts for future development. Since TQM is a continuous journey, it is necessary to develop the baseline against which the growth and development can be compared. Hence, the first use of assessment data is to create a baseline on the status of various items of the school. The assessment of institutions throws significant light on their strengths and weaknesses. Understanding these strengths and weaknesses provides a logical basis for prioritizing areas of intervention for development. Simultaneously, the assessment data also provides clues on the methods of intervention. Just as quality is a continuous journey, so is the case of institutional assessment, which is carried out periodically. This, on the one hand, shifts the baseline and, on the other, facilitates setting new targets and new mileposts.

Conclusion

The assessment of an institution is not as difficult as accepting the outcome of the assessment. The institutional assessment brings to surface many known but not articulated realities as much as it unveils many unknown elements of the institution. Since the purpose of institutional assessment is not to categorize the institution as 'bad' or 'good', but to understand the relative strengths and weaknesses for the sole purpose of development, it is important to involve as many functionaries as possible in the assessment. And, a participative process is the cardinal principle of TQM. Further, the responses of different categories of people will paint different pictures of the same institution. It has to be understood and accepted that none of the pictures is either correct or incorrect; people perceive the same institution, even the same component of the institution, differently. What is important, in the context of quality management, is to understand and acknowledge the perceptual differences and make deliberate efforts to reduce the perceptual gaps.

Participative Management and Team Building

6

Introduction

Involvement of all, customer focus, and continuing quest for excellence are the three pillars of total quality management (TQM). We have moved a step further by reconstructing 'internal and external customers' of conventional TQM as perceners since education is a team game—a partnership involving parents, teachers, community, employers, and students (self-regulated learner). Involvement of all can be achieved only through participative processes; the percener concept can be validated and upheld only if all get collectively involved in the search for excellence. For TQM then, participative management and team building are non-negotiable.

This new participative management paradigm fits in well with the horizontal organizations possessing a collegial culture. In fact, the existence of a democratic culture in the larger socio-political scenario and an outdated bureaucratic structure in educational institutions is a paradox. The new social culture generates a special demand for participative processes in management. It also contributes to the optimization of capacity of the organizations through synergy among individual and group energies. Teams can be the most useful outcome of participatory processes; they can also be the instrumentalities for participative management. Participatory management and teams are, thus, natural allies of TQM.

Participatory management

For effectiveness of an institution, activities must be managed in participatory style (Rossmiller and Holcomb, 1993; McLenighan, 1990). Several studies indicate teachers' preference for participatory management and dissatisfaction with the absence of feedback, autonomy, and task-related interaction (Frase and Sorensen, 1992). Porter (1990) found that over 81 per cent of the respondents in a survey of librarians felt that participatory management increases job satisfaction; 75 per cent indicated that participatory management improves performance.

The principal of an institution plays an important role in developing the culture of participation in management. He or she adopts a facilitative style of sharing decision-making responsibilities on issues related to school management and administration (Haskin, 1995). Conley and Bacharach (1990) made a strong plea that 'a collegiate, professional work environment can only be created by adhering to a participatory managerial philosophy that respects teachers and professionals and decision makers, and considers specific relationships arising between teachers and administrators'. Emerging research literature on participatory management in education—both by itself and as part of TQM literature—indicates that participatory management is a viable alternative to conventional management (Sheane, 1993).

Democratic decision-making and participation exist as values in most educational institutions, though they have not become part of an institutional culture. During my three-year long work on TQM in education with a large number of educational institutions at the school and higher educational level, almost every head of institution claimed to have a 'very participatory approach' in the management of his or her respective institution. This was not necessarily how the teachers and the non-academic staff perceived the situation. Probing deeper revealed something interesting. In order to run the institution, tasks were distributed among people. This was construed to be 'participation' by the principal. However, the organizational decisions were not taken in consultation with the teachers and other staff, resulting in the staff perception that the organizational management was not participative. From the angle of institution building and quality management, a participative process must necessarily include both rights and responsibilities with regard to organizational diagnosis, policy decisions and development initiatives, strategic planning, implementation, and evaluation.

In the chapter on institutional assessment, particularly under the section on SWOT analysis, I have indicated how the staff of the institution should be involved in identifying the strengths, weaknesses, opportunities, and threats of that institution. In the process of such diagnosis, there may be conflicts due to variations in perception. The constructive resolution of such conflicts may require the adoption of managerial processes such as collective bargaining. I have tried this in several institutions, with success.

In my experiments, following the SWOT analysis, I would first ask the participants to list 20 areas for improvement in the institution. Data analysis indicated, across institutions, that the onus for development was thrown at others, particularly at the principal and college management. I deliberately insisted on this long list of 20 so that the participants would exhaust listing what others should do, and finally look at themselves. This can be tried out since it provides in-depth organizational diagnosis to a great extent. During my experiments, however, I changed my methodology and asked the teachers to suggest three development initiatives or ideas for improvement that could be implemented in the given condition. I encouraged them to brainstorm with each other in search of ideas and validation of their ideas. It took them some time, but this methodology was more productive. The ideas thus generated and fed back to the participants led to another round of discussions. In almost all cases, the institutions were able to decide on a few development ideas. Such ideas could be termed as incremental or as kaizens.

In the next stage, my questions to the participating teachers would be: 'How are you going to implement your ideas?' Who will be responsible? What would be the time schedule for implementation? What kind of minimum resources and support would you need to implement the idea and what is the source of the resources? What kind of problems are likely to be faced in implementing such ideas? How are you going to overcome such contingent problems? How would you know at the end of your implementation whether you actually succeeded? How would you monitor progress? Who is going to evaluate it?' Instead of answers spoken aloud and individually, I insisted on their resolving the questions collectively and on paper. This often led to the formulation of some kind of road map or strategic plan.

Such activities were carried out in a series of short, two- or three-hour workshops held over a period. This participative approach was not free of conflicts or problems. For example, in a very large senior secondary school, teachers identified office management as the weakest link, both to the collated response to the Mukhopadhyay's Institutional Profile Questionnaire and the SWOT analysis. Initially, the principal disagreed on the basis of his own experience about response from the office. I asked the teachers to shift from perceptions to narrate incidents to substantiate their views about weak office management. As they narrated several incidents with mutual corroboration, the principal woke up to new knowledge about his office. This led to the identification of new and innovative ideas for improving office management, including monitoring and evaluation by a team of teachers.

There are several instances of involvement of parents in development initiatives in schools and colleges (Mukhopadhyay, 2004). The obvious advantages of such participatory management are the involvement of all and ownership of the innovative ideas among the various perceners, particularly teachers and principal. This also adds to the diversity of ideas, which need not be the monopoly of the head of the institution. Further, by involving one group of teachers to monitor and evaluate the project implementation by another group, enriches mutual learning and facilitates the development of the learning community in schools and colleges. More than the technique in participatory management, the stumbling block may be the values and attitudes. Participatory management anticipates not only the participation of the principal but also the delegation of authority to the perceners. The latter is indeed a rarity. On the other hand, teachers may be found incapable of accepting and justifying the delegation, primarily because they are not developed and mentally empowered to exercise the rights with responsibility. As a result, participative management faces initial hurdles in the form of the attitudes of both principal and staff. It requires deliberate, continuous, and determined efforts to overcome such hurdles. More than anything else, it takes time. Interestingly, as the staff members learn to work in participative processes, themes emerge on the basis of the values, beliefs and work styles within departments and sometimes across departmental boundaries.

Team building

'Team-work throughout any organization is an essential component of the implementation of TQM for it builds trust, improves communication and develops independence' (Oakland, 1988). Murgatroyd and Morgan (1993) argued that to implement TQM, an organization has to be a learning organization, for which it is necessary to build teams. It is also necessary to share, test, and refine learning on a continuous basis. The team provides an important platform where new learning can be articulated, tested, modified, refined, and finally examined for the real value of learning. Taking a leaf out of the Club of Rome report, *No Limits to Learning* (Botkin, Elmandjra, and Malitza, 1979), maintenance learning equips us to solve known problems through known ways; innovative learning equips us with methods of coping with and solving problems so far unknown. The report argues that we know how to deal with wars with conventional weapons, but are almost clueless about dealing with nuclear war. When teams as learning organizations articulate, challenge, test, and refine learning, they try either to cope with solving problems unknown to them or solve known problems through methods hitherto unknown. Thus, it offers a framework for innovative learning.

Peter Senge (1990) differentiates between the impact of individual learning and that of team learning. In his view, 'Individual learning, at some level, is irrelevant for organizational learning. Individuals learn all the time and yet there is no organizational learning. If the teams learn, they become micro-cosmic for learning throughout the organization. Inside gains are to be converted into action. Skills developed can propagate to other individuals and to other teams. The team accomplishments can set the tone and establish standard for learning together for the larger organization.'

Murgatroyd and Morgan (1993) argue that teams are self-managing and autonomous; they learn to set their own goals, working methods, and means to assess achievement or failure. Such autonomy and self-management is the seed of the process of continuous quality improvement and self-renewal. As the teams develop the skills of self-renewal, the institution becomes a self-renewing organization. The quality journey is safe in such organizations.

Educational institutions have several diverse functions. Though teams concentrate primarily on one area, they are affected by other functions in the institution. For example, a team of teachers innovating on science education will be influenced and affected by the team working on student assessment and evaluation. The teams have the advantage of examining issues across various functions, for they are not only interrelated but also interdependent. Studies (Mukhopadhyay, 1989) indicate principal centricity in innovation and change in institution. As a result, institutions grow and decay with the coming in and going out of the principal. Teams protect against such eventualities; participative processes and teams provide the basis for organizational self-renewal and sustainability of change. This is also achieved through transformational leadership that facilitates team building.

There are, and there can be, several forms of teams in educational institutions. One such team is the project team. A project is a time-bound activity. Project teams can undertake small or large projects. Sallis (1996) argues, 'Ad hoc and short life project and improvement teams are key elements in the delivery of quality improvement. Teams have the added advantage of involving maximum number of people in the total quality process. Teams become the engines of quality improvement.'

For TQM and continuous improvement, the trick is to design a series of small projects with some common purpose and focus, even with marginal overlaps, that are easy to implement. They can add up to substantial gains and change for the institution. Should the projects be planned properly, these hold the potential to effect qualitative improvement in many areas.

Let us take an example. A group of three teachers teaching social studies in three sections of grade 8 or in three grades—say 6, 7, 8—decide to deal with 10 per cent of the syllabus through seminars by teams of students. They jointly identify the topics and prepare the students, who present the seminars. They, either as a team or as individuals, depending upon their engagements in the time table, observe each seminar. Wherever necessary, they assist the team presenting the seminar. At the end, they administer a pre-designed test on the topics. They also review the experience with the students and amongst themselves. They may find that students learn better, are more interactive with their peer seminarians, are motivated to prepare well for the seminar, enjoy the sessions, and so on. Teachers may find that preparing the students for something other than normal classroom management was a new and exciting methodology. The project can be extended, modified, and disseminated to other teachers.

However, most institutions practise the course team approach. Miller, Dower, and Inniss (1992) saw course teams 'acting as conduit of information to management on changes necessary to improve provision'. Whereas the academic departments are responsible for transacting the academic curriculum, the others are responsible for (a) time-tabling (thus using the time of the teachers and non-teaching staff, such as laboratory assistants); (b) use of audio-visual aids and other instructional resources; (c) quality of instructional processes; and (d) perhaps, marginal supervision and monitoring. Together, they form course teams. There are yet other possibilities where teachers of different subjects come together to deal with a subject.

There have been some interesting experiments in forming teams by creating matrix structures. The Technical Teachers' Training Institute (TTTI), Bhopal, has a department each in civil, mechanical and electrical engineering, education, and educational management. There are several other functional areas like student evaluation, research, audio and visual media, curriculum development, etc. The disciplines are organized as departments with a designated head. The functional areas are organized as task forces with an elected leader. These are the two axes of the matrix (Table 6.1).

People appointed in the departments as professors, readers, and lecturers choose any two work areas from curriculum development, evaluation, or research. Since the members of the task forces come from various departments representing various disciplines, inter-disciplinarity becomes a characteristic of each functional area in the institute. Since the membership of each individual faculty member is in two task groups, each group was

Table 6.1   Matrix structured organization

Task areas → Departments ↓	Curriculum development	Media	Evaluation	Research
Civil				
Mechanical				
Electrical				
Management				
Education				

fully aware of the activities and experiences of other task forces. One of the professors (head of civil engineering) as a member of the research task group became a fine scholar and trainer in research methodology. The task groups also provided opportunities for leadership development among those who were otherwise not in leadership positions, such as heads of departments. In the process, within two years, the TTTI developed formidable teams in evaluation, curriculum development, research, etc.

Diversity of roles in teams

Just as a team comprises several members, it also comprises several skills and role expectations. Mergerison and McCann (1985) offered some of the comparatively more acceptable roles.

- *Informing or advising:* to ensure that the team has all the necessary and relevant information, it is necessary to develop a mechanism for identifying and retrieving information from various sources
- *Innovating:* to accomplish new and so far unknown tasks as well as old tasks in a more cost-effective manner
- *Promoting:* to communicate and promote ideas within the team so that the ideas may not get lost
- *Developing:* identifying its detailed components as well as methods of implementing each component with linkage with one another to make an innovative idea more implementable
- *Organizing:* organizing people, activities, and resources so that the plan is implemented
- *Producing:* another related skill
- *Inspecting:* required, in a team, to internally ensure quality of process and output
- *Maintaining:* ensuring sustainability of the team spirit so that the team as a whole moves forward

- *Linking:* developing and managing positive linkages among all team members involved in planning, executing, and evaluating; only through linkages and understanding of interdependence can this mutual responsibility be discharged properly and the task accomplished

Development of teams

Team development, from incubation to maturity, is a long process. It is not necessarily trouble-free. Referring back to the experiences in the TTTI, I delineated certain stages of team building. In the first two or three meetings, everybody expresses their viewpoints about what should or should not be done, about what was in the best interest of the institute, about how people should behave, about how activities for the task force should be chosen and carried out and so on. From these few initial meetings, there is hardly any tangible output. What really happens is the generation of numerous ideas, the challenging and verification of ideas, the growth in mutual understanding of group members: their values, beliefs, styles of communication, and cognitive and non-cognitive styles and qualities. In effect, these meetings lay the foundation for the formation of teams.

After some initial meetings, the task groups sit down to decide who will lead the group. The leadership does not usually follow hierarchy. It goes more or less by whether someone is acceptable as an academic leader of the group.

In the next stage, the groups identify actual projects for implementation. Projects identified or developed are prioritized and screened in terms of feasibility and implemented. In the task group meetings, they exchange information on the status of projects and review them collectively.

This four-stage development of teams through task groups in the TTTI coincides well with the four-stage process of forming, storming, norming, and performing proposed by Tuckman and Jensen (1977) (Figure 6.1). In the fourth stage, the team has to decide to conform to the activities or transform. It looks for new ways of doing old things and also doing new things in new ways.

In fact, in and after the performing stage, the teams get into the trap of conforming rather than transforming because transforming requires a new cycle of storming, forming, and performing. In conforming, the very purpose of teams as building blocks for quality management gets lost. For TQM, teams have to be transforming on a continuing basis. From that angle, the development of teams is a spiralling phenomenon (Figure 6.2) rather than a linear curve.

The net learning from our experiences and also from relevant literature is this: a team cannot be built overnight, nor is it an accident. It has to be carefully planned and nurtured over a period until it matures and becomes autonomous and self-directive. In the process, training and capacity building for team building become necessary inputs.

Important requirements and tools of team development and management (nurturing) are training, capability building of the team as a whole, and empowerment of its members.

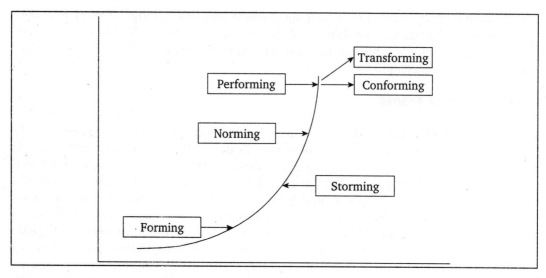

Figure 6.1   Stages of formation of teams

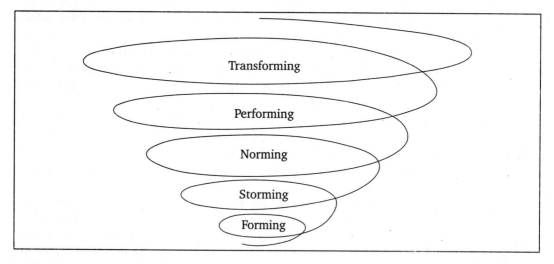

Figure 6.2   Spiral curve of team formation

TQM institutions need to invest in training on team effective working. There are several alternative ways of organizing training for teamwork. The best possible way is on-the-job training where teams can review their experiences and gain learning. The foundation stones of team building are mutual understanding, recognition of each others' strengths, and mutual respect. For hands-on training, teams need to develop a culture of openness where members feel free to discuss, without fear of conflict or misunderstanding. Team building can be substantially facilitated by carefully designed interventions by well-trained, experienced specialists.

Maturity and self-direction

According to Murgatroyd and Morgan (1993), team maturity is the basis for self-management and self-direction. As a team goes through the process of development, it learns many new skills and also counters many new problems on the way. Both failure and success experiences of the processes and products contribute to the team maturity. The maturity is indicated by its capability for self-learning and self-direction. Instead of blaming others—either within the group or outside—as and when the group learns from its experience and corrects itself to ensure achievement, it is on the path of development. There are some outstanding examples where an institution has been able to maintain its output as well as quality without either a head or a deputy head for months, even years. In such cases, the groups and teams have learnt to direct themselves. This ensures the endless journey of quality.

Effective and ineffective teams

A team by itself is not the panacea for all ills. Effective teams achieve better results compared to ineffective teams. Across literature, there are some common criteria that determine team effectiveness. Woodcock (1979) provided a list of nine characteristics.

1. Sharing mission and vision
2. Open communication
3. Trust and mutuality
4. Creative conflicts
5. Appropriate working methods
6. Appropriate leadership
7. Review and reflection
8. Empowering individuals
9. Linkages with other teams

Morgan adds 'fun' and 'celebration of successes and failures' as two other characteristics of an effective team. Should we superimpose Woodcock's and Morgan's contribution to our experience, the following attributes sharply differentiate an effective team from a relatively ineffective one:

- Mission
- Ambience: equality and collegiality
- Open communication
- Trust and empowered membership

- Power-based leadership
- Appropriate working methods
- Linkages outside the team
- Celebrations

Mission

When prospective team participants set the agenda or mission for themselves, they own it. Resultantly, the mission moves all members in a common direction and steadily cements their relationship. Thus, a mission binds people together in a team. The team becomes focused and the members move together. Effective teams clearly define their missions.

Ambience: Equality and collegiality

Teams are made of equals. Hierarchy is counterproductive. Effective teams depict equality and collegiality in practice.

Open communication

Effective teams practise open communication so that articulation, review, examination, refinement, and mid-course corrections, wherever necessary, may happen without fear. Open communication reduces the possibility of concealment of information by the information-rich, thereby reducing the divide among its members, indeed, the way the beavers work in the case of a breach in a dam (Blanchard and Bowles, 1998). Open communication also offers 'creative conflicts' (Woodcock, 1979).

Trusted and empowered membership

Effective teams allow arguments, disagreements, and contradictions with full trust in their members. They evince a culture of 'agree to disagree'. Effective teams recognize both the potential as well as contribution of individuals and carefully nurture the potentialities. Effective teams not only utilize their members but also empower them.

Power-based leadership

Since teams abhor hierarchy, they flourish with power-based leadership—a leader who uses inter-personal skills, rather that the position of authority, to influence the team and mobilize it towards mission accomplishment.[1] Team members ascribe one amongst them as a leader where, the premium is on leadership skills instead of on hierarchy.

---

[1] We will deal with this concept of power versus authority in greater detail in the chapter on leadership (Chapter 9).

Appropriate working methods

Guided by a mission and power-based leadership, effective teams develop appropriate working methods characterized by the following:

- Access for all members to relevant information
- A time frame for the completion of every activity
- Each member's familiarity with the interdependence of activities
- A specific responsibility to each individual
- Maintenance of good records of activities and/or discussions

There can be differences in working methods from one project to another. The important attribute is a team's maturity to collectively develop new and alternative methodologies.

Linkages outside the team

Teams are the building blocks of an organization. The blocks cannot stand independently and still make a building. Teams must be linked to one another. Effective teams make it a point to link up with other teams. It is through such linkages that synergy can be created for TQM.

Celebrations

Effective teams ensure joy, fun, and camaraderie at work. Individuals spend a considerable amount of their days and a large part of their lives in the organization. Fun adds spice to life and strengthens emotional bonding among team members. While it is not very common, many progressive institutions have introduced activities like a birthday party for the teacher, teachers' picnic, outings to the movies, etc., to build fun, joy, and comradeship at the workplace.

Morgan recommends the celebration of both success as well as failure. An effective team, open in communication, review, and reflection, is also open to learning from experience. Failing essentially provides an opportunity to learn from the experience: how not to fail, and how to build success on failure (Pearn, Mulrooney, and Payne, 1998). Hence, looking at failure with the same interest and enthusiasm accorded to success is an important indicator of an effective team.

Conclusion

There is very little doubt about the desirability of participative management in organizations. There is, however, a major gap between desire and action. Further, developing participative management also requires certain convictions, competencies, and strategies. More often than not, what is missing is the conviction itself—that participative management is a significantly better approach to management of organizations than managing organizations by designated managers. Beyond convictions are the techniques, skills, and strategies of developing participative management. Here are a few tips.

1. In meetings, ask the employees to state their agenda of action rather than telling them what they should do.

2. In subsequent meetings, ask the employee-participants to mutually discuss their agenda of action. Play the role of chairman but do not steal the show. Try to facilitate the discussion and optimize the participation and contribution of employees.

3. Allow and encourage participating employees to design and develop strategies for implementing their plans of action. Create occasions where they can share their strategies of implementation with their colleagues and get mutual feedback.

4. Allow and encourage participating employees to design a mechanism for monitoring their actions and also evaluate the results of their actions. Once again, you steer all that without imposing yourself.

5. Having gone through these four stages of involving participating employees into designing their own actions, implementation strategies, and monitoring mechanisms, raise with them the organizational or departmental issues. Please be careful; you are actually inviting them to discuss departmental or organizational policy issues. To begin with, they may or may not find it comfortable to discuss organizational policies. Many of them may refrain from discussing because they consider this to be the domain of their principals. It would take time to build such a culture.

The important point in developing participative management processes is to understand that there is a taxonomy involved in participative processes as well. The participation in action, namely carrying out activities as decided by others, is in the same category as maidservants participating in day-to-day household chores. The maidservants do not take any decisions; hence, they do not psychologically own the responsibilities. Similarly, in a majority of educational institutions, teachers are told (and dictated) what to do, how to do, and when to do. They are also told the mechanism of monitoring and the person to monitor. They hardly have a say in organizational policy matters. This is called the 'maidservant syndrome'. Meaningful participation is when employees are involved in decision-making—more importantly in organizational policy-making—in their own work space.

The key strategy for changing from the current style of participation to meaningful, active participation is to change from critical statements and affirmative dictations to learning to form interrogative sentences. In simple terms, instead of assigning the job to the employee, ask him what he/she wants to do? How does he/she want to do it? When does he/she want to do it? How would he/she like to be monitored? When and how would he/she like to be evaluated? Switching over from the current bureaucratic style of management to a democratic and participative style of management is not a smooth transition. It will be resisted by teachers, supervisors, and bosses. The reasons are not difficult to find.

Teachers are used to non-participative management; they do not need to take responsibility because they are not decision-makers. The decision-makers identify themselves with their decisions rather than the processes and quality of decisions. If they don't take decisions at their own level, they lose the very purpose of their 'administrative existence'. Participative management extends the sense of worthwhileness of action into larger number of people in the organization. As more people learn to take decisions, they are likely to appreciate the worth of their actions and also their own work for the organization.

Human Resource Development for Quality Institutions

7

Introduction

For total quality management (TQM) and institution building, nothing can be more important than the human resources in the organization. It can be pointed out that salary cost alone accounts for between 85 per cent (in higher education) and almost 97 per cent (in primary education) of the total institutional budget. Educational institutions are human systems. Hence, the quality of an educational institution—school, college, or university—is only as good as its people.

Educational institutions are knowledge enterprises (Mitra and Mandke, 2003). They perform the roles of knowledge creation, knowledge warehousing, and knowledge vending. And this very knowledge is exploding, not just expanding. Since the objective of TQM is to strive for excellence on a continuing basis, it is necessary to develop mechanisms for need-based human resource development (HRD) on a continuing basis. No wonder, all major gurus of TQM have recommended HRD as a necessary component of TQM.

What constitutes HRD, particularly for educational institutions? That is the moot question. It probably begins with selecting the right kind of people for the institution—the right people in the right jobs. Yet, it has to move beyond this static proposition; the agendas of HRD, of TQM, and of institution building have to accommodate continuous upgradation of professional competence, commitment, motivation, and inspiration.

Staff selection and placement

Given the employment scenario, it is important to recognize that the turnover in the education sector is very low. All those recruited, usually in their mid-20s, are likely to retire from the same institution in their early 60s, averaging a work span of nearly 35 years. Selection makes a tremendous difference to whether we induct assets or liabilities into the organization. This is the basic foundation on which HRD can be built up. There is adequate literature on scientific methods of personnel selection. Let us flag only a few important issues.

- Empirical evidence reveals that the personal interview is the least dependable tool for selection. In the hands of untrained interviewers—as most of them in universities, colleges, and schools are—it can spell disaster. It is only by accident that some right people get selected despite such untrained selectors on selection committees. It is necessary to use multiple selection tools such as tests, group activities, dependable references, etc., and then undertake a personal discussion. Like in an arranged marriage in the conventional Indian joint family, detailed backgrounds of both the bride and groom are examined, it is necessary to assess not only the aspirant's scholarship in the concerned subject and other cognitive qualities but also emotive qualities, ethics, and values.

- Unlike other professions, teaching is a profession that influences through knowledge creation, preservation, and dissemination. The process of influencing, by all evidence, is a cognito-affective process. Hence, just excellence in academic subjects and performance in a university examination may be necessary but far too inadequate to be sufficient to become a teacher. It is necessary to understand the values, ethos, and culture that a person brings to the institution with his/her appointment. Let me narrate an incident of staff selection to illustrate this point (Box 7.1).

BOX 7.1 SELECTION IN THE NIEPA

During a visit to New Delhi, an outstation professor met Prof. Moonis Raza, then director of NIEPA, at the insistence of a common friend. Within a few minutes of their first meeting, Prof. Raza invited his visitor to present a seminar to the faculty, which he followed up with a formal invitation. The professor came to Delhi and presented the seminar, but Prof. Raza could not attend. Within a fortnight, the professor received another invitation from Prof. Raza to help NIEPA design a module for a group of trainees from Sri Lanka. Prof. Udai Pareek, eminent management scientist, was also present. After about a month, he was again invited to implement the module. This time, Prof. T.V. Rao, another reputed management scientist, was present. On both occasions, Prof. Raza invited his guest faculty for lunch, and alone. So, they spent more than an hour together every time.

Hardly had the professor realized what was happening that he received a letter from NIEPA saying that it was looking for a professor of management, and would he be 'kind enough to send his biodata'. Subsequently, he was called for a 'discussion' with a group of experts, along with other candidates, and was offered appointment. Almost all the senior faculty members came to NIEPA through a similar process.

I asked Prof. Raza about this elaborate process of staff selection. His response was exemplary. According to him, bringing a full professor is like transplanting a full-grown tree. 'If we don't choose the right tree for the right soil, either the tree will die or it will damage the soil. A lecturer is like a small sapling that knows how to adapt to the soil; also the soil knows how to nurture it'.

The Indian Institute of Management, Ahmedabad, follows a similar rigorous process of one-to-one discussion with three/four senior faculty members followed by a faculty seminar.

- The other important point is the ethics of personnel selection. Over the years, the selection process has lost credibility primarily because it is governed much more by extraneous reasons than concern for the institution. To reciprocate the obligations of the benefactors, academically weak but well-connected candidates get preference over the meritorious. Such recommended candidates often bring in wrong values. Quality institutions can ill afford such unethical practices. Institution building and TQM cannot be founded upon poor ethics or wrong human values.

Understanding others

The starting point in planning HRD is to understand the intellectual, emotional, social, and moral qualities of the teachers and other staff. It is equally important to understand the relative strengths and weaknesses of each staff member. There are several ways in which such understanding can be accomplished. Individual staff members can be described in terms of their personality attributes e.g., Cattell's 16PF or Eysenck's Introversion-Extroversion, ego states and life positions of Transactional Analysis School, and *Satwa, Rajas,* and *Tamas gunas* enunciated in the Vedanta. In the current context, it may be useful to understand the staff through some institution-related attributes of confidence, commitment, and competence. These three qualities can be represented as depicted in Figure 7.1.

Although commitment–confidence–competence have been arranged in a sequence, it is not very easy to decide whether confidence leads to commitment or vice versa. Competence is based on both commitment and confidence since competence can be developed if commitment exists. Thus, commitment is the basis for the development of the other attributes. Let us elaborate these three attributes.

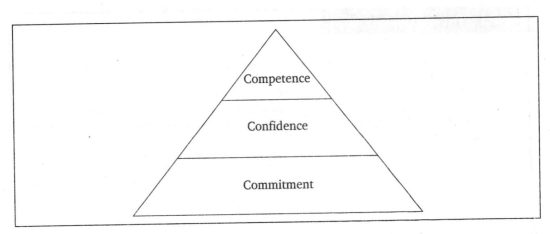

Figure 7.1   Commitment–confidence–competence triangle

The identification of competence and key performance areas has been done through job analysis of teachers by several investigators including Lalithamma (1977) and Panjwani (1982). Dave (1998) provides a comprehensive framework for understanding a relatively similar triangle of commitment–performance–competence (Boxes 7.2, 7.3 and 7.4).

The realms of commitment, competence, and performance are interrelated. Indeed, performance is the function of competence and commitment. Based on Dave's theoretical construct and earlier studies on job analysis, we can derive eight key performance areas.

BOX 7.2   FIVE COMMITMENT AREAS

1 *Learners:* love for the learners, readiness to help learners, concern for their all-round development, etc.
2 *Society:* awareness and concern about the impact of teachers' work on the degree of advancement of families, communities, and the nation
3 *Profession:* internal acceptance of the role and responsibility of the teachers' profession, no matter what circumstances one entered it under
4 *Excellence:* care and concern for doing everything in the classroom, school, and community in the best possible manner; the do-it-well attitude—'whatever you do, do it well'
5 *Basic human values:* genuine and consistent practice of professional values such as impartiality, objectivity, intellectual honesty, national loyalty, etc. (the role model aspect)

BOX 7.3   FIVE PERFORMANCE AREAS

1 *Performance in classroom:* including teaching and learning processes, evaluation techniques, and classroom management
2 *School-level performance:* including organization of morning assembly, celebration of national, social, and cultural events, and participation in school-level management
3 *Performance in out-of-school activities:* including such educational activities as field visits of learners, observation tours, etc.
4 *Performance related to parental contact:* including such matters as enrolment and retention, regularity in attendance, discussing progress reports, improving quality of achievement, etc.
5 *Performance related to community contact and cooperation:* including such issues as Village Education Committee (VEC) work, joint celebration of certain events by the community, eliciting community support in school development, etc.

BOX 7.4   TEN COMPETENCE AREAS

1 *Contextual competencies:* to provide a wider view of the development of education in society and teachers' role in it
2 *Conceptual competencies:* concepts of education and learning, psychological, sociological, and neuro-physiological aspects of education, etc.
3 *Curricular and content competencies:* according to specific stage of education, such as primary, upper primary, and secondary
4 *Transactional competencies:* general, by subject, by stage
5 *Competencies in other educational activities:* planning and organizing morning assembly, etc.
6 *Competencies related to teaching–learning material (TLM):* classical TLM, new educational technology, local resources, etc. as well as preparation, selection and use
7 *Evaluation competencies*
8 *Management competencies*
9 *Competencies related to parental contact and cooperation*
10 *Competencies related to community contact and cooperation*

---

1 *Planning:* planning the teaching schedule for the year, planning of units and lessons for course coverage within a specified time frame, planning laboratory activities, co-curricular activities, examination and evaluation, etc.
2 *Guiding:* though not officially designated, teachers help students—both inside and outside the class—in academic and personal problems
3 *Teaching:* classroom teaching, tutorials, group activities, home assignments, laboratory practicals, field trips, etc.
4 *Examination:* setting question papers, preparing examination schedules, invigilation, evaluating answer scripts, tabulating marks, declaring results, etc.
5 *Management:* management of curricular and co-curricular activities, classroom management, management of laboratory and library, field trips and educational tours, house activities, conduct of terminal, annual, and Board examinations
6 *Human relations:* relationship with principal, colleagues, students, parents, supervisors, alumni, other professionals (e.g., teacher educator), etc.
7 *Professional development:* reading, writing, lecturing, attending training programmes, seminars, conferences, extension lectures, etc.
8 *Extension and social service:* extension lectures, writings and publications, leading and participating in social action programmes, community development, etc.

These competencies can be classified into three categories and represented in a 3-D model (Figure 7.2).

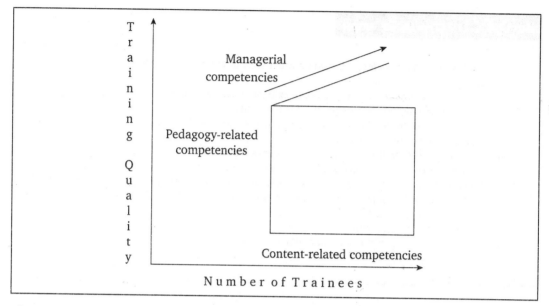

Figure 7.2   3-D model of training areas

Content competencies

Although, in teacher education, the emphasis has primarily been on training in pedagogy, all communication and pedagogy can be built only on a sound knowledge of the contents of the teacher. Knowledge and mastery of content, though not 'sufficient' is the 'necessary condition' for good teaching. The upgradation of content knowledge has become all the more necessary since knowledge is expanding at exponential rate. Recent studies on teachers indicate gross content deficiency of teachers. Hence, refresher courses on contents have been introduced as in-service education for all levels of teachers: primary, secondary, and higher education teachers. Content upgradation is a major aspect of HRD.

Education- or pedagogy-related competencies

Indian education is plagued by two major maladies: massive quantum of dropouts and underachievement. There are at least two facets of underachievement: (a) a large number of students fail in the examination; and (b) those that pass, pass with a fragile knowledge restricted to lower order cognition. Research reveals the contribution of school/college-related factors to the perpetuation of these two maladies. The major challenge lies in the development of sustainable learning with higher order cognition. This will necessitate a paradigm shift in the instructional processes in the institution calling for adoption of multi-channel learning set on the foundation of a constructivist paradigm. Given the new scenario, where learning habits and skills are changing, pedagogy-related competencies assume a new dimension and much greater significance. Take the case of EDUSAT, the satellite launched on 20 September 2004. It will facilitate two-way video-conferencing, resulting into nation- and state-wide virtual classrooms. Several pedagogical skills will be required—both at the teaching end as well as the reception end—to take full advantage of the learning network generated by EDUSAT.

Managerial competencies

These comprise organization of activities, relating institutional activities with community celebrations, parental contact and interaction, etc. In the TQM context, where participative management through team building is the hallmark, each teacher needs a new set of managerial skills of visioning and sharing vision, collective decision-making, working together, etc. In the context of multi-channel learning environments, the challenge is in management of instruction and learning (Mukhopadhyay and Parhar, 2001). Thus, there is a need for building managerial competencies among teachers.

Understanding others will necessarily include understanding the strengths and weaknesses of each individual teacher vis-à-vis the 3-D model of content–pedagogy–management. This should also help identify the training and development needs of each individual in the institution.

Quality management is a function of performance on different tasks. Performance, however, is the effect of a combination of willingness and competence. This combination of willingness and competence provides us a new opportunity to understand the people in the organization, through the Can do–Will do matrix.

Can do–Will do matrix

The competence (can do) and willingness (will do) parameters for each of the three dimensions—content, pedagogy, management—can be plotted in a matrix. People vary in the degree of their competence as well as willingness vis-à-vis a particular task. Both competence and willingness are distributed over a continuum; hence each can be assessed on a 5- or 7- or 9-point scale. A 5-point or 9-point scale will yield as many as 5×5 (25) or 9×9 (81) cells in the matrix, depicting as many combination of staff attributes. Though apparently more scientific, such a large number of categories is difficult to handle. To make it feasible, these two dimensions can be dichotomized, offering four possible combinations (Figure 7.3).

This matrix provides four categories of teachers, those who

1. can and will do (the safe and trusted lieutenants of an institution
2. cannot but will do (motivated but lack competence)

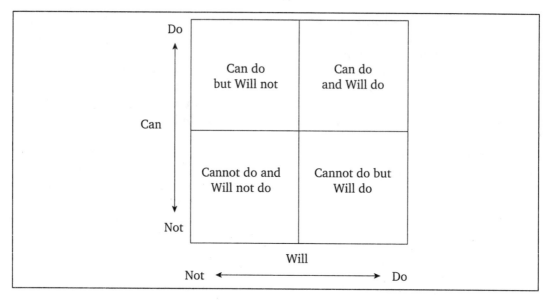

Figure 7.3 Can do–Will do matrix

3. can but will not (competent but unwilling)
4. cannot and will not (neither motivated nor competent)

From the perspective of HRD for building a quality institution, the following is the analysis:

1. Members of the first group search and find their own ways and fend for themselves. Self-regulated learners, they make use of any opportunity to upgrade themselves. They actually do not need much external help. The best help is to remove the road-blocks on their chosen path of development—(principal) just walk ahead of them, detect landmines, and remove them.

2. Members of the second group, since already motivated, can be developed faster. The deficiencies for each individual teacher need to be identified; tailor-made pro-grammes can be designed for each one. With the development of competence, this group will slowly move over and join the first group and strengthen the institution.

3. Members of the third group are the most risky. Competence without motivation to contribute is a competent negative force, and harms organizational health and development. There are numerous incidences where people in this category dis-courage others. In a girls' high school in a village, the principal made efforts to encourage teachers to increase their reading habits and range. Some of the new and young teachers took to reading beyond the routine school textbooks. They faced continuous criticism and bullying by two senior staff members, 'Oh! Are you going to become professors?!'

4. Members of the fourth group are definite liabilities. They lack both motivation and competence. It is difficult to motivate them and since they are not motivated, it is difficult to build competence in them. According to the situational leadership theory, this group belongs to the immature category. Direct instruction (telling) should work, at least partially. It is useful to assign them simple tasks and use 'authority' to ensure timely accomplishment. It is important to insist on completion; if need be, concede quality to begin with. As they learn to complete tasks on time, the element of quality can be introduced. For every task accomplishment, they must be rewarded with appreciation. As a matter of strategy, it is important to emphasize initially the development of competencies. Take one simple skill at a time and then move on to integration and complicated skills. Micro-teaching for improving classroom instruction is one such measure. As the skills and competencies develop, strategies appropriate for the other two groups can be applied.

In TQM, everyone must strive for quality. Hence, the challenge is to enlarge the 'will and can do' group and reduce the others. Participative decision-making is the key to people's involvement, and hence the key to creating willing and competent workers. This is an area of decision-making on facts. The principal can maintain a private diary and rate each colleague on competence, commitment, even confidence on a five-point scale. Give them the development input and rate them every quarter, half-yearly, and annually, based on data and facts (classroom observation, observation on co-curricular activities, etc.).

Although our emphasis so far has been on teachers, TQM perspectives must include all other employees as well. A college principal, at the end of a three-week management training programme in NIEPA, commented, 'NIEPA faculty is competent and committed. That was expected. What impressed me most is your Class IV staff. If you asked them to get something done in five minutes, they were right there in two minutes with the work—amazing responsiveness!' Yes, in NIEPA, faculty members are happily sold out to the commitment and competence of some of the junior employees. Let me elaborate. Group D staff is assigned the duty of facilitating railway reservations for the participants and internal staff. As soon as a staff member receives a requisition for reservations, he comes with a computer print-out indicating availability of tickets on various trains plying that route. He has picked up the skill of browsing the Internet to visit the Indian Railways website and check the reservation status. NIEPA has allowed and encouraged him to 'play' with the computer.

Thus, the non-teaching staff can be a great resource. Without its involvement and contribution, TQM would remain a daydream. It is necessary to carry out job analysis and training needs assessment and design development strategies for the non-teaching staff members as well. They really support the academic staff; but for them, the performance of even the competent academic staff can be dramatically low.

Building competence: HRD strategies for TQM

There are three basic requirements for implementing TQM, as far as the staff is concerned.

1. Quality consciousness
2. Striving for individual excellence
3. Teamwork

Any HRD strategy must contribute to more than one of the above goals, if not all three. In order to comprehensively cover all three targets, it would be necessary to develop a strategy that uses more than one method. Let us examine the following four approaches to HRD

1. Induction
2. On-the-job training
3. Participation in training programmes
4. Participation in open and distance education programmes

Induction

Induction is an important investment on staff. However, more often than not, induction escapes the principal's attention. There is often a great hurry to assign routine institutional tasks to the new incumbent. It is important to invest time on proper induction. Bharat Heavy Electricals Limited provided 18 months of pre-induction training to newly recruited, bright young engineers. Successful candidates in the Indian Administrative Service (IAS) and allied services undergo lengthy pre-induction programmes. Teachers are trained but just training is not enough. A new recruit should understand and get accustomed to the culture of the institution. Let me share an interesting case of induction (Box 7.5).

Two messages emerge from this incident. First, the new incumbent had ample opportunity to understand and adapt himself to the culture and ethos of the institution. He had enough time and opportunity to socialize, and get accepted by other colleagues. Second, a person will be on a job for nearly 30 years. If he does what he wants to do, he will contribute far more and better than if he is asked to do what he does not want to do. Further, if he has to contribute for the next 360 months, is it not worth spending one month on inducting him into the institutional culture? There are several methods of inducting a teacher into an institution.

- The principal introduces the institution: its culture, practices, programmes, specialities, etc.
- The candidate is provided pre-induction training. For example, the Indira Gandhi National Open University (IGNOU) has a regular provision for pre-induction training for its newly recruited academic staff.

Box 7.5   CASE OF AN INDUCTION

After submitting the joining report, the young teacher in a technical teachers' training institution went to the principal, asking for assignment of duties. The principal advised him to spend the next one month talking to the faculty, visiting the library, sitting in the classes, working in the laboratories, workshops, studio, wherever he liked including gardens, etc., and of course, going to the staff club. The principal's only expectation was that the new teacher should maintain a diary and time logbook for the month. Also, he was free to meet the principal whenever he needed; the principal would be available. The teacher met the principal only twice during the month.

At the end of the month, the new teacher visited the principal. The principal asked him what he was interested in. The new teacher, a civil engineer, expressed his desire to work on educational filmmaking. The principal called the head of the media department and informed him about the interests of the new staff member. He was advised to pick a theme from civil engineering and make films. The young teacher of those days is one of the leading filmmakers in education today.

- The newly recruited teacher can develop a schedule and, with permission, observe other teachers taking classes to learn about the existing and accepted teaching practices, classroom composition, and student ethos. Similarly, he can observe other activities such as library visits, laboratory practicals, co-curricular activities, etc.
- A young teacher can be attached to a senior teacher to assist him or her in arranging or creating instructional aids and materials, share and participate in the classroom proceedings in the team teaching format, assist him or her in setting question papers and assessing answer sheets, etc.

On-the-job training

Before an HRD programme is developed, it is important to diagnose the strengths, weaknesses, as well as potentialities of each staff member. Against each of the eight performance areas mentioned above, a profile can be drawn for each teacher indicating his or her relative strengths and weaknesses. The profile of eight areas of competencies (can do) may not be the same as the profile of commitment (will do). For a teacher, in some areas, the commitment and competency can match and be complementary whereas in some other areas there may be a gap (Figure 7.4).

This profile can be the basis for developing individualized development plans. Again, these plans should have data indicating the capabilities of a teacher vis-à-vis the eight identified areas. The initial data will provide the baseline on which developments can be compared over the years.

HRD has to be on a continuing basis. On-the-job training is an important methodology and has several forms. One of the ways is attachment of the new incumbent to senior teachers who guide him/her in all areas of functioning. Other methods are staff workshops,

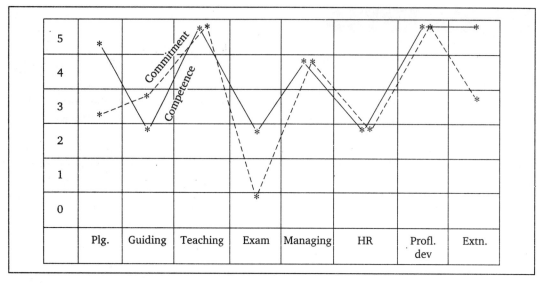

Figure 7.4   Can do–Will do profile of a teacher on eight areas of performance

planning and executing individualized development plans, job allocation followed by observation, support, and corrective feedback, cooperative learning programmes and projects, etc. Let us examine a few in greater detail.

Counselling interview

A widely-used approach is the counselling interview with the teachers. The principal, vice-principal, or even senior teachers can discuss, at an individual level, and provide constructive feedback on the competence in various areas. The only objective of such a counselling interview is to provide development support, and not to find fault with the teacher. The principal may have to handle the situation carefully at least to begin with. The principal may fix up one or two meetings with each teacher in a year depending upon the size of the institution. But before such meetings are conducted, enough data about various aspects of the teacher's activities must be collected. The data must be verified with the teacher.

Group activities

The counselling interview should encourage a teacher to participate in discussions in groups and receive feedback. Once such confidence is developed, it is possible to start group activities. A group of teachers, who share one subject say in undergraduate classes, can work together to plan the curriculum and develop unit and topic plans. They can visit each other's classes as and when they are free, plan the examination, and also plan counselling of slow learners across the sections. This process would obviously create opportunities for sharing each other's strengths and weaknesses, and a self-correcting mechanism can be set in motion.

Counselling and group processes have to be supported by professional inputs in content, pedagogical, and managerial skills as also self-awareness skills. The institution can organize lectures, seminars, and workshops on various content areas to deal with new developments by inviting scholars from local colleges, universities, national laboratories, industries, etc. Similarly, an institution can organize short workshops on educational technology, preparation of software, etc.

There is an interesting practice among the private schools of Delhi. As the school reopens after summer break, teachers join the schools two days ahead of their students. These two days are for staff workshops conducted by experts. Staff members develop their annual instructional plans and consolidate the individual plans to develop the departmental plan.

Journals for staff development

Journals provide an important opportunity for continuing education. Professional journals bring in new ideas tested through empirical research and also provide follow-up support for training. Hence, creating provisions for subject journals and educational/pedagogical journals in institutions provides support for in-house staff development. Besides subject journals, wherever available, three types of journals should be subscribed to:

1. Education in the broader context for widening the horizon, e.g., *Perspectives in Education*
2. Educational technology for improving instructional practices, e.g., *Journal of Educational Technology: Media and Technology for Human Resource Development*
3. Educational management with focus on institutional management, e.g., *Management of Education*

Indian journals of a standard equivalent to the international standard are usually of low cost. Also, they are more relevant to Indian schools. Three to four journals are available for about Rs 1,000 per year. For a school with 25 academic staff members, the annual investment per head is as low as Rs 40; it is still lower for school with a larger staff. An unconventional but effective strategy is to place these journals in the staff room rather than in the library. It requires special effort to go to the library and procure a journal. If it is placed in the staff room, a teacher turns the pages at leisure and may read an article that interests him or her.

Face-to-face training

Another approach to staff development is taking advantage of formal inservice programmes offered by various resource institutions at the state and national levels, like the Academic Staff Colleges, Institute of Advanced Study in Education (IASE), colleges of education, State

Councils for Educational Research and Training, State Institutes of Educational Technology (SIETs), National Council for Educational Research and Training (NCERT), NIEPA, as well as international institutions. There is now a large number of private institutions offering staff development programmes.

To derive comprehensive benefits out of all such programmes, it would be necessary for the principal to collect information on all such events and disseminate it to the teachers. Collecting training calendars of state and national institutions, identifying programmes that are likely to be relevant and contribute to the development of knowledge, skills, and attitudes of the teachers, vice-principals, and principals, and negotiating with them for the requisite berths are the first steps. It is important that the principal himself or herself attends training and development programmes at regular intervals. On completion of each training programme, there should be a debriefing session where the trained teacher makes a presentation to the faculty followed by a discussion. This will enrich both the trained teacher and other colleagues.

Wherever there is a chain of institutions, e.g., DAV schools, Ramakrishna Mission schools, Christian missionary schools, etc., programmes can be specially designed to suit their specific needs. Because of the network, the programmes will be feasible and cost-effective. For example, the DAV has set up an organization for HRD. Similar institutions have been established up by the Delhi Public School Society, Bharatiya Vidya Bhavan, etc.

Conferences and seminars are other important forums for learning. It is not necessary to write and present a paper every time one attends a conference. Conferences transact a large number of papers. Within a short span of three or four days, participants get exposed to 30–40 papers documenting contemporary research and thinking in a particular area. Besides, there is also the opportunity of interacting with peers and experts from other institutions, and listening (communication skills) to experts and guests. Finally, depending upon the affordability, institutions should consider deputing staff—teachers as well as principals—to international programmes. This provides an important exposure to the external world, bringing about a change in outlook.

Open and distance education

Open and distance education has thrown open new opportunities for continuous staff development. Several institutions offer flexible, short-term programmes. There are also postgraduate programmes in content as well pedagogy-related issues in education. There are also a number of short modular courses with significant relevance to institutional management. Educational institutions should take full advantage of such programmes.

Several institutions, other than open and distance education institutions, which deal with staff development are exploiting the use of distance education methodology. The NCERT, for example, has conducted several programmes for primary teachers and teacher educators through interactive television, supported by print material (Maheswari and Raina, 1997). I have conducted several of NIEPA's training programmes on management, including TQM in education, through this methodology too. Each such programme had a capacity of 400 participants. Full advantage should be taken of such programmes, since these are less expensive but more effective. EDUSAT plans to offer a massive opportunity for staff development through distance education.

Commitment and motivation

There may be a grammatical difference between commitment and motivation. For practical purposes, commitment implies affiliation and attachment to work or profession. This depends on the perception of the worthwhileness of the work one is engaged in. Although many teachers may have joined the profession by default or as a last choice, many others chose this profession because they thought it was worthwhile, and they continue to show their affiliation to all that they do. First key to developing commitment is to inculcate the sense of worthwhileness in what the employee does. There is the famous parable of the three stonecutters in a temple complex. When questioned what they were doing, each responded differently.

- 'I'm breaking stones.'
- 'I'm making a sculpture.'
- 'I'm constructing a temple.'

Although all three were actually cutting stones, they had differing sense of worth and pride in what they were doing.

Recently, a dedicated social activist while conducting a staff development programme for primary school teachers asked them, 'Why do you teach?' After a lot of debate and discussion, they discovered that they teach because they have the responsibility of developing the right citizens for the country. In their own statements, teachers hardly ever realized that they were engaged in such worthwhile work. In another instance, a professor was conducting technical sessions in a refresher programme for senior IAS officers. He did well. As a token of appreciation, two participating officers asked the professor why did he not join the IAS, which is by far the most important profession. The professor politely responded, 'I work in the mother profession—teaching. We produce engineers, doctors, lawyers, industrialists, ministers, bureaucrats, and what not. I am in the best profession under the sun. Indeed, next to God with her grace. I would have joined another profession if I could not make it to teaching.' This displayed a strong sense of worthwhileness in teaching.

Motivating is more difficult than building competencies. There are no formula solutions to this problem. It is, however, important to recognize that no human being can survive on this earth without motivation. People can differ in their locations of motivation. A teacher, who is extremely motivated and interested in his work in the institution, might prove a lousy householder. There are teachers who display high motivation as long as it is reading and teaching, but are completely disinterested in assessing answers scripts of students. Then there are teachers who are reluctant workers in the institution but great householders or community leaders. The challenge lies in shifting the motivation to the work situation.

Our experience teaches us that the Involvement–Responsibility–Recognition Cycle (IRRC) works with such people. The hallmarks of management strategy are the following:

- Involve them in decision-making
- Make strategic interventions so that they accept the responsibility of their decisions and implement them
- Recognize their contribution initially, in private and in public, even if it is not significant

IRRC has been found to work with many individuals. This should fetch dividends by way of moving at least a few from the third group to the first one. 'Gung Ho'-ing (Blanchard and Bowles, 1998) is a tested technique of inculcating willingness or motivation in work.

The second key to motivation development is independence. As discussed, educational institutions suffer from the maidservant syndrome. A maidservant takes care of all the work in the house without either authority or independence; she is given detailed and complete instruction about what to do, when, and how. No wonder she does everything with the missing zeal. Similarly, teachers and other staff members in schools, colleges, and universities are handed down the curriculum, syllabus, time table, textbooks, and examination schedule, without any provision for independence. Little do we realize that the commitment and willingness of the head of the institution is largely influenced by the independence he/she enjoys. This independence must be taken forward to generate willingness among the staff as well. Ricardo Semler's *Maverick* provides an eye-opener in this regard.

The third important key to generate willingness and motivation is 'cheering up'. Educational institutions must practise celebrating success as well as learning from mistakes. Human systems in general, and educational endeavours in particular, seem not to recognize their mistakes and/or unwilling to correct the malady; instead, they resort to blaming others, the 'system' being the victim most of the time (Pearn, Mulrooney, and Payne, 1998). Deriving inspiration from the training of the killer whale (Blanchard, 2002), commitment can be built up by using appreciation and positive feedback for desirable action, by ignoring and not criticizing errors. Seeking positive strokes is part of the human psyche. The strength of positive strokes should be fully exploited by using appreciation for even small achievements and contribution by the teachers towards the institutional growth. This motivates them to repeat the action to derive further positive strokes; in the process, it also bolsters confidence.

Inspiration

A large amount of literature on institution building is now emerging with the concept of spiritual or inspirational leadership. Lance Secretan's *Inspirational Leadership* is an important title on this theme. The main contention of such literature is to reconsider the relationships between people in the organization; 'controlling and motivating' is the old story where the new story is 'inspiring'. Compared to motivation being a psychic attribute, inspiration is the soul quality. Difficult to clearly spell out, inspiration is what happens to us when we remember names like Jesus Christ, Mahatma Gandhi, Nelson Mandela, Martin Luther King, Mother Teresa, and perhaps a primary or secondary school teacher unknown to the larger public.

The key to inspiration is to help awaken within the individual an understanding about his/her real self. Inter-faith research indicates that human beings are made in the image of God. Accordingly, his or her full potential is divine or perfection. As Lance Secretan contended, if we can see God in everyone, we don't need to manage them; we need only to help them to recognize that they are potentially perfect. The development of such recognition and self-esteem should create a self-propelling force within the individual. And, that's inspiring. The only limitation of this concept and approach is that it is not mechanical, it cannot be done by strategy. Only an inspired person can inspire others.

HRD blueprint

We have presented the concept and approaches to HRD for TQM in educational institutions. In order to fructify the ideas, it is necessary to develop a HRD blueprint. The following are the steps involved in developing the blueprint:

1. Let each teacher and employee engage himself/herself in an exercise of job analysis, rather task analysis. Each individual can use a work-time log sheet to document his/her day-to-day activities.
2. Let every teacher and employee identify the skills and competencies required to perform in each of the work areas identified. Further, let each one identify his/her relative strengths and development needs vis-à-vis his/her work areas.
3. Tabulate the training needs for all teachers and employees on a master sheet vis-à-vis each functional area (Table 7.1). This should provide enough data for clustering the teachers and training areas, e.g., a group of teachers may need training in content; the other on teaching skills, and may be some others need both.
4. Discuss with the staff the master sheet, and collectively decide the strategy of development—what skills will be developed through on-the-job-training, where and in which programme can one be deputed for formal training, and what can be done through organized and unorganized distance education programmes.

Table 7.1   HRD blueprint for TQM

Functions → / Teachers ↓	Planning	Guiding	Teaching	Examination	Management	Human relations	Professional development	Mode and length of training
A								
B								
C								
D								
E								
F								
G								
H								
I								
J								
K								

While preparing the blueprint, the following important considerations must be kept in mind:

- **Time scheduling:** annual calendar with a long-term framework since all the training needs cannot be achieved within one calendar year
- **Cost of development:** schedule to be managed within the limited resources of the institution
- **Affordability to spare a teacher:** negotiation between developmental needs of a staff member and the institution being able to afford to spare him/her from the institution
- **Sustainability:** one-time development effort to be followed up for sustainability
- **Review:** review of staff development at multiple points; first immediately after the development activity/training, followed by review every quarter, and an annual review to derive best advantage of the investment in HRD
- **Annual feature:** just as TQM is continuous search for quality, HRD in TQM is also continuous; hence make HRD planning, execution, monitoring, and evaluation an annual feature

Conclusion

The theme of HRD for TQM is developing quality consciousness among one and all in the institution. The entire exercise should be directed towards building awareness for quality as a culture. This will necessitate personal mastery over all the functions listed earlier. Meticulous attachment to the concept of the 'best' in all endeavours is a necessary prerequisite of TQM.

Importantly, the long-term goal of HRD for TQM cannot be restricted to development of technical and managerial skills and competencies. The goal in the beginning is to convert each one into an empowered doer who takes charge of the situation. From empowered doers, the teachers and staff members must move on to become continual thinkers. Only continual thinking can transform institutions into learning organizations; and only organizations that learn continuously can improve continually.

For continuous quality improvement, which is synonymous with institution building, it is important to recognize that HRD activities must go beyond the mechanics of training needs assessment, providing training, training evaluation, etc. The real challenge in HRD is inspiring the staff beyond development of competencies and even beyond motivation. The principal with his/her expression of positive concern about the staff and its professional development as well as the ability to personally influence the staff holds the key to success in developing human resources for institution building and quality management.

The solution to the quality challenge can be achieved to a great extent by helping teachers recognize the worth of what they do and by inspiring and cultivating work values.

Decision-making for Quality Management 8

Introduction

As breathing is to living, decision-making is to management. It is a part and parcel of management. It is the quality of decisions that either make or break organizations. Decisions are based on impressions and perceptions, and sometimes on facts and information. Often, the manager's decision is influenced by impressions based on one or two incidents. These impressions are developed by either listening to others or by observing a phenomenon or a person himself or herself. Some managers are a little more careful; they verify the impressions with others. This helps them develop a better perception of the situation on which the decision is to be taken. However, there are very few occasions where data and facts are collected before taking decisions. In this chapter, the main emphasis will be on decision-making based on facts. This is necessary since total quality management (TQM) aims at continuous quality improvement; it needs to base its development strategy on baseline information. Hence, data and information are necessary foundations for decision-making for continuous quality improvement, as also for institution building because decisions based on information and data provide transparency in management. Let us examine various ways of taking decisions in organizations.

Decision on files

Decisions are taken on files, in meetings or in one-to-one interaction/discussion. In the formalized bureaucratic system of management, there is an elaborate process of decision-making on files. Decisions taken in meetings as well as in one-to-one discussion are placed on file. In fact, till it is 'on file', there is no sanctity of the decision. The files move from one end of the hierarchy to the other, through specific steps. A typical sequence of decision-making in a bureaucratic system is as follows:

1. Head in the hierarchy notes on files, 'Please put up' and marks it to, say, the Administrative Officer (AO)
2. The AO records, 'Comments please' or simply signs, and passes it on to the Section Officer (SO)
3. The SO, in turn, initials it and marks it to his Assistant or the UDC
4. After the Assistant or the Upper Division Clerk (UDC) makes his or her propositions, he or she marks it to the SO
5. Usually the SO forwards the file to the AO with comments like 'Agreed'; some are overenthusiastic and paraphrase the same proposal, once again
6. The AO repeats what the SO has done and forwards to the boss who is, under rules, the 'competent authority'
7. The usual noting of the boss is 'As proposed'

This passing the buck style of decision-making is diagrammatically represented in Figure 8.1.

Some clever boss in the bureaucracy, who wants the decision in a particular fashion but is keen to hide his or her involvement, briefs the subordinate orally how and what to

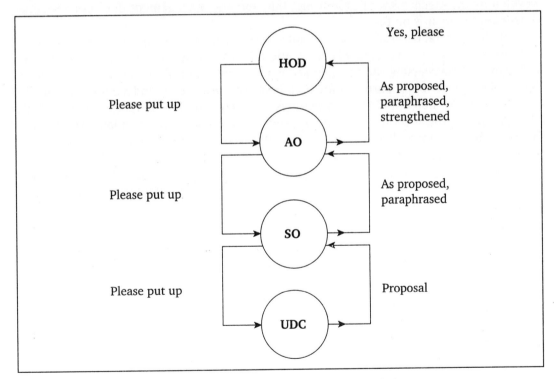

Figure 8.1   Passing the buck decision-making model

propose. This bottom-up approach to decision-making is safe for the bosses, but suffers from poor quality since the quality of the decision actually depends upon the quality of the person at the lower end (Devi, 1996) who proposes, and not on the others in the hierarchy. In educational institutions, this creates serious problems. For example, when training material was being produced in a management training institution for a programme on TQM in education, it was decided to process all papers on computers and take printouts on a common format. Down the line, a clerk decided that since some of the papers that were photocopied from printed material, were readable, though not easily, these could be photocopied without processing. There was no concern for quality of the product although this would send wrong signals to the participants about quality consciousness and concern. The main problem with such decision-making is the lack of vision and understanding of a perspective at the point of origin of a decision.

The second, but rare, approach is when the idea is mooted at the top end with a larger vision and passed on to the channel for 'comments' or 'please examine'. The file comes back with the comments; usually the comments are provided justifying the proposal on the basis of rules and regulations. There are wide variations in the quality of decisions, depending upon the source of its origin (Devi, 1996). Whatever be the origin of the proposition or the mechanism of processing, bureaucratic management does not recognize a decision unless it is on file.

There are several occasions when we take decisions in formal and even informal meetings and discussions. The relatively conventional format is when a meeting is held under a designated chairperson, the member secretary or convener of the meeting initiates and moves the agenda items, participating members give their views, and a decision is arrived at. Decisions are noted and the proceedings are recorded. The member secretary drafts the minutes of the meeting, gets the approval of the chair, and circulates the minutes among other members. If no comments are received, it is construed as approved by all members. Then the resolution gets the status of an organizational decision.

The third mode is the informal discussion. A note beginning with 'Discussed with you' usually follows this. The decision has actually been arrived at the informal chat. The note formalizes the decision.

What is important is that in organizational decisions, there are formalities irrespective of whether the actual decision was arrived at on file, in a formally convened meeting, or in an informal chat. The decision is invariably formalized on file.

Decision situations

There is more than one type of decision situation in an institution: (*a*) routine or conventional; (*b*) unconventional; and (*c*) rare and creative. Careful analysis of the files reveals that a very large majority of the files warrant routine decisions, e.g., staff leave, salary disbursement, purchase, admission, examination, etc. Many principals, who are competent and have developed a knack for management, take very little time to dispose of such files.

There are situations where unconventional decisions are taken on conventional matters. This needs, on one hand, dynamism on the part of the decision-maker and, on the other, a kind of systemic thinking and perspective. Let me cite a case to illustrate the issue.

A member of the staff of a regional institute put up a leave application for a personal visit to Chennai. The principal called the staff member and asked him whether he could take on the responsibility of some outstanding work of the institute in Chennai at the Directorate of Education. The staff member happily agreed to accommodate the assignment within his personal leave.

The principal asked him to send a tour plan for approval. The staff member confirmed that he would do the official work within his personal visit. The principal insisted that he should put up an official tour plan along with his personal leave application for two or three days.

The argument of the principal was that for the outstanding work in the Directorate, either he would plan a visit himself or depute someone else. The institute would incur expenditure on travel anyway. Now that a senior staff member was going to Chennai and was willing to undertake the responsibility, why should the institute not spend on his travel and also sanction the number of casual leaves that he needed so that he may attend to his personal work in Chennai as well?

The routine decision would have been to sanction personal leave to the applicant and depute another person to go to Chennai for the outstanding work. The dynamism in the decision-making is in combining the two, thereby saving the absence of one more staff member from the institute while simultaneously sending out the signal that the institute cares for and values its staff. The decision very likely motivated the staff greatly.

Though there are very few dynamic decision-makers, they take many such decisions because they often see many more alternatives to the same situations than what conventional-thinking people see.

Rational decision-making

In the above case, the head of the institute had several choices. He knew his options and exercised the choice judiciously. Indeed, scientific decision-making is in identifying the alternatives and picking the right one. This is the basis of rational decision-making. The approach to rational decision-making has been competently dealt with by Kepner (1965) in *The Rational Manager: A Systematic Approach to Problem Solving and Decision Making*. For our purpose, we will bring only tips of the thesis. There are basically two parameters in rational decision-making: search for alternatives and conditions that the decision must satisfy. In fact, this particular dimension of conditionality brings in rationality and the issue of decision-making based on facts.

Any major decision-making situation offers several alternatives. The best choice or the best decision depends upon whether it fulfils all or the maximum number of conditions. The conditions can also be divided into two categories: necessary and desirable. A decision must fulfil all necessary conditions. The best decision is the one that fulfils, besides all the necessary conditions, the maximum number of desirable conditions as well. Just to illustrate, let us take a hypothetical case of buying a house.

> The buyer has spelt out his or her requirements with clear specifications. She has also spelt out what must be there, and what extra facilities she would prefer; call them necessary and desirable, respectively. A property dealer offers her information on three houses. The buyer plots the information and data on a sheet of paper (Table 8.1).
>
> Both House Numbers I and III fulfil all necessary conditions. House Number II does not, so it is out of consideration. House Number I fulfils two of the four desirable criteria, while House Number III fulfils three. Hence, the buyer decides to go in for House Number III.

It should be noticed that in order to arrive at this decision, the buyer needed considerable data and information to examine whether the alternatives fulfilled the conditions. Management in the TQM context emphasizes this very approach of making decision based on facts rather than on perceptions or impressions.

Table 8.1 **Rational decision-making: Hypothetical case of buying a house**

Conditions	House I	House II	House III
Essential			
Drawing-dining room: 15 × 20 ft	15 × 20	18 × 20	17 × 22
3 bedrooms: 12 × 12 ft	12 × 12, 12 × 12, 12 × 12	14 × 12, 14 × 12, 12 × 12	12 × 12, 12 × 12, 12 × 12
1 attached toilet	Yes	Yes	Yes
1 more toilet	Yes	2	Yes
Kitchen: 8 × 10 ft	8 × 10	10 × 12	10 × 8
Cost: Rs 15 lakh (max.)	14 lakh	15.75 lakh	14.5 lakh
Desirable			
Balcony	Yes	Yes	Yes
Servants quarter	No	Yes	No
Garage	No	Yes	Yes
Lower cost	Lower by 1 lakh	More by 0.75 lakh	Lower by 0.5 lakh

Decision based on facts

There are many incidents in the life of an organization, when a decision needs to be based on facts, e.g., location of girls' hostel in a co-educational institution, construction of a new library and learning resource centre, centre for information technology, etc. For such once-in-a-lifetime decisions, rational decision-making is the right approach.

There are other areas that are directly related to quality requiring frequent and/or periodic decisions. Let us examine some situations where the quality and data are importantly interlinked and can indicate the quality now and also whether the quality is improving or deteriorating over a period. Such areas can be chosen on the basis of what are considered indicators of quality by the members of an institution. Let us assume that academic skills of learners, performance in class, school and external examination, performance in sports and games activities, punctuality, discipline, and morality are some of the accepted indicators of quality. Each issue needs data and information before a rational decision is arrived at.

1. ***Learning skills:*** Reading, listening, observation, and writing are the major learning skills. These facilitate the development of the skill of learning to learn. An institution that sets out its mission to improve instruction and academic performance has very little choice but to build basic learning skills. The first important requirement is to ascertain the current status of learning skills. This would imply measuring reading speed and comprehension, listening comprehension, writing speed and legibility, etc. For example, during management development programmes that I conduct, the principals of schools and colleges show their ignorance about the average speed at which students read with comprehension. Also, they are completely oblivious of the speed at which they write. Similarly, other attributes like achievement motivation, attitudes, values, sociability, reasoning abilities, etc., can be measured and data stored. Measurement of such and other characteristics of a batch of students, as they move from one standard into another, will indicate whether their skills are improving; also who has improved to what extent. Such measures carried out annually or biannually provide strong indicators of the direction of the movement.

2. ***Transition rate:*** Transition rate, as a concept, means the number of students moving from one standard into the next. Obviously, the better the institution, the larger is the proportion of such transition. In order to ascertain academic quality, it is necessary to calculate the transition rate from one year to another. Only data can indicate the following:

   - That there can be inter-grade variation in the transition rate in the same year
   - That the transitions rates can vary between two years for the same grades
   - That, within the same grade, the transition rate can vary from one section to another

The perceptive principal would see this as an indication of what transpires in the classrooms, in the examination hall, and so on.

3. **Number of classes in a year:** As mentioned earlier, every educational institution has a stipulation of the number of working days and classes to be taken according to the time table. Data can be collected on the number of classes taken per subject, per grade, and per teacher. This can be used to check whether the institution is fulfilling the process specification, a component of quality management. There would be variations in the number of classes taken among the grades and even within the same grade among the subjects. The difference will also be between the actual classes taken and the classes supposed to be taken. Such data and information will help in taking decisions.

4. **Daily attendance:** Attendance in classes is another important feature for improvement of quality. It would be interesting to figure out the average attendance per class. One of my own four-year-long research projects, with more than 6,000 primary grade children, indicated that there is a seasonal variation in attendance in the rural areas (Mukhopadhyay, 1998). While the average attendance is about 79 per cent across the year, the average attendance is relatively low during the monsoon and harvesting seasons and high during autumn, spring, and summer. The average attendance, besides seasonal variation, also indicates the teacher quality, management efficiency, and attendance of students.

5. **Classroom teaching competence:** The classrooms are usually very secretive. Only students experience what and how a teacher teaches. One of the important critical success factors in quality management is improving the classroom teaching competence of the teachers and the classroom processes. The supervisors observe classrooms without any structured observation schedule, resulting into some impressions and perceptions coloured with biases and personal prejudices of the observers. On the contrary, classroom proceedings can be observed on the Classroom Teaching Competence Scale (CTCS). There are several such observation instruments including one by Mukhopadhyay and others (Appendix I). Let us say that a school or college decides to observe each teacher four times a year on this scale (Table 8.2).

Table 8.2 Scores on CTCS for five teachers

Observations → Teachers ↓	O_1	O_2	O_3	O_4	Average
I	46	48	51	53	49.5
II	64	61	58	57	60.0
III	44	34	47	42	41.25
IV	55	53	56	55	54.75
V	35	37	40	38	37.5

The data indicates comparative performance of teachers as well as consistency and/or improvement of a particular teacher over the months. Teacher II gets the highest average score of 60 whereas the lowest average of 37.5 is scored by Teacher V. Further, Teacher II is consistent in scores in various lessons. Compared to that, the scores vary from 34 in one lesson to 47 in another in case of Teacher III. Teacher I demonstrates steady improvement from one lesson to another. Detailed analysis by component will indicate a teacher's relative strengths and weaknesses in various skills of classroom teaching. Similar data can be collected on the use of other instructional methodologies.

6. **Results analysis:** Results are often given to the students by subject. At best, they are compared with the best score in the class. Although such a marksheet can be good enough for a student, it is not enough for the teachers or the institution. There can be different types of analysis. First, for each subject, grade, and section, the mean, mode, and standard deviation can be calculated. The raw scores will automatically indicate the range, from the lowest to the highest score. While the mode indicates the score that the majority of the students clusters around, standard deviation provides very important information on the dispersal of scores. Plotted in a graph, the results indicate the trend of the marks (Figure 8.2). These graphs indicate that the scores in science are normally distributed. The scores in social sciences are negatively skewed; more students have performed better. In mathematics, the scores are positively skewed, indicating that more students have fared badly.

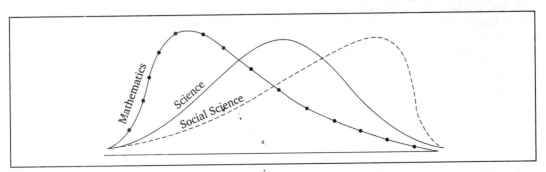

Figure 8.2 Curve representing distribution of marks

Just as these are the curves on three subjects of the same class, such curves of the same subject across various grades can also be plotted. Those will indicate inter-class differences in performances in a subject facilitating decisions on where to plug the holes.

In the university or Board examination, student performance can be analysed in terms of percentiles to elicit a comparative picture: where do the students stand vis-à-vis all the candidates in the Board?

7. **Sports and games:** Sports, games, and other co-curricular activities are important dimensions of school quality because they influence the character building of

students. Usually, the activities conclude with award distribution. Hardly any data is maintained on performances in different sports, games, etc. Only data can indicate whether there is any performance improvement. An institution can maintain records of participation of each student in such activities along with preferred items of participation and performance therein. For example, in a track event, say the 100 m sprint, the range of 'timing' and the best 'time' can be ascertained. It is only such data that will offer opportunities for taking decisions on modes of further improvement through effective training.

These are only a few examples. Data can also be generated on infrastructure and resources like instructional material, audio-visual aids, learning resource centres, and libraries.

Steps in creating data

The primary reason for collecting and collating data is to develop a basis for taking a decision on the basis of facts. For example, an institution might be quite satisfied with the way examinations are held—smooth and trouble-free. But inside the examination hall, there can be copying, either unnoticed or ignored. This obviously does not indicate quality, though the process may be smooth. The quality-conscious manager would like to ensure that if there are 20 cases of unfair means in a year, it should come down to 10 in the next year, and perhaps zero the year after.

Fact-based decision-making, hence, requires a sound mechanism of generating valid and reliable data. The major steps involved in generating valid and reliable data for decision-making are detailed here.

1. Choice of tools

First, there have to be certain *instruments* for collecting data. The instruments can be tests, inventories, questionnaires, interview schedules, observations schedules, etc. The instruments can be developed in-house or readily available instruments can be adopted/adapted to suit the institution's needs. The CTCS, mentioned earlier is one such instrument, which has been tested for reliability and validity. There are tests, scales, and inventories for measuring study habits, reading and listening comprehension, reasoning abilities, attitudes, values, etc.[1] It is important to choose a well-constructed and tested instrument since quality of data can be only as good as the instrument itself. The important consideration in

---

[1] There have been several efforts in collecting well-documented information on various types of tests and measurement instruments. Most follow the *Handbook of HR Instruments* by Udai Pareek. The *Handbook of Social and Psychological Instruments* edited by Udai Pareek and T.V. Rao is another handy document; a revised version has recently been edited by D.M. Pestonjee.

decision-making on facts is to identify the areas where the institutions need data and facts for decision-making.

2. Data collection

The second step is collection of data. Data can be collected from several sources. For example, the data on results, number of classes taken, and average attendance can be collected from the available records in the institutions. For other areas like reading and writing speed and comprehension of students, classroom teaching competence of teachers, attitude of teachers towards students, etc., it will be necessary to administer tests and the questionnaires. There are many occasions when the principal discusses with teachers and counsels them, or teachers discuss the students' problems with them. Usually, such discussions are unstructured and not recorded. Should these be conducted on a structured schedule—on a series of pre-identified questions—and be recorded, it will generate trend data that can be used for decision-making. Alternatively, the principal and the teachers could maintain detailed notes on their discussions. This will help review progress in the next event of discussion.

An important issue in data collection is to create valid and reliable data. The validity of the data depends on the kind of questions asked. Should the question be asked directly on the issue on which data is required, it will provide valid data. The question of reliability and dependability is whether the same question will get the same response, if repeated. Depending upon the situation, the respondents may have to be taken into confidence before data is collected. This is particularly important where the data on individual performance is concerned.

The final issue is of the respondents. Data for decision-making for quality management should be collected from all stakeholders in the institution: members of the managing committee, principal, teachers, non-teaching staff, students, parents, and old students. Wherever possible and relevant, it is good to collect data from more than one source. Data from multiple sources provides the opportunity for cross-checking and verification for generating more dependable bases for decision-making.

3. Data storage

The third stage is data storage. Since TQM essentially emphasizes a long-term perspective and looks for continuous improvement, it is only on a comparative basis that one can see whether quality is improving. Hence, data will be needed for comparison over the years. It has to be stored and preserved. The data can be stored manually on files or electronically on computers. It is obviously useful to store data on computers for easy retrieval; computers can also be used to carry out necessary analysis. In fact, computerized data management has given rise to the concept and practice of the Management Information System (MIS). Considerable amount of professional literature has been developed on the subject

(O'Brien, 1999). This has also been termed as a Decision Support System; the MIS with the facts in its store supports decision-making, indeed fact-based decision-making.

4. Data analysis

The fourth stage is data analysis to find the trends. Data analysis may require a wide range of application of statistics, from very simple descriptive statistics, like central tendencies, dispersal, percentage, and frequency distribution to extremely complicated predictive methods like regression, analysis of variance, analysis of covariance, factor analysis, etc. The predictive analyses are necessary for generalization in research. For purposes of decision-making on facts, simple descriptive methods that can provide not only the current position but also the trend should be adequate. For example, 'percentage' is usually used to describe the performance of students. If the percentages are compared between the years, it provides a clue whether the students' performance is moving forward or deteriorating or maintaining status quo. By computing simple critical ratio, one can also test whether the differences in percentages are significant or not.

However, in certain situations, one may actually need certain types of analyses. For example, if there is a perception in an institution that performance in social sciences is related to students' language capabilities, it can only be verified by computing the coefficient of correlation between scores in language and social sciences. This can be further used to examine whether there is a causal relationship between language abilities and performance in social sciences. Should the answer be positive, one must take a decision on enhancing the quality of language instruction. Here comes the question of judicious choice of analysis to be carried out.

5. Data presentation

The fifth stage is data presentation. The data can be presented in more than one form. Most common forms of data presentation are tables and graphs, especially tables with two axes each depicting one set of variables. For example, in Table 8.3, the Y-axis has one common variable (the year) and the X-axis carries the mean scores in English, Hindi, Science, Mathematics, and Social Sciences. The cells accommodate data. Tables can have raw scores or percentages and other forms of processed scores.

Tables can also have qualitative information in the form of either statements or qualitative codings (Table 8.4). Such tables provide a quick comparative picture of the staff on any other area.

Data can also be meaningfully presented through graphs, which, being visual, make for more effective communication. There are a number of alternatives to present data in graphic mode, such as histograms, bar charts, columns, pie diagrams, scatter grams, lines, curves, etc. The presentations can also have 3-D effects. Let us examine some sample presentations (Figures 8.3, 8.4 and 8.5).

Table 8.3 Mean scores of 10th standard Board examination

Year	English	Hindi	Science	Mathematics	Social Sciences
1997	44	48	52	55	42
1998	48	44	57	51	38
1999	39	47	44	46	47
2000	42	53	49	48	49

Table 8.4 Qualitative information on teachers

Attributes → / Teachers ↓	Punctuality	Interest in students	Preparation for teaching	Interest in school activities	Inter-personal relationships
Suman	Always makes special effort to be punctual	Takes keen interest	Makes full preparation for every class	Does not show much interest	Not very good; rather isolated among teachers
Vijaya	Generally on time	First to jump in with help if there is a problem	Takes it easy, rather casual	Always ahead of others to volunteer; also competent	Very good; popular among teachers and students
Jasbinder	Rather irregular	Not much	Really prepares for teaching	Reluctant, except in co-curricular activities	Good; especially with other teachers
Abdul	Always effortlessly punctual	Selective; takes interest in students personal problems; guides and counsels well	Does not make any special preparation for classes	Selective; takes interest in administrative matters and library only	Average; does not have either great friends or arch rivals in the staff
Robert	Occasionally late; feels ashamed	Keen about student activities, but lacks skill in handling them	Well-prepared; makes fresh preparation every time	Reluctant; not interested beyond his routine duties	Rather isolates; remains in one corner of the staff room, engaged in some reading

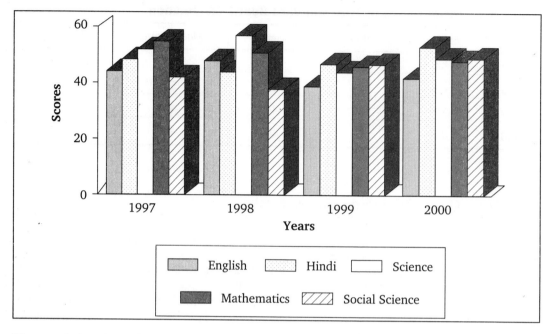

Figure 8.3   Bar chart of mean scores in Board examination

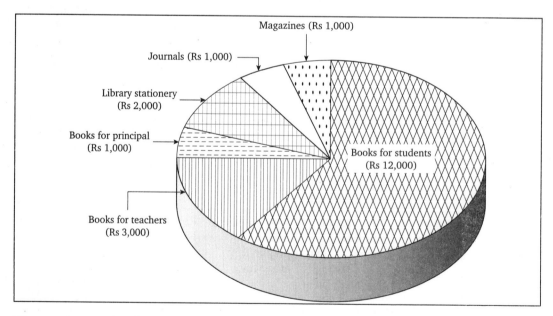

Figure 8.4   Pie diagram of expenditures

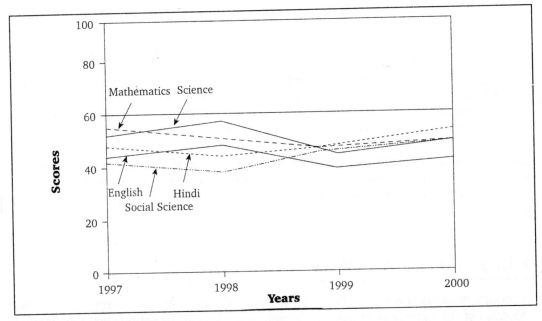

Figure 8.5   Line charts

There are many more interesting ways of presenting data (Kaufman and Zahn, 1993; Wainer, 1981). Such graphic presentations can be made by using appropriate computer software. For example, electronic spreadsheets effectively convert data into graphics. Other specialist software includes Harvard Graphics.

Data culture and skills

Various such analyses can provide a sound basis for both collective and individual decisions. Also, facts are the only bases to indicate whether or not there is any progress in the institutional quality. The conventional decision-maker will normally brush aside any scientific or innovative method of decision-making. But then TQM is an innovative approach and not cut out for the conventional heads of institutions. It can only be appreciated and experimented with by those who are open to new ideas and practices, who are dynamic, and who are competent to manage quality. It does require lot of competence to design instruments, collect and store data, analyse it, and make a presentation of the results. These are largely the skills of a researcher. This implies that TQM and decision-making on facts demands that each institution has to build in a research component into its functioning.

The skills needed for creation, management, and processing of data have to be brought within the range of the academic staff. It is not necessary that the principal himself or herself learns all the technicalities of instrument designing to statistical analyses. He or she needs to know a good smattering of the approach. A dynamic principal would ensure development of the necessary research skills in a few of the staff members or recruit one who has such a background. For example, a teacher with an M.Ed. degree or postgraduate degree in sociology or psychology usually brings with him or her basic knowledge and skills of research methodology. While a majority of the teachers can master the basics of statistics and data processing, a teacher of mathematics or statistics or econometrics is likely to pick up faster due to his or her background in quantitative techniques. TQM institutions can develop a team comprising individuals who are good in instrument development and/or adaptation, data generation, computerization and data analysis, report preparation, etc.

Ethics in decision-making

Although decision-making on facts can substantially improve the quality of decisions, adoption of this innovative practice in decision-making depends entirely upon the ethics of the decision-makers. Although in normal circumstances, heads of institutions are expected to take decisions in the interest of the institution, this does not necessarily happen; in fact, it does not happen in most institutions. There are several alternative claimants to the advantage of the decision. Actual decisions are influenced by various such considerations. Let us compare two cases to illustrate the point. In a highly reputed university, the Vice-Chancellor received a request from a well-known professor for permission to leave the country to join an Indian delegation for about 10 days. The university has a rule stipulating the maximum number of days a professor can be out of the university in a year, decided by the faculty and approved by the statutory authorities of the university. The concerned professor had already exhausted the number of permissible days to be out of the country. Despite the fact that the professor was drafted by the Government of India, the Vice-Chancellor did not approve and stood his ground; unless the rule was changed, he would not be able to permit the professor to leave the university and coursework at his/her hand. In sharp contrast, there are several instances where scholars are routinely permitted by the heads of universities and institutions to leave their coursework and research responsibilities in their own departments and universities for foreign visits and assignments. Although such decisions set wrong precedents for others, heads of institutions resort to such decisions for want of ethics and concern for the organization.

Contemporary research on institution building and leadership provides enough evidence that violation of ethics of decision-making costs the institution heavily; instead of institution building, it facilitates organizational degeneration. Those heads who nurture the ambition of institution building must be concerned and careful not only about the skills and competence of decision-making, but also its ethics.

Conclusion

Decision-making is part of the life of a principal. He or she takes innumerable decisions every day of the week. Such decisions can be classified into two broad categories: routine and non-routine. The non-routine decisions can be classified into three categories: reactive, responsive, and proactive. The proactive and responsive decisions are indications of the dynamism in decision-making.

The crux of the question in the TQM context is the quality of the decision, and involvement of others in the decision. Proactive and responsive decisions provide the basic foundation for TQM. Rational decision-making and decision-making on facts require a different orientation—a shift from emotional (spur of the moment) to rational decision-making. It will also be necessary to develop a 'data culture' in the organization and develop a set of skills that are normally available with trained researchers. Importantly, data culture facilitates participative decision-making, for it offers everything for everyone to see. It is transparent, fact-based and hence more scientific. However, the foundation of decision-making for quality management and institution building must be based on ethics and values.

Leadership for Building Quality Institutions 9

Introduction

Leadership is all about influencing—motivating and inspiring people to create vision and achieve it. Vision can be total quality. Total quality management (TQM) is a never-ending journey. It is a tryst with quality. It is a passion, a pride (Peters and Austin, 1985), indeed an obsession. It is a journey involving all, with a focus on the perceners. The challenge in building a quality institution is in creating the passion, the obsession, and the tryst with quality involving all in the organization. That whipping up of the passion in the organization, and guiding and carrying all in that journey is the challenge of the leadership in the TQM organization.

A leader is 'someone who acts as a guide' *(New Webster's Comprehensive Dictionary of English Languages)*. Accordingly, the principal—the leader of a school or a college—is a guide for quality transformation. Drawing from Case's (1993) analogy of a leader as a venture capitalist and chief coach-cum-coordinator, Westerman (1994) calls upon us to turn the conventional hierarchical pyramid (describing organizational hierarchy) 'on its side so that the top of the pyramid is on the left and everything else flows to the right' (Figure 9.1). This graphic expression reinforces the idea of the leader as a coach and coordinator; it also ensures flow of direction in the form of mission from the leader (Westerman, 1994).

The principal is challenged to create the culture of quality that penetrates to the smallest elements, processes, and systems of an institution. It is a common experience that under the same set of rules and regulations, with the same set of teaching and non-teaching staff, and with students from similar backgrounds, an educational institution degenerates or maintains status quo, or rises to prominence with a change of principal. This is also borne out by large number of research studies on management of change in education (Mukhopadhyay, 2004). Delors Commission contends, 'A good school head who is capable of establishing effective teamwork, and is seen as being competent and open minded often achieves major improvement in the quality of his or her school' (UNESCO, 1996). While ordinary, non-quality institutions can afford non-leaders as heads, quality institutions cannot move ahead without appropriate leadership.

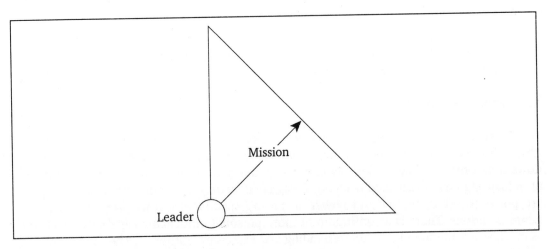

Figure 9.1   Leader as coach and coordinator

Concepts in leadership

There are some popular, well-established concepts associated with organizational leadership. These are labelling of leadership, power–authority grid, and styles of leadership with associated concepts such as style preference, style flex, and style effectiveness.

Leadership labels

There is more than one typology. One such categorization is 'designated' versus 'ascribed' leadership. Where leadership position is by designation, e.g., principal of an educational institution, it is called 'designated' leadership. Where a person is chosen by peers to lead, he or she is an 'ascribed' leader, e.g., office bearers of teachers' associations. The challenges of the designated leader, namely, the principal is to emerge also as ascribed leader and mobilize other ascribed leaders in the institution in accomplishing institutional missions. We will return to this later while dealing with the power–authority grid.

A popular classification of leadership is the authoritarian–democratic–laissez-faire trilogy. An autocratic leader takes the decision himself or herself and hands it down to 'subordinates' for implementation. The social setting of such institutions is hierarchical and non-collegial. The democratic leadership style is reflected by consultative decision-making in a comparatively collegial atmosphere. In such a case, the principal uses his or her position as first among equals; he or she consults others on important matters and facilitates a collective decision. The laissez-faire leadership is indicated when things are left to happen, often characterized by absence of initiative, absence of intervention, interference, monitoring, etc. However, in another form, the laissez-faire style is delegative; in this case, it is not left to chance, but a conscious decision to delegate is taken.

To avoid a personality cult and autocratic tendencies, there are structural innovations for participative decision-making. Creation of a staff council, representation of teachers, non-academic staff, and parents on management committees, etc., are some structural precautions against the trends of authoritarianism.

Authority and power

Two other important concepts related to leadership behaviour are 'authority' and 'power'. Although these two terms are used interchangeably, they imply different things. 'Authority' flows from official position (designated leader) and 'power' flows from personal qualities of influencing others (ascribed leaders). Designated leaders use authority; ascribed leaders are power-based. Authority and power, in an organizational setting, are not black and white situations. There is a continuum of more personal influencing capability or 'power' as much as a continuum in the understanding and exercising 'authority'. The zone of overlap (Figure 9.2) between power and authority is the most effective event of leadership.

Designated leaders, who are high on power, tend to use more of their personal influence than official positions for accomplishing organizational missions. Designated leaders, such as principals, who are weak in exercising personal influence depend more on the authority of their position and use dictatorial styles. Issuing memos, serving show-cause notices, throwing tantrums, and admonishing subordinates are some indicators of such tendencies. Some are low on both power and authority, for instance, the laissez-faire ones who leave things to happen. Leadership for building quality institutions warrants enriching and use of the power element of the power–authority grid for influencing.

In the Indian paradigm, human nature is governed by three qualities: *sattvik, rajasik,* and *tamasik*. According to this theory, every individual has all the three qualities but in different proportions; also for the same individual, at a given point in time, one quality may be dominant over the other two.

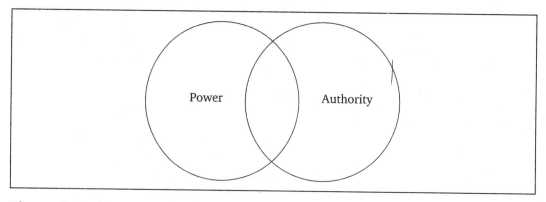

Figure 9.2   Power–authority grid

1. *Sattvik* quality stands for knowledge, illumination, and sense of duty without attachment
2. *Rajasik* quality stands for action, high energy, urge to dominate, and material possession
3. *Tamasik* quality implies lethargy, inertia, ignorance, and lack of interest

The dominance of the *rajasik* quality is likely to make one an authoritarian leader; the *tamasik* quality is likely to make a person laissez-faire, and the *sattvik* quality is likely to make a person democratic and delegative. Western theories of power and authority fit into the Indian paradigm very well.

Baddaracco and Ellsworth (1989) offer another typology guided by one of three philosophies: political, directive, and values-driven.

1. The ***political*** leader is a strategist; he/she adjusts his/her vision of the future and mutually defined goals with the inherent resistance to change within the organization and is aware and conscious of such resistances.
2. The ***directive*** leader directs an organization towards a well-defined goal based on a SWOT analysis (assessment of organizational strengths, weaknesses, opportunities, and threats); he/she takes key decisions personally. He/she relies upon structure and system to control decisions while challenging conventional wisdom.
3. The ***values-driven*** leader is a pace–setter, leading by example by walking the talk. He/she demonstrates values for the followers emphasizing overall organizational purposes rather than their self-interest.

One of the important contributions to the understanding of leadership is the situational leadership theory by Hersey and Blanchard (1992). They identified four styles of leadership based on the combination of leader's concern for task and concern for relationship. The style takes shape through the interaction of these two concerns. Although the concern for task and the concern for relationship form a continuum, the authors dichotomized each of them into high and low. Accordingly, they identified four styles: directive (high concern for task but low concern for relationship), coaching (high concern for task and high concern for relationship), supporting or participating (high concern for relationship but low concern for task), and delegating (low concern for both task and relationship).[1]

---

[1] The styles of leadership can be measured using the LEAD questionnaire developed by Hersey and Blanchard. This comprises 12 situations that occur in organizations. There are four possible responses, representing one for each response. The respondent is to choose one of the responses that represents his/her way of decision-making in those or similar situations in the college or school. I have used this tool for data feedback to literally hundreds of college and school principals for training in leadership development. Rarely do principals choose the delegative style; very few choose the directive style either. Frequently chosen styles are either coaching or participating with greater concern for relationships, risking the task accomplishment and hence the achievement of missions.

In the *directive* style, the leader tends to dictate. In the *coaching* style, the leader primarily acts as a coach to ensure goal accomplishment. This is an important style for heads of institutions when introducing innovation and change. In the *participating* style, the leader involves himself or herself along with the followers in actually carrying out the tasks with the main objective of keeping people happy. In the *delegating* style, the leader trusts his/her followers and allows members to take responsibility along with rights to innovate, change, and redefine their roles.

Everyone in a leadership position has a personal style indicated by the preference in various situations. What distinguishes a leader is his/her effectiveness in choosing a style according to the demand of the situation, thus demanding flexibility. Moving from the directive to the delegating style through coaching and participating styles is guided by the task maturity of the followers; but follower task maturity is what the leader perceives. The perception itself emerges from the leader's own world view. This theory is situated 'here and now', living from moment to moment. Also, it takes a static view of the leader–follower relationship (Mukhopadhyay, 2004).

Three important concepts associated with Hersey and Blanchard's situational leadership theory are style preference, style flex, and style effectiveness.

1. *Style preference:* indicated by the frequency at which a leader opts for one of the four styles; the most frequently chosen style indicates the style preference of the leader.
2. *Style flex:* indicated by the flexibility with which one can change and adopt styles as required by the situation to be effective; a leader with strong style flex adopts all four styles; indeed, he or she moves easily among the styles. This is measured by the number and the frequency of choice of styles by an individual.
3. *Style effectiveness:* indicated by the right choice of a style according to the situation; for example, a situation that demands telling style, the leader chooses telling style. This indicates effectiveness. However, in a situation that demands delegation, if the leader still chooses the telling style, it becomes counterproductive or ineffective.

While these concepts of leadership have significant implications for day-to-day management of institutions, leadership in TQM institutions needs a fresh look.

Leadership in quality institutions

We would recollect the three major principles of TQM.

1. Percener orientation
2. Involvement of all
3. Quest for continuous improvement of quality (not one shot)

One who is anchored in perceners' needs and expectations can inspire the quest for continuous improvement of quality or incite the passion. One who can achieve quality through involvement of all is eligible to lead a TQM institution. Thus, drawing from the three pillars of TQM, a TQM leader is characterized by the following attributes:

Percener focus

- Conscious of responsibility to perceners
- Identifies various categories of perceners
- Sensitive to their expectations
- Makes deliberate efforts to ascertain and appreciate percener expectations

Involvement of all

- Inspires colleagues in the quest for quality
- Involves all in developing vision and quality management
- Empowers colleagues to innovate and take risks
- Promotes sense of equality
- Removes bottlenecks

Continuous improvement

- Personally innovates
- Demonstrates constancy of purpose towards quality
- Walks the talk
- Plans long-term strategies
- Reviews and resets systems

Ten of Deming's 14 cardinal principles of TQM have implications for leadership:

1. Create constancy of purpose for improvement
2. Adopt new philosophy
3. Improve constantly and forever the system of production and service
4. Institute training on the job
5. Improve quality and productivity, and thus constantly decrease cost
6. Institute leadership
7. Drive out fear so that everyone may work effectively for the company
8. Break down the barriers between departments
9. Institute a vigorous programme of education and self-improvement
10. Put everyone in the company to work to accomplish the transformation

The challenge to leadership in a TQM context is that of adopting a new philosophy, a philosophy of a quality culture and all other associated processes and systems that ensure generating a quality culture. Deming exhorts leaders to create constancy of purpose for quality improvement and create systems for involving everyone in the organization in quality management. The most significant challenge is 'instituting leadership', implying moving away from management to leading. It also implies creating and mentoring leadership at all levels. Similarly, Sallis' (1996) indicators of quality institution also have a series of implications for leadership.

- Has a strategy for quality
- Has a quality policy and plan
- Senior management is of leading quality
- Improvement process involves everybody
- Quality facilitator leads the improvement process
- Plans for the long term
- Has a distinctive mission
- Treats colleagues as customers

The principal, as a leader, is challenged to develop a distinctive mission with a long-term plan with a set of quality policies, plans, and strategies. Other important challenges are involving everybody in an environment of equality. Also there is the challenge of 'leading from the front' and 'walking the talk'. While these challenges are derived from Sallis' identification of attributes of quality institutions, he concludes that leaders in TQM organizations should do/have the following:

- Have a vision of total quality for his/her institution
- Have a clear commitment to the quality improvement process
- Communicate the quality message
- Ensure that customer needs are at the centre of the institution's policies and practices
- Ensure that there are adequate channels for the voice of the customers
- Lead staff development
- Be careful not to blame others when problems arise, without looking at the evidence; most problems result from institutional policies, not staff failure
- Lead innovations within their institutions
- Ensure that organizational structures clearly define responsibilities and provide the maximum delegation compatible with accountability
- Be committed to removal of artificial barriers whether organizational or cultural
- Build effective teams
- Develop appropriate mechanisms for monitoring and evaluating success

Peters and Austin (1985), on the basis of their research on excellence, prescribe MBWA or 'Management By Walking About' as the leadership style for quality revolution. MBWA implies visibility of leadership and their understanding and feeling for front-line processes of the institute (Sallis, 1996). In the context of education, they identified the following attributes of leadership:

- *Management by walking about*
- *For the kids:* close to the customer or customer focus
- *Autonomy, experimentation, and support for failure:* encouraging innovation and risk-taking
- *Create a sense of family:* sense of belongingness among parents, students, teachers, support staff, etc.
- *Sense of the whole, rhythm, passion, intensity, and enthusiasm:* essential personal qualities of a leader

Spanbauer (1992) emphasized the empowerment of teachers through involvement in decision-making, and delegation of more powers and autonomy as leadership traits in a quality-based institution. Chowdhary (1996) distinguished between a professionally managed institutional model and a TQM institution (Figure 9.3). The professional model places emphasis on the performance of the individual whereas TQM emphasizes the system. However, what Chowdhary classified as the 'professional' model is the conventional administration of an institution in a hierarchical culture. This model allows and promotes maintenance of status quo.

Professional		*TQM*
• Individual responsibilities • Professional leadership • Administrative authority • Professional authority • Goal expectation • Expectation • Rigid planning • Response to complaints • Retrospective performance appraisal • Quality assurance	*Versus*	• Collective responsibilities • Managerial leadership • Accountability • Participation • Performance and process expectation • Flexible planning • Benchmarking • Concurrent performance appraisal • Kaizen

Figure 9.3   Professional versus TQM model

Source: Chowdhary (1996).

Leading an institution to maintain status quo and leading an institution to foster continuous growth and development are two different paradigms altogether. In the latter, leadership has to continuously evolve and unfold to its full potential. Hence, the emphasis is on transformational leadership (Frazier, 1997). Compared to a transactional leadership that works for 'maintaining a status quo by exchanging an assurance of a secure place of work for a commitment to get the job done' (Abu-Duhou, 1999), transformational leadership emphasizes on the capacity to engage others in a commitment to change (Burns, 1978; cited in Abu-Duhou, 1999). In institution-based management for TQM, transformational leadership is necessary to change the culture of the system so that principal and teachers not only share but also commit to the same set of values. Frazier enumerated the following as the attributes of transformational leadership:

- Creating great vision: beginning with the end purpose in mind
- Modelling the values of the vision
- Trusting and enabling talents of followers: becoming vulnerable to others' strengths
- Driving out fear: creating an environment for learning
- Maintaining constancy of purpose

The most remarkable feature of a transformational leader is mentoring leadership by trusting and nurturing leadership qualities in others and/or augmenting the capabilities of ascribed leaders who are not designated to any position. The mentoring of leadership may apparently make oneself vulnerable to others' strengths, but that is a contradiction in itself; a transformational leader is never static on his or her own position. As he or she nurtures new leadership to maturity, he or she shifts his or her own position by inculcating new skills and competencies and moves from manual to knowledge or thinking leadership, turning the focus from institutional management to institution building.

Daniel Goleman et al. (2002), the emotional intelligence guru, made a refreshing contribution to the understanding of leadership and the dynamics of the relationship between leader and his/her follower in his books, *Primal Leadership* and *The New Leaders*. His basic thesis is 'leading with emotional intelligence' by generating resonance with the followers. Accordingly, he classified leadership styles into resonant and dissonant.

- The **visionary** leadership style is the most positive, as it moves people towards shared dreams when changes require a new vision and a clear direction
- The **coaching** style is highly positive since it connects personal goals with organizational vision
- The **affiliative** style makes a positive impact by connecting people with each other
- The **democratic** style also exerts positive impacts since it values people's inputs and gets commitment through participation

Goleman et al. classified **pace-setting** and **commanding** styles as dissonant styles although such styles are relevant and can be effective in certain situations like high-quality results from a motivated group or to kick-start a turnaround.

Inspirational leadership and spiritual leadership concepts of Lance Secretan (1999) and a few other authors brought in a new dimension to the thinking on leadership. Secretan discards visioning and strategic planning as old-style leadership. He also discards the classification of leader and follower. He dumps the word 'follower' for 'percener', not just as a new word but as a new expression—changing from follower to percener or partner, from an unequal to an equal relationship. He contends that each one is a leader and proves his point by raising different situations and roles in life; thus leadership is hidden in everyone. A.P.J. Abdul Kalam, the scientist President of India asks the same question: 'Why wait for someone else to lead, why not lead yourself?' (Kalam, 2002). The old style ends with motivating, new-style leadership is about inspiring beyond motivating. Secretan asks: 'What caused followers to dedicate themselves with such passion to the vision of Christ, Gandhi, Confucius, Martin Luther King, Mother Teresa and Nelson Mandela?' They were inspired not motivated. We know that Martin Luther King did not say, 'I have a strategic plan!' and Mother Teresa didn't have a quality programme. She didn't need one. 'Inspiration does not depend on power relationships; on the contrary, when we are inspired we are truly empowered. To inspire others, we must create an environment in which people sense a power beyond another human, a higher power, a divine influence that wells up from deep within causing them to be infused with a breath of God. In other words, we must become as effective at engaging the energy of the soul (inspiration) as we have become in engaging the energy of the personality (motivation).' Secretan's theory gets summarized into two questions: 'Why can't we see God in others? (implying then we don't need to manage), and leader to percener question 'I am your leader, how can I serve you?' instead of the old-style question, 'I am your leader, how can I teach you?'

I must flag the issue of women in leadership. This is throwing new insights into how leaders lead for institution building. Almost all the leadership theories are based on research on male leaders. With the increasing number of women assuming leadership roles, there is an emerging women's voice in leadership theory. Dewan (2004) provides a comprehensive review of the research and writings on the theme. A competent summarization of this issue has been done by Latchem and Hanna (2001). The issue is more of the impact of difference of the male and female brains: the logical–rational versus the empathic–emotional attributes of males and females in their leadership styles. Goleman and Secretan build an effective bridge. Leaders with a large female brain are endowed with greater potentiality of developing resonance; they are more competent in actualizing emotional intelligence for leading. Also, the 'mother-being', naturally endowed with empathy and concern for others, makes mothers spiritually richer and inspiring (Mukhopadhyay, 2004). Leaders, both male and female, endowed with logic, reasoning, and other such cognitive attributes of the male brain are likely to be more successful with situational, transactional, even transformational leadership styles. However, most women principals seem to adopt lower order leadership styles attributed to male brain phenomena, perhaps due to social value loading in favour of male styles and dominance.

Institution building for quality management

'Institution building implies the process of developing certain capabilities which makes the organization continue with not only its ongoing operations but also innovate and continuously improve on its performance. To that extent, institution building is developing the process capability of the organization for self-renewal and traversing the path of continuing change.

'The differences in the developmental experiences among the schools, colleges and universities are primarily due to the differential emphasis on and different processes of institution building. Large majority of the institutions do not experience any deliberate and planned effort in institution building. Few institutions that experience growth and development indeed experience institution building. It continues to grow with or without change of its personnel; change happens automatically' (Mukhopadhyay, 2004).

According to Pareek (1981), institution building has been used with two meanings. 'One meaning refers to the process of development of some institutions by an outside expert institution, as total systems, including the development of values and norms which is relevant for the type of work the institutions have been doing. The second meaning in which the term is used relates to the internal development of an institution to be able to play its role effectively'.

Institution building needs vision and sharing of vision, involving and empowering staff, removing roadblocks and encouraging risk-taking, and creating and developing leadership at all levels. The following are some major qualitative requirements of a leader for a TQM institution:

Visioning

Institution building must be guided by a future vision. Transformational leadership is characterized by visioning and involving other perceners in collective visioning. The vision should be comprehensive and indicative of the road ahead. It must be shared, if not collective, so that everyone is involved in organizational creativity, like the passionate working of several creative artists on a mural or collage. Yet, it is important that the leader himself models the value of the vision, translating into action the philosophical aspect of the vision for others to emulate.

Encouraging risk-taking

Quality management and institution building are functions of successful implementation of innovations leading to the development of a culture of change. Anything beyond management of status quo cannot be risk-free. Leadership for building quality institution involves the ability to take risks—calculated risks. Innovations upset dynamic equilibrium in institutions; hence it brings in resistance. One of the challenges of a quality management leader is driving out the fear by creating an environment for risk-taking. The leaders encourage perceners, 'Do not worry! I am there to take care of the problems. Go ahead and innovate.' He transforms an institution into a learning organization.

Removing roadblocks

An entrepreneur leader identifies the roadblocks and bottlenecks and tears them down to facilitate the movement for those who innovate. It is a difficult skill. First, it requires perceptiveness to understand the problem that others face or the courage to explore such problems. Second, it needs a proactive mindset to facilitate others. Third, it is the reverse of ego-centred management where 'I' is at the centre.

Commitment to change

Kurt Lewin's Field Force Analysis facilitates the understanding of organizational equilibrium. While most people like to stay in a stable position, the leader of a quality institution indicates the commitment to build momentum for continuing change. The principal's role is to see that the organization keeps searching for the new equilibrium, moving upwards with every swing of the see-saw. In practical terms, the leader must innovate himself and also encourage and support colleagues to innovate and take risks.

Empowering colleagues

Quality being a continuous journey involving everyone, the leader of a quality institution invests in capacity building and staff empowerment. On one hand, the leader invests in carefully chosen and focused training programmes for the staff; on the other, he fosters a culture of equality through colleagueship in contradistinction to the hierarchical management in ordinary institutions. Training in technical skills and promoting collegiality by involving all in organizational decision-making are important investments in empowering colleagues.

Mentoring leadership

The transformational leader makes a serious bid to expand his tribe. He engages in trusting and developing the managerial capabilities of colleagues. The managerial skills bring them the confidence required to lead the sub-systems of the institution, e.g., departments, offices, the gymnasium and sports division, etc. The mentoring of leadership prevents organizational decay in case of change of guard and also provides sustainability to organizational self-renewal. Mentoring leadership implies delegating tasks, assigning responsibilities with rights, organizational decision-making (including visioning) and organizational policy formulation.

Ascribed leaders, within the organization, are important elements that can either build or destroy organizations. Argyris (1993) called them power agents. He maintains, 'These informal leaders exert power and influence over their peer groups, through competence and knowledge, personality, interpersonal skills, rewards and favours, or cohesion.' Apparently, this could become a challenge to the principal himself or herself. The first step is to identify these ascribed leaders within the informal groups. Alternative and/or collective leadership may render a leader vulnerable (Frazier, 1997) and irrelevant. But becoming deliberately vulnerable to the strength of others is the real test of leadership. It is, at this stage, that the leader transforms himself or herself into thinking and visioning leader rather than being bound by task–relationship dynamics. In this context, a saying on leadership by Lao Tzu, a famous Chinese philosopher of the 6th century B.C., is worth recollecting:

A leader is good when his presence is felt.
A leader is better when his absence is felt.
A leader is best when neither his presence nor absence matters.

Before I conclude, let me reproduce what I learnt from my research on leadership for institution building in education as leadership attributes, styles, and actions of leaders who can be classified as institution builders (Mukhopadhyay, 2004). Institution builders as leaders have the following qualities:

- Are good classroom teachers
- Pursue scholarly pursuits; are self-regulated learners
- Are men and women of higher human values
- Derive strength from personal styles and qualities rather than official positions
- Are people of natural creative instincts
- Enjoy involved visioning, often incremental
- Are rarely 'strategic' but natural and genuine
- Act like 'fathers', including women principals who are highly task concerned and obsessed with production emphasis but genuinely and deeply concerned about the staff's personal well-being
- Inspire the staff
- Despite a well-developed personally preferred style, are resilient without sacrificing core values

While these are some common denominators, there are qualitative differences within these parameters among leaders in schools, colleges, universities, and national institutions. The differences lie much more in the cognitive domain—intellectual prowess and style. The processes of power building and inspiring that they follow are similar.

Conclusion

Often we come across a question: 'Are leaders born or can they be made?' There is no straight and easy answer. Leadership is part of personality, hence it is shaped by environmental exposure in the early years of life; some qualities may be inherited. However, behavioural modification is a tested technique in management. Leadership behaviour can also be modified to make it more effective through sustained efforts. However, it cannot be induced externally; it can come only through self-concern. In other words, leadership qualities can be inculcated only if a leader makes deliberate sustained efforts. In a way, the implicit message is that the full potential of leadership is hardly known. Planned and deliberate efforts to inculcate leadership qualities can optimize the potential.

Research on leadership for building quality institutions offers an interesting hierarchy or taxonomy. Situational leadership is the foundation, functioning on 'here and now' basis, hand to mouth. The next stage is transactional leadership through empowerment of followers; transformational leadership moves one step further to inculcate leadership traits and values in others creating a second line of defence and organizational mechanism for collective leadership. These leadership styles are supported by cognitive skills. Primal leadership banks on emotional intelligence, effectively motivating followers towards achievement of missions and goals. Beyond motivation, a psychic quality is inspirational leadership that inspires (a soul quality) perceners to generate their own goals and missions and strive towards achieving them thus making conventional positional leadership meaningless and redundant. The way I understand it now:

> Leaders inspire;
> who cannot inspire, motivate;
> who cannot motivate, transform;
> who cannot transform, inform;
> who cannot inform, manage;
> who cannot manage, control; and
> who cannot control, leave it to fate.

And, it is a hierarchy, a taxonomy. For TQM and institution building, leaders must transcend lower levels of leadership and may have to begin with a minimum transformational style.

Strategic Planning for Total Quality Management

10

Introduction

Total quality management (TQM), for Frazier (1997) is continuous quality improvement (CQI). CQI is not merely terminology; there are significant implications of the concept. The emphasis here is on 'the continuity' of efforts in quality improvement; indeed, quality as a never-ending journey. As a matter of practice, 'quality' does not conventionally figure in list of items to be managed in an educational institution. Quality management surfaces like dolphins, as and when there is a crisis or a sudden thrust due to change in guard in the institution or external challenges and threats, e.g., coping with the challenge of globalization. In sharp contrast, TQM promotes philosophy of planned development. This would imply that just a 'here and now' approach or situational management is not adequate. The institution needs a future vision of where it intends to go in the next five or 10 years.

The vision and foresight have to be converted into goals and activities; methods of accomplishing them have to be spelt out. Hence, planning becomes a necessary ingredient in adopting TQM in educational institutions. Almost every author has used the phrase 'strategic planning' rather than 'planning'. Why strategic planning? What does it mean?

Strategic planning

The word 'strategy' has a connotation of methods adopted primarily in war. The Hindi meaning of the word, 'strategy' is *ran-niti* (*ran* for war and *niti* for approach or principle). But what might be the reason for importing the word 'strategy' from the lingua franca of war in the field of management of industry, service, or education?

In war, strategy is focused on a single target: win and win, no plan to fail. It does not even romanticize the concept of 'learning from failure'. The second and associated agenda is to win at the least cost to human life, equipment, and money. Third, war must be won within the shortest time. Fourth, war plans to strike at the most vulnerable point of the opponent with the greatest strength. Fifth, the timing of the strike is extremely important in war strategy. Sixth, skilful deployment of army, navy, and air force is crucial so that they may complement each other and create synergy on the war front. There can be many other components of war strategy. But how are they relevant to education, and the management of quality? By extrapolation, we may interpret the following:

- Strategic launching of TQM as an attack on poor quality
- Protecting an innovative effort like TQM from failing
- Achieving total quality at the least cost
- Improving quality in the shortest time; reducing the incubation period and take-off time
- Finding a safe entry point; using the kaizen principle to identify an area where success can be ensured and future effort and success built upon
- Timing and sequencing of events in TQM to get the best benefits
- Ensuring deployment of the best human resources and teamwork to ensure continuous improvement

Strategic planning would then imply developing a long-term plan with built-in medium- and short-term plans to achieve organizational missions and goals in the shortest time and at the least cost by deploying available resources and optimizing human capabilities. In this chapter, we will review some existing models of strategic planning followed by a model proposed for Indian institutions.

Strategic plan models

There are several strategic plan models. Murgatroyd and Morgan (1993) proposed an interesting framework within which planning parameters can be fitted. They built four generic models based on two parameters—access and service—by dichotomizing both 'access' and 'service' into open and niche access, and basic and enhanced services respectively. Open access institutions are such institutions where anyone can walk in and take admission if he or she fulfils necessary qualifications. There is no restriction on the basis of merit, caste, creed, religion, gender, language, economic class, etc. Niche access institutions are those where entry of students is controlled on predefined criteria. Whereas average government and government-aided schools are open access institutions, fee-charging private schools, girls' schools, and denominational schools are niche access institutions. Schools that offer usual courses along with usual co-curricular activities can be classified as broad or basic service institutions; schools that specialize, say in sports or creative arts or science education, can be categorized as enhanced service institutions since they also provide basic services. Authors have presented the four generic models in the form of a visual (Figure 10.1).

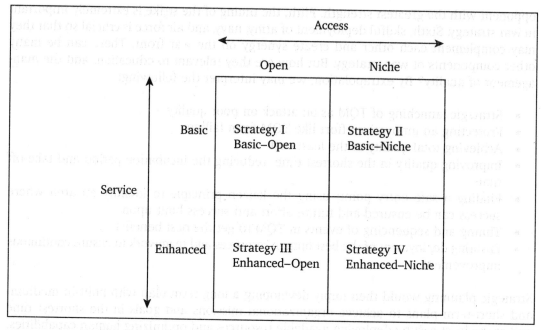

Figure 10.1   Four generic strategies

Basic–open

Most Indian schools and colleges belong to this category since they, under rules, allow admission to all irrespective of caste, creed, religions, gender, etc. At the secondary education level, almost 130,000 schools and over 14,000 colleges belong to the basic–open category. Any strategic plan model for this category will, hence, be applicable to most Indian institutions. Although admission remains open, the strategic planning for TQM would emphasize quality improvement of basic services. Basic services can be curricular and co-curricular for the students; and satisfaction and recognition for the teachers and other staff. Based on the institutional assessment, preferably organizational diagnosis and SWOT analysis, a school may choose one or more areas for development. For example, an average performing school decides to ensure that all students enrolled in school will pass the Class 10 final examination. The strategic plan will demand focus on the identified issue and on developing strategies to achieve the same.

Enhanced–open

In this model too, admission is open to all. The institution may decide to focus on one area or the other: academics, sports and games, cultural activities, NSS, Scouts and Guides, or Junior Red Cross. Within academic areas, a school may decide to excel in science. For example, Madhyamgram High School of West Bengal is an average institution with open entry. It has lifted the Subroto Cup in the National Inter-school Soccer Championship several times. This has been possible because of its major emphasis on soccer. Thus, soccer or games is the enhanced service in the school. Thaker's High School in Ahmedabad, an otherwise average institution, has bagged several state, national, and international awards in science club activities (Mukhopadhyay, 1981). The enhanced service area in this school is thus science education. In all such institutions, there is special emphasis on certain activities in which the school excels. That it excels in it year after year indicates planned effort through which they reach the top, and stay there.

Basic–niche

Niche institutions are the ones where admission is restricted on one or the other criteria. There are not many such schools. This category features more higher and professional education institutions. For example, the Indian Institutes of Technology (IITs), the Indian Institutes of Management (IIMs), and most other prestigious technical and management institutions provide admission only on merit. The District Institutes of Education and Training (DIETs) in many states also admit candidates on merit alone.

The institutions that provide selective admission but offer basic services belong to this category. English medium private schools, Kendriya Vidyalyayas, Navodaya Vidyalayas, Ashram Schools, Sainik Schools, and Central Tibetan Schools belong to the basic–niche category. They may expand and diversify basic services. For example, Mother's International School of Aurobindo Ashram, New Delhi, admits children on merit, offers the usual curricular programme prescribed by the Central Board of Secondary Education, and offers a wide range of co-curricular activities under the guidance of qualified and competent trainers. Within the basic services, it offers several diversifications like as many as 24 different trades in Socially Useful Productive Work (SUPW) or pre-vocational education. For the development of leadership qualities and social sensitivity, the students work with the neighbouring community, raise funds for social causes like care of the old, disabled, and so on. Over the years, the school has built a strong tradition of quality in sports and games too. In this case, there is an overall upgradation of quality in all its departments. The school is strategically well placed. Since the admission is on merit, there is a quality control in the student input. Because of the rules that govern the teacher recruitment and their service conditions, the minimum qualification of teachers is fixed. The school management fully exploits its academic and social reputation to attract talented teachers.

Enhanced–niche

The niche character is common with Strategy III. The difference is the emphasis on enhanced service. However, there are major variations in the character of 'niche' institutions.

For example, a girls' or a boys' school is a niche institution since it is a single-sex institution. But between the two single-sex institutions, say two girls' schools, one offering open admission (e.g., Udang Girls' High School, a usual government-aided institution) and another on merit basis (e.g., Jesus and Mary's Convent, an English medium private school) are qualitatively different. The major difference is that the schools with selective admission on merit use more than one 'niche' criteria and have already achieved quality basic services and are now ready for enhanced services, whereas schools with open admission struggle to provide the minimum basic.

A school with selective admission can focus on one or another area of school activity. For example, a fee charging private institution with quality basic services decided to enrich its students in information technology. It has mobilized resources from parents and the community with the target of providing one computer to each child. Similarly, a girls' school is a niche school as it offers admission to girls only, otherwise admission is not selective. While it provides basic services at average level, it excels in sports. Over the years, it has developed a tradition of excellence in sports and games for girls.

These four generic models provide a sound basis for identifying and classifying an institution into one of four categories. This provides the institution an opportunity to examine the focus of TQM within the larger framework of the service mix—whether to continue in basic service or turn to enhanced service; also whether to set up a sequence of enhanced services over a time frame. The model also offers schools the choice to shift from one category to another, and accordingly choose strategic plans.

Kaufman (1992) offered a four-stage model of strategic planning:

1. Scoping
2. Data collection
3. Planning
4. Implementing and evaluating

Scoping

TQM can target at mega (societal concern and linkage), macro (institutional), and micro (department/team/individual) levels. The first stage of strategic planning is to define the scope of TQM in the institution. Experiments with TQM in classroom transaction (Hansen and Jackson, 1996) or in staff selection (Cole, 1995) are instances of micro scoping dealing with one component of schooling. All efforts of holistic organizational development are cases of macro scoping (see case on Chowgule College in Mukhopadhyay, 2004). Wherever a school or a college goes beyond its boundaries to include social action to transform a community, it demonstrates the case of mega scoping (see case on Udang High School in Mukhopadhyay, 2004).

Data collection

The second stage of strategic planning is collecting data and information on a variety of issues that intrinsically determine the adoption of TQM in institutions. Data and information are needed on the following:

- Ideal vision
- Beliefs and values
- Current missions
- Ideal and current results
- Needs

One section of the MIAS (see Appendix II) calls for data on enrolment with gender disaggregation, teachers and non-teaching staff, budget and financial provisions, inter-grade transition rate, details of the physical infrastructure and facilities, excellence in academic and non-academic areas, etc. It is important to collect trend data. In one of my recent TQM exercises with a school, it realized that the enrolment and performance of the school in both academic and non-academic areas had gone up phenomenally but the number of classrooms and teachers had remained unchanged over the last five years. Only trend data can provide such revelations. For the purpose of decision-making on facts and as a prerequisite to strategic planning, it is necessary to develop an inventory of items in various aspects of schooling where data is necessary. The next step is to define the nature and source of data and frequency of updation. All such areas with defined interrelationships can create the Educational Management Information System; it can be planned well to develop the facility for Relational Database Management System.

Planning

Planning constitutes five important activities.

1. The first and foremost is the identification of matches and mismatches. There are areas and activities that can complement (matches) one another. Others can contradict (mismatches) one another. It is important to identify them and make deliberate efforts to reconcile the differences.
2. Reconciliation is the second stage of planning.
3. The third stage is developing collectively the short- and long-term missions to guide actions.
4. The fourth stage is carrying out a SWOT analysis to identify strengths, weaknesses, opportunities, and threats. On the basis of the SWOT analysis and mission statements (both short- and long-term), the strategic move is to decide institutional policies and rules for decision-making. The focus is on rules and practices in

decision-making rather than on decisions per se; this is important in all participative management processes.

5. The final stage is developing strategic action plans that will translate the missions into reality.

Implementing and evaluating

This is the final stage, comprising the following primary stages:

- Putting the plan into action
- Carrying out formative evaluation
- Carrying out summative evaluation
- Continuing or revising, as required

Table 10.1   Strategic planning process

Stages	Questions
Mission and vision	• What is our purpose? • What are our vision, mission, and values?
Customer or learner requirements	• Who are our customers? • What do our customers expect of us? • What do we need to be good at to meet customer expectations? • What do our learners require from our institution? • What methods do we use to identify learner/customer needs?
Routes to success	• What are our strengths, weaknesses, opportunities, and threats? • What factors are critical to our success? • How are we going to achieve success?
Quality performance	• What standards are we going to set? • How are we going to deliver quality? • What will quality cost us?
Investing in people	• How should we make the best use of our staff? • Are we investing sufficiently in staff and staff development?
Evaluating process	• Do we have processes in place to deal with things that go wrong? • How will we know if we have been successful?

The four-stage mechanism of strategic planning with all its sub-components provides a working model. Sallis (1996) raised some guiding questions while proposing a six-stage strategic planning model (Table 10.1). Such questions are linked to each stage. Let us review the questions and the planning stages. The response to such and similar questions can be the building blocks of a strategic plan.

The three models proposed by Murgatroyd and Morgan, Kaufman, and Sallis offer three different orientations to the concept of strategic planning for implementing TQM in organizations. Interestingly, these three models can be integrated to provide a fourth eclectic strategic planning model (Figure 10.2).

By implication, each category of institution—basic–open for example—needs to define its scope and methods of data collection, planning, implementing, and evaluating as much as it must define its mission and vision, customer focus, routes to success, quality performance, and methods of investing in people. Ideally, a strategic planning model should combine all three models.

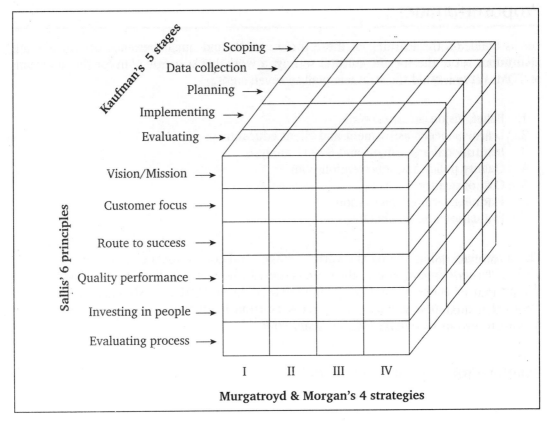

Figure 10.2   3-D eclectic strategic planning model

There are, however, certain commonalities among the three models. Kaufman's concept of scoping is the process of visioning at a spatial level. Sallis takes the grammarian view of reductionism of vision into mission. This is referred by Kaufman in the next stage of data collection. Similarly, there are some common elements in the planning stage of Kaufman model, and routes to success questions of Sallis' model as much as evaluating in both models is common. Investing in people, deciding standards, and cost of quality are parts of strategic planning and implementing. Although both Kaufman and Sallis models are presented in generic forms (equally applicable to all institutions), there is a need to examine their comparative relevance to different types of institutions as mentioned by Murgatroyd and Morgan. In the Indian context, for example, planning capability is likely to be better in basic–niche institutions. The enhanced institutions may not necessarily be conscious of their type and specialities.

Proposed model

Let us build, on the learning of these three models and our experience of educational institutions set in the specific cultural setting, a workable strategic plan for the adoption of TQM. We will build the strategic plan in seven steps.

1. Belief, vision, mission, goals
2. Learners' needs assessment and client education
3. Institutional assessment and SWOT analysis
4. Quality policy and intervention plan
5. Cost of quality
6. Planning for implementation
7. Evaluation and feedback

The interrelationship among the various stages and components can be seen in Figure 10.3. The model incorporates all seven stages. It, however, indicates that vision needs the input of concept of quality and understanding of TQM as a strategy. Similarly, in deciding quality policy, inputs are necessary from leadership concepts and practices, human resources development, and teamwork.

Belief, vision, mission, and goals

Belief
Belief guides actions. Although there are no formal mechanisms in educational organizations for articulating belief, there is ample evidence in our utterances of what we believe.

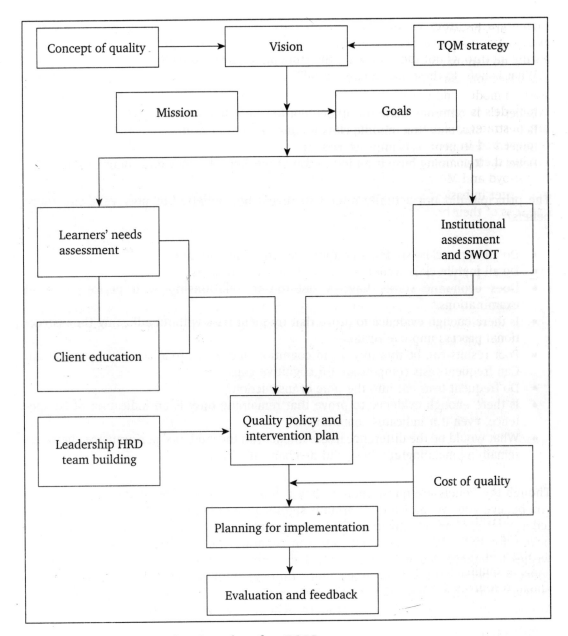

Figure 10.3   Strategic planning for TQM

Let us examine an episode. After undergoing a capacity building programme on resource utilization, a participating principal visited me and said, 'The programme was really excellent. Everybody taught so well. But, Sir, we have lot of problems in our school. All our students come from middle-class homes only. Hardly, 46 per cent pass in the Board examination. Our teachers take tests every two months; they remain really so busy in testing all throughout the year. Still, the students perform so badly.'

What beliefs do these statements reveal?

Belief 1   Good programme for others, not for me (I'm a non-learner).
Belief 2   Students from middle-class homes cannot perform.
Belief 3   Frequent tests improve results.
Belief 4   Remaining busy is an indication of teacher efficiency and commitment.

The principal did not actually intend to reveal her beliefs. But how valid are these beliefs?

- Do all upper-class students perform well in examinations?
- Do all middle-class students fare badly in examinations?
- Does economic status have a one-to-one relationship with performance in examinations?
- Is there enough evidence to prove that frequent tests without adjusting the instructional process improve results?
- Poor results can be due to gaps in cognition and poor articulation in examination. Can frequent tests compensate for cognitive gaps?
- Do frequent tests eat into the time of instruction?
- Is there enough evidence to prove that remaining busy is an indication of competence, even if it indicates commitment?
- What would be the difference in the impact (on the students' performance) between remaining meaningfully busy and mechanically busy?

Though the beliefs are questionable, they colour the vision. The saying 'you are what you believe you are' indicates enormous significance of beliefs in the life of an individual as well as of an organization. One strategic plan, hence, is to understand and share beliefs for two advantages. First, one can separate the actual belief from what one wishes to believe. Second, sharing the belief provides the foundation for developing collective belief founded on much more rational thinking. For example, if everyone believes that 'this school will be the best in the state' (common among schools like Mother's International School or Modern School), everyone is likely to work towards that *vision.*

Vision

Vision is built on a set of beliefs about the organization, its people, environment, culture, structure, facilities, etc. Visions are of two types: near and distant. The distant vision is the dream or imagination. In Swami Vivekananda's view, imagination has a great role in life. An institution should continue to strive to reach that imagined status. Such a vision is not limited by time and quality. 'Best' is relative and there is a continuous shift in the 'best'; for, the 'good' ones are moving towards 'better' and the 'better' ones towards the 'best'. Even if being the best can be time-bound, staying there is a timeless endeavour.

I had a meeting with the staff of a teacher education institution that was implementing TQM; I asked, 'Can you be the best in the country?' The immediate response was 'No, how can we?' To the subsequent questions by other members of the group, the assertive responses were 'We have by far the best staff—both competent and motivated', 'We have the best of students selected through rigorous admission tests', 'The students come from good homes with reasonable financial affordability', 'The college has good physical infrastructure, educational technology facilities, good linkages with other institutions, etc.' When I asked, 'Then, what's missing?' The almost unanimous response was: 'We can't believe that we can be the best.'

Short-term vision has to be built to contribute to the generation of the distant vision. The distant vision can be divided both on components and time into short-term visions. The strategic point for TQM is to set a shared vision. Vision is a creative endeavour, not everybody is endowed with it. Hence, one may develop a vision if one is creative, and share or validate the vision with others. Alternatively, through brainstorming and vision building workshops, one can develop a collective vision for the institution. We will return to visioning methods later in the book.

Mission

Mission is the end-of-the-road target for the institution. Missions are futuristic and directional—statements of purpose of an institution. However, most institutions do not have a documented articulation of a mission statement. In fact, sometimes mission statements are almost meaningless. Let us see some examples.

- Most students will achieve mastery over all subjects.
- Students will demonstrate the values of cooperation, honesty, respect for elders, etc.
- Students will excel and achieve their full potential in physical, mental, emotional, intellectual, and inner-life development.

Goals

Through reductionism, goals are missions unbundled. Goals are like mileposts; each contributes to the achievement of the mission. Goals determine the activities, programmes, and processes of an institution. Also, goals determine the way a programme is to be offered. Let us see how a mission needs to be unbundled into institutional goals.

Mission statement

Most students will achieve mastery (learning) over all subjects.

Goals (in behavioural terms)

Teachers will

- explain the concept of mastery learning
- cite experiments and research on mastery learning
- describe instructional design for mastery learning
- plan experimental projects for mastery learning
- implement mastery learning projects
- institutionalize mastery learning strategies

Students will

- cite examples of achieving mastery (learning) by other students of comparable backgrounds
- exude confidence that they can achieve mastery learning
- adopt new learning strategies
- demonstrate mastery learning; 80 per cent of the students securing 80 per cent marks (popularly called the 80/80 matrix) in all subjects

All the goals, except the last, are enabling goals but important. The statement of goals indicates that a mission is a summation of goals. Hence, missions and goals are integrally related. This logical relationship between mission and goal holds equally good between mission and vision.

Hence, the first step in strategic planning for TQM is to state the long-term vision and spell out the missions and short-term goals and targets.

Learners' needs assessment and client education

There are two different strands: what the learners 'need' and what they 'want'. Need is 'hygienic', want is 'motivating'. There is a growing belief among many teachers that most students want certificates, not knowledge or skills. This could have been adequate a few years ago when the number of graduates was limited and jobs were related to qualifications. Now that every job and entry to every professional course is based on entrance tests, certificates have turned out to be admit cards for competitive selection tests for jobs and admission to institutes of higher learning. It is only knowledge and skills that can hold graduates in good stead. Accordingly, the focus has now to be shifted to the learners' needs from wants. The major difference in the learning outcome is the difference between fragile and sustainable learning. While both fragile and sustainable learning can lead to higher performance examination, TQM stands for sustainable learning.

The assessment of needs will depend upon the goals and targets—to offer basic or enhanced services. On the basic services, there is a need to assess learning difficulties. For example, it is estimated that nearly 2/3rd of the students fail in mathematics and English in the Board examination. There can be diagnostic tests to identify where the difficulties are and appropriate remedial action can be worked out. Longitudinal assessment of learning difficulties, say, in mathematics will indicate that the failure in the Board examination is the effect of cumulative learning difficulties over various grades before the candidate is sent up for the Board examination in Class 10.

I was associated with an innovative experiment in a few municipal primary schools in Mumbai slums. After taking graded tests, the schools labelled Grade 4 children into Grades 2, 3, and 4 equivalent competencies in mathematics. Similar exercises were done for Grade 3 and 2 too. The schools reconstructed its instructional practices in mathematics by clubbing children on their competency levels across grades to which they belonged. As it was done in case of language of science education, the composition of each class became different. Within three years, the students achieved reasonable homogeneity on minimum levels of learning in mathematics in each grade.

Learners' needs assessment should be both in academic and non-academic areas. To get a meaningful assessment of learners' needs, it is necessary to involve the learners as well as their parents. Should the institution produce 'employable graduates', e.g., teacher training institutions, vocational education institutions, etc., it is equally important to consult the employers.

In India and other developing countries with unabated population growth rate, there are more buyers of education than the system can offer, and there are too many graduates than the employment market can absorb. On the other end of the continuum, are the new specialized fields like electronics, biotechnology, nano- science and technology, etc., where there are far too few qualified and competent people in the market. Under the circumstances, schools and colleges need to develop well-designed mechanisms for client education—educating them about future employment and the entrepreneurship market, gate passes to successful living (e.g., learning not only 'to know' but also 'to do', 'to live together' and 'to be'; UNESCO, 1996). This is not unusual; every consumer product industry keeps updating its potential customers. This will be evident from the advertisements and promotional literature of computer or automobile industries, particularly since the market has been opened up and competition has become fiercer.

Two important areas of client education are the relationship between sustainable learning and performance examination, and the emerging employment market as skill- and quality-oriented, not necessarily qualification-oriented. Thus, the basic issue is to assess the needs of the 'clients' and, in the process, it is necessary to consult multiple categories of customers: students, parents, community, employers, etc.

The second important step in strategic planning, then, is to clearly assess learners' needs and also what they want to learn. In order that they are able to assess and articulate their needs and wants, TQM institutions must offer opportunities of education to the students and their parents about what to expect from education.

Institutional assessment and SWOT analysis

Every effort in TQM or change management in institutions must be preceded by institutional assessment primarily to diagnose strengths and weaknesses of the organization. Institutional assessment can be carried out in more than one way. Mukhopadhyay's Institutional Profile Questionnaire (MIPQ) is a simple tool that helps generate an institutional profile indicating stronger and weaker areas of an institution. It is good to use a well-designed instrument to collect information on various aspects of an institution. Also this provides the baseline information against which you can measure progress of your school or the college. The SWOT analysis, a qualitative technique can be used for organizational diagnosis. SWOT is a familiar and popular acronym in management in general, and organizational diagnosis in particular. SWOT stands for strengths, weaknesses, opportunities, and threats. The main thesis is that for quality improvement, the institution should do the following:

- Identify and encash on its strengths, and strengthen them further
- Identify its weaknesses, and initiate deliberate action to reduce them
- Identify its opportunities, exploit them, and convert them into strengths
- Identify its apparent and potential threats and try to eliminate or reduce their intensity so that they may not harm it or aggravate its weaknesses

I have used the SWOT analysis exercise with several hundred principals of schools and colleges during my management workshops (sample SWOT sheet—Table 10.2). Strengths and weaknesses are easily recognizable. Principals find it rather difficult to identify opportunities and threats, as they are often hidden.

Table 10.2   SWOT analysis of an educational institution

Strengths	Weaknesses
• Good building facilities • Strong dramatics and sports activities • Strong social action activities • Enthusiastic management	• Poor academic results • Poor staff quality • Inadequate sports and games facilities • Lack of recognition for social action programmes
Opportunities	Threats
• Multiple use of building • Excellence in dramatics and sports activities • Enthusiastic and supportive local community and alumni • Fund mobilization for innovative activities	• Teachers union activities and low staff morale • Exodus of talented students for better sports facilities • Loss of image, from high-profile socially sensitive to conventional • Withdrawal of community support

A SWOT analysis is a participative process of organizational diagnosis. There are several ways in which this is actually carried out.

- The SWOT analysis can be carried out by asking participants to fill in blank SWOT sheets. The responses in the S, W, O, and T quadrants can be collated and presented for discussion and consensus building.
- The SWOT can be identified through an open discussion with the staff. Many institutions have tried hands-on consultation without the help of any structured questionnaire. Deft handling can give good results in this approach too, with the risk that a few articulate members may hijack the discussion, leaving out the large silent majority.
- The SWOT analysis can be built on data collected through questionnaires and tests. For example, some members of the staff, selected on certain criteria, can respond to the MIPQ. The data thus generated can be collated to figure out staff perceptions of organizational strengths and weaknesses. Such a profile can then be presented back to the staff for further debate so that a consensus emerges.

A SWOT profile becomes more acceptable when it is built through participative process, instead of any individual's exercise, howsoever brilliant he/she might be. I have found better results in a three-step process of SWOT.

1. Administer an institutional assessment instrument
2. Tabulate the data to draw a profile
3. Present the profile to staff for discussion and develop consensus

Thus, the third important step in strategic planning is to carry out organizational diagnosis either through the administration of a reliable instrument (questionnaire) or through a consultative process leading to the collective generation of a SWOT sheet.

Quality policy and intervention plan

Following the SWOT is the decision on quality policy. The starting point depends upon two considerations: what is the current status and position of the institution, and where does it want to go? While TQM is applicable to all categories of institutions, the critical decision is on the quality policy. The most fundamental questions are the following:

- Is the institution in a crisis, facing threat to its reputation, if not existence?
- Is the institution in normal running condition?
- Is the institution already good?

The quality policy will obviously differ according to the condition of the institution. The quality policy for the institution in crisis will be to come out of the crisis so that normalcy is restored and the stage is set for development. The quality policy for the institution in normal running institution is to build quality, moving from the average to the good. The quality policy for a good institution is to achieve higher goals, and distinguish itself as a great institution. For a great institution like Takshashila or Nalanda in ancient India, the IITs and IIMs of modern India, and Harvard, Oxford, and Cambridge of the West, the quality policy would be to sustain and search for further excellence. The journey must go on.

Responses to the following questions using the access service paradigm of Murgatroyd and Morgan (1993) can offer an alternative way of locating an institution for deciding the quality policy.

- Do you follow open entry or admit on merit alone?
- Have you been able to achieve minimum levels of learning—say, average transition rate of 80 per cent and above, or average pass percentage at Board/external examination of 70 or 75 per cent?
- Have you been able to offer an average level of facilities and learning opportunities in co-curricular activities?
- Have you been able to develop a satisfactory relationship with the local community that 'supplies' the students to your institution?
- Have you been able to achieve an average level of classroom instruction?

Answers to these and other questions should guide the decision on quality management policy. While every type of institution can offer enhanced services in one area or another, a strategic policy is to build general services to a certain minimum level and then take on to enhanced services that would distinguish an institution from others. Despite the emphasis on all-round development, the foremost demand of the students and parents is academic excellence. If the institution is an open-admission school, you may consider identifying areas that are critical to success in academic quality improvement. If you have already achieved minimum basic quality and your institution is on the move ahead, it is time to decide on specialization. The point to be noted here is that enhanced services or specializations are to be built upon minimum basic services; they are not alternatives.

As a consequence to organizational diagnosis and institutional assessment, the strategic plan warrants defining the quality policy of the institution.

In the broader context of quality policy, specific interventions are chosen. Kaizen, as a principle and practice, provides a sound instrument of intervention.

Kaizen

Kaizen is a Japanese term used to depict a particular approach to TQM. TQM is massive and holistic; it is, however, seen as a product of a large number of smaller interventions. Sallis (1996) defined it thus: 'The philosophy of TQM is large scale, inspirational and all-embracing, but its practical implementation is small-scale, highly practical and incremental. Drastic intervention is not the means of change in TQM.' TQM is incremental and success-oriented; it builds success on success. Kaizen professes identification of relatively innocuous, but important area for intervention; then slowly build on the achievements. This provides sound entry point for TQM in an organization and also builds up strength against resistance to innovation. The strategic issue is identifying critical areas where intervention is likely to succeed and make significant contribution to the missions and goals. Let us take an example (Box 10.1).

Box 10.1   A KAIZEN ON STAFF DEVELOPMENT

The Principal of a college of education in Mumbai arranged for a few audio-cassette recorders and some blank cassettes. He told his academic staff that he wished to develop a collection of audio lessons in the library. He asked the teachers, whosoever was willing, to take a cassette recorder and blank cassettes to the class and record their lectures. The teachers were also asked to take the cassette and the recorder, if needed, home and listen to the recorded lecture. Should the teacher himself/herself be satisfied, the cassette could be deposited with the librarian. If the teacher were not satisfied, he/she would erase it and re-record the next class. The teachers were not expected to get feedback from any other person, including the principal; however, the teachers were free to consult anyone they liked.

Besides the development of the collection of audio lectures, classroom instruction improved substantially. Every teacher took auto-feedback. In fact, during the first four months, no audio cassettes were deposited in the library, despite the cassette recorders and cassettes being issued by the teachers.

This was a simple intervention but one with long-term implications. On one hand, the library was getting enriched with new form of instructional material for reinforcement of learning to those who needed to repeat or missed class. On the other hand, it was improving the quality of classroom instruction.

Kaizen is an important component of quality policy. Intervention planning has to be based on overall quality policy. In this regard, the following issues and action points are worth considering:

- Develop long-term (seven to 10 years) as well as medium-term (three to four years) and short-term (one year) policies
- Prioritize areas of intervention and sequence them logically; for example, if you decide to improve academic performance of students, you may have to first upgrade the teachers
- Identify one significant but easy to intervene area so that success is ensured
- Identify areas where intervention can have multiple and multiplier effects
- Involve people in developing the quality policy
- Make full use of learning from SWOT; for example, a school with average academic performance should continue to strengthen its strong social interface tradition along with its new emphasis on academic quality improvement
- Identify resources needed to successfully implement the quality policy; identify the sources and mechanism of mobilization and your strategy for optimal utilization of resources
- Ensure that the quality policy is a written/printed document and everybody has access to it

- Provide for periodic review and mechanism for modifications within the quality policy and strategic plan

An important strategy is to raise relevant questions vis-à-vis quality management in the institution. The answers to such questions should draw up the list of intervention areas and activities. To translate strategic planning with involvement of all, I have a form or blank (Table 10.3) useful.

Table 10.3   Institutional planning form

Target year	Goals	Activities	Responsibility	Monitor	Resources
2010					
2009					
2008					
2007					
2006					
2005					

This form has been used to develop a perspective plan for a school. This is usually done by a group of teachers in a committee and the draft perspective is presented to the entire faculty. On the basis of discussion and consensus, the perspective is finalized.

I experimented with another implementable strategy with several institutions, for intervention in quality management. The principals were asked to identify three improvements that could be made in the given condition, implying no requirement of additional resources for reference to the larger system. Subsequently, they had to take certain decisions and tabulate them (Table 10.4).

Table 10.4   Planning format for a short-term intervention (a kaizen)

Activities			
Responsibility			
Time frame			
Possible problems			
Possible solution to each problem			
Criteria for success			
Methods and means upon entering			
Desirable resources			
Remarks			

Among many interesting results of this experiment, the story of a DIET in Punjab is worth recollecting. The idea of the principal was to develop an attractive campus in a situation where there is no provision for maintenance and the institute is in bad shape. The idea was unbundled into a few activities like clean classrooms, clean laboratories and corridors, clean courtyard with flower garden, and shady trees. The students were divided into small teams; each team was responsible for maintenance of one area. Each teacher offered to be the adviser to one team. Following the tradition of *kar seva*,[1] the students and teachers decided to spend half-an-hour everyday on these activities. For gardening, students required certain basic implements, which they brought from their homes. Within three to four months, students decided to pool resources to buy some implements which were not very expensive. Now, the institution had its own gardening implements. Teachers were not found wanting; they too joined in by making small contributions to the students' initiatives. Come spring, the dry, drab, 'unclean' institution was sparkling and welcoming students, teachers, parents, and guests with flowers blooming all over the campus.

This was just one of the three ideas, and had an enormous impact. Such exercises can be repeated within the institution by calling all teachers to identify two or three possible improvements. Each idea for activity can be strategically planned in the format given above. Some can be done individually, some implemented in groups, and some others done by the institution as a whole. This will satisfy the important criteria of TQM, namely CQI and participation of all.

Cost of quality

There is a common belief that quality is expensive and can be achieved only when there is large resource flow. This is a myth. *Quality is free* is the title of the book by Philip Crosby, an international TQM guru. Let us see a simple case.

The average unit cost per year in secondary grades is approximated at Rs 1,500. If a school's average transition rate is about 60 per cent and the student strength is 1,000, 400 students stagnate every year. The annual cost of stagnation is a whopping Rs 0.6 million where the annual budget is Rs 1.5 million. Similarly, as mentioned earlier, the annual national loss due to failure in the Board examination is about Rs 90,000 million. Indeed, quality can be free if these losses due to failure are prevented.

Performance is a multivariate phenomenon, ranging from home-related and person-related to school-related factors. There are school-related factors that might account for and explain more than 60 per cent of the phenomenon of stagnation and non-performance.

---

[1] Gurudwaras are spotlessly clean, all the time, everywhere. The devotees who visit the gurudwara take upon themselves the responsibility to clean the place, manage and clean the footwear of visitors, offer water, etc. All such service amounts to serving God. Such activities are called *kar seva* (*kar* for hands, *seva* for service).

Should the school-related variables be controlled, there will be significant reduction in stagnation and wastage. Our own experiment in the cluster of villages around Udang reduced the primary school dropout rate from 49 per cent to 17 per cent by changing the school processes to make them more interesting for the children through music and sports. There are many Indian studies on mastery learning (Hooda, 1982; Yadav, 1984) that have demonstrated that a large majority (about 80 per cent) of the students can demonstrate mastery over the subjects with only a modification of the instructional processes.

The critical importance in TQM is cost consciousness so that efficiency of every bit of investment may be assessed in terms of its contribution to quality improvement and management. From this angle, effective resource utilization is more important than the quantity of the resource. The human resource, the salary alone, costs over 90 per cent of the annual budget of a school and over 80 per cent of the annual budget of a college. Unless human resources are optimized—quantitatively, where all teachers take all classes scheduled for them; and qualitatively, where all teachers update themselves with reading and researching which they are already paid for (preparedness cost)—any amount of investment will be infructuous.

Another element is the optimal use of physical resources: library, laboratory, audio-visual aids, sports and games facilities, gymnasium, etc. It is important to identify the resources; some are obvious, some latent and unnoticed. The strategic plan for quality must accommodate and exploit resources.

Cost consciousness and cost management are two other important components of cost of quality issue. Very often, we are not cost-conscious. For example, what is the hourly teaching cost of a school teacher vis-à-vis the hourly cost of another employee at an equivalent level? Let us calculate (Table 10.5).

The additional Rs 94 (Rs 181–Rs 87) is paid to a school teacher for preparation and professional upgradation through self-study. There are arguments that teachers do much other work. The fact remains, that all that is preparatory to teaching and hence, this is the practical hourly cost of teaching. The argument is that a teacher needs to prepare to be effective in the classroom, in student assessment, indeed in all the eight areas mentioned earlier in the book. Indeed, the additional Rs 94 per hour is invested in the teacher for preparation. Whenever the teacher goes without preparation, the preparatory cost of Rs 94 remains unutilized. This approach of costing actual cost of teaching and teacher utilization is corroborated by the International Institute of Educational Planning, Paris (IIEP, 1990).

A series of similar costs can be calculated. The issue of quality revolves around the return on investment (RoI). Now, the hourly cost is the same for two teachers in the same school. But the teacher who regularly prepares and teaches according to plan gives better RoI than the one who takes it casually. Cost consciousness implies developing sensitivity about costs and likely returns keeping the quality in focus. Cost management is the natural corollary to cost consciousness. Cost management implies investment decisions. For example, for improving academic quality, where should you invest—on staff development or instructional material or audio-visual aids or alternative instructions or all? The investment

Table 10.5   Comparative cost per hour of teacher and non-teacher employee

Items	Non-teacher employee	Teacher	Remarks
Number of working days in a year	261–33–10–12 = 206	220–12–10 = 198	
Number of hours per day	8	6 periods × 40 minutes = 4 hours	
Working hours per year	1,648	792	A teacher earns Rs 94 more than a non-teacher employee of equivalent level per hour.
Annual salary	144,000	144,000	
Cost per hour	87	181	

Notes: 1.   As per stipulations, schools are expected to work for 220 days in a year including examination days. Schools have eight periods per day of 40 minutes each with one short and one long recess. Teachers usually carry a burden of about 30 periods a week or about 6 periods a day.

2.   Non-teacher employees in the government, business establishments, and industries work five days a week and enjoy 33 days of earned leave compared to the summer and autumn vacation of teachers. Both teachers and non-teacher employees enjoy 10 casual and 12 medical leaves.

decision depends upon the estimation of RoI for improvement of quality. A few statements are valid for all Indian institutions. Academic staff is the most critical factor for success and we are not deriving enough from it. Also, we are not investing enough in staff development. Most institutions offer conventional programmes contributing to maintenance learning, not innovative learning (Botkin, Elmandjra, and Malitza, 1979). Strategic planning must accommodate a detailed mechanism of human resource development.

Strategic planning for TQM must have cost consciousness and RoI estimates for every investment made, either as a routine or as an innovative programme.

Planning for implementation

Fancy statements like 'we are good planners but bad managers' are made by armchair planners who are miles away from grass-roots realities. No plan is a good plan unless it can be implemented and managed. TQM as a philosophy does not offer any cosy corner for romanticizing planning. Plans must be implementable. Planning for implementation is that component of strategic planning which details out the activities, time frame, resource allocation, monitoring details, and indicators of success. In other words, planning for implementation looks for answers to a series of questions associated with each of the seven stages of planning. Questions pertain to activities, indicators of success, resources, and monitoring. Just two sample questions for each of the four criteria, for each of the seven stages, are given in Table 10.6.

You will notice that questions have also been raised on planning for implementation. These are only sample questions. Each TQM institution must be able to raise relevant questions on the basis of its own background and personality.

Evaluation and feedback

A strategic plan is incomplete without the mention of the frequency and mechanism of evaluation and feedback. The basic purpose of evaluation and feedback is quality assurance, not quality control. Evaluation does not mean passing judgements on success or failure. The purpose is to assess the distance travelled from the place of origin and distance remaining to the destination. These are directly linked to the milepost concept mentioned earlier. Thus, evaluation has to be formative; it should provide, besides achievement, the weaker aspects of the plan implementation—warning signals on prospective disasters so that mid-course corrections can be planned and executed. The frequency of evaluation should depend upon the kind of activity planned. It can be carried out monthly, quarterly, or half-yearly for the annual plan, annually for the short-term plan, and biannually for the long-term plan. It is extremely important that the strategic plan contain details of frequency, evaluation methods, and persons responsible.

For successful planning and implementation of TQM, it is necessary to plan the mechanisms of evaluation and feedback including the persons responsible for this.

Conclusion

A strategic plan is, more or less, the culminating point of all discussions so far on TQM. We have reviewed three different models and proposed a model that should fit in an Indian situation. What is important is to identify the basic pattern and style of the institution and adapt the model. In the process, an institution may develop a plan that is unique. The real indicator of success is a strategic plan that reflects that uniqueness of the institution.

Table 10.6   Sample questions for developing planning for implementation

Seven steps in strategic planning	Activities	Indicators of success	Resources	Monitoring
Belief, vision, mission	What are the activities to be undertaken for developing a shared vision of the institution? How will the vision be unbundled into missions, goals, and activities?	Do you have a vision and mission statement? How feasible is the vision and mission?	What financial resources are required? What expert resources are needed?	How would you monitor the process of development of vision, mission, etc.? How would you ensure the quality of vision, mission, etc.: their worthwhileness and achievability?
Learners' needs assessment and client education	What activities will be undertaken to assess learners' needs? How would you educate your customers?	Do you have a document on learners' needs? Do you have a report on customer education and its results?	What financial resources are required to assess learners' needs? Who will carry out the learners' needs assessment and customer education?	How would you ensure timely accomplishment of learners' needs assessment and customer education programmes? How would you ensure quality and reliability?
Institutional assessment and SWOT	Which tool would you use to assess your institution? When and to whom would you administer it? How would you develop a SWOT sheet?	Do you have an institutional profile? Do you have an agreed upon SWOT sheet?	What financial resources are required? What kind of expertise is required to carry out institutional assessment and SWOT, and where will you get that expertise from?	How would you ensure timely accomplishment of tasks? How would you ensure quality of assessment and organizational diagnosis and their acceptability among staff?

(Continued)

Table 10.6   *(Continued)*

Seven steps in strategic planning	Activities	Indicators of success	Resources	Monitoring
Quality policy and intervention plan	When and how would you develop your quality policy? How would you develop intervention plans and ensure that these contribute to the achievement of quality policy?	Do you have a statement of policy, e.g., standard to be achieved? Do you have a set of activities identified to achieve the policy?	What financial resources are needed to develop the quality policy and intervention plan? Where would you derive those financial resources from?	How would you ensure timely development of the quality policy and intervention plan?
Cost of quality	How would you work out the differential contribution of investment items on quality? How would you estimate financial requirements for implementing the planned intervention?	Do you have a cost analysis of spending on various aspects of the institution vis-à-vis contribution to quality? Have you worked out the cost estimation for each activity planned quality management?	How much time do you need to assess the differential contribution of investment from quality management? Who will carry out the cost studies?	How would you ensure that intervention plans indeed contribute to and lead to a fructifying the quality policy?
Planning for implementation	What will be the mechanism for developing a plan for implementation?	Have you agreed upon a PERT chart for implementing the strategic plan?	What financial resources are required to implement the plan? Who will be responsible for which activity?	Does the implementation plan take into account the cost of activities? Are responsibilities fixed for each activity to an individual or a group?

(Continued)

Table 10.6   *(Continued)*

Seven steps in strategic planning	Activities	Indicators of success	Resources	Monitoring
	How would you identify the factors that can be the roadblocks in implementing the strategic plan?	Do you have a document identifying risk areas?		
Evaluation and feedback	What tools would you use for evaluation and feedback? What would be the frequency of such evaluation? How would you ensure that evaluation is objective, and not covered with self-fulfilling prophecies?	Do you have a documented plan for evaluating activities? Do you have a document on how the feedback will be given and how mid-course corrections will be carried out?	What financial, human, and time resources are required to evaluate and give feedback?	Do you have a schedule for evaluation? How would you ensure that evaluation is neither a fault finding nor a self-fulfilling prophecy?

Implementing Total Quality Management

11

Introduction

Most educational institutions run on a routine, often without a plan of development. Any developmental efforts are usually piecemeal approaches. Total quality management (TQM) urges for long-term planning, which is also dynamic, since the plan is subject to continuous review and revision. It is important to ensure acceptance and internalization of the concept of TQM, and its theoretical constructs. It is not necessary that people use the term TQM, which may be construed as 'jargon', 'old wine in new bottle', 'another management fad', etc. A similar approach to TQM has been termed Continuous Quality Improvement or CQI (Frazier, 1997), Return on Quality or RoQ (Weller, 1996), and Quality Management Plus or QMP (Kaufman and Zahn, 1993). What is important is absorbing the basic spirit of the movement—the concept of quality in education and techniques and strategies of its management on a continuing basis.

Managing change

Managing change is an extensively researched area, both in India and abroad (Mukhopadhyay, 1981, 1989; Rogers and Shoemaker, 1971; Havelock, 1973). There are several dimensions and a few basic contentions in the management of change. First, change is the function of successful adoption and institutionalization of innovation. An innovation passes through several stages during adoption. The management of change amounts to steering an innovation through the various stages till an innovation is institutionalized. The members of an organization react differently to the same innovation. Several agencies and processes are involved in the adoption of innovation. It is also important to recognize that resistance is the natural company of innovations. In this case, TQM is the innovation—a new approach and strategy for the management of quality, and hence management of change. Each kaizen is an innovation. It will be useful to examine how innovations are adopted in organizations.

Adoption of innovation

The adoption of innovation happens through a five-stage process (Rogers, 1962).

1. *Installation* signifies the first implantation of the idea in the mind of a potential individual adopter or an adopting organization
2. *Trial* signifies the mental exercise of assessing feasibility, planning for adoption, and also assessing adverse consequences
3. *Adoption* is the actual translation of the idea at the field level: pilot or full scale
4. *Evaluation* is the assessment of the process efficiency of adoption and impact of the innovation; evaluation in this case is not summative, the basic intention being corrective to final adoption
5. *Internalization* is the mechanism of subsuming an innovation into the system, rendering it out of the 'zone of innovation'

Thus, TQM as a new philosophy and innovative strategy for quality improvement will go through these five stages. These stages, however, are not sacrosanct; each one actually comprises several micro-stages.

As soon as an innovation is diffused into the system, it generates different reactions among potential adopters. Some reject the idea outright on the ground that it cannot be implemented or is unnecessary. Some keep toying with the idea for some time, and then give up as soon as the challenge of implementing the idea is understood or some other conventional activity creates a demand on them. A few began the mental trial primarily to find out the ways and means of adopting it, and actually implement the new idea. In another classification, adopters have been classified into innovators, early adopters, adopters, late adopters, and laggards.

We can relate the classification of people according to the reaction to innovations with the can do–will do typology presented earlier in the book (Figure 11.1).

Those who are competent and willing are either innovators or early adopters. The competent but unwilling as well as incompetent and unwilling are the laggards. The willing but not competent persons largely belong to the categories of adopters and late adopters. Willingness becomes the determining factor. As TQM is introduced in a school or college, teachers and non-teaching staff react differently. A perceptive principal can identify the innovators, early adopters, adopters, late adopters, and laggards.

There are certain structural aspects of adoption of innovation. First, there must be certain sources from where new ideas for quality education and quality management can flow into the adopting school or college. An important requirement, hence, is to be connected to the sources of ideas. Such sources may be sister institutions, professional bodies, professional literature, resource institutions, etc. The second structural issue is the communication of innovation: methods, techniques and power of communication, credibility of the communicator, etc. The third element is the characteristics of the innovation itself.

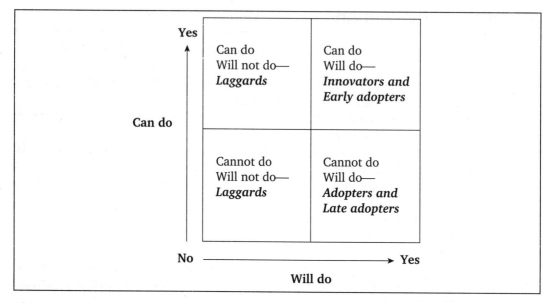

Figure 11.1   Categories of adopters on Can do–Will do matrix

Innovations that are complex, relatively abstract, or take too long to achieve results are likely to be resisted and rejected; kaizen works better. Management of resistance warrants anticipating resistance and planning for its resolution.

Resistance to change

Resistance is the law of innovation. In fact, the dynamics of change comprises two sets of forces: one set of forces released by innovators and early adopters, and the other set of forces released by the laggards and late adopters. Lewin's (1951) classical force field analysis theory contends that prior to the intervention of innovation, these two sets of forces maintain a state of equilibrium. This equilibrium gets disturbed by the introduction of innovation. The fate of an innovation depends upon the equation of these two contesting sets of forces. Several attributes of the individuals in the organization as well as the qualities of the organization have been identified to be responsible for resistance to innovation, e.g., conservativeness, sense of insecurity, fear of failure, low self-esteem, inability to sense needs, unwillingness to work, inadequate exposure to new ideas and media, poor contact with progressive organizations and individuals, etc. Similarly, role conflict, lack of training, lack of clarity of innovation, lack of technical competence, non-availability of literature, lack of access to guidance, work load, fatigue from innovation, unrealistic time targets, etc., are some other characteristics of individuals who tend to resist innovations.

Organizational factors pertain to both external and internal mechanisms. External factors are demand for change in social relations, threat on dynamic equilibrium of the system, lack of openness, lack of permeability from one layer of organization to another, localness, lack of communication and linkage with resource systems, etc. Internal factors are division of labour, hierarchical organization, reward for traditional behaviour, interference of higher management, closed organizational climate, physical distance between sub-systems, inadequate financial and physical facilities, organization size (especially small), directive and autocratic leadership, cohesive small groups, lack of autonomy and involvement in decision-making, peer criticism, sense of imposition, vested interests, etc. These resisting forces are potential dangers to the adoption of TQM.

TQM and management of change

TQM is one approach to management of change. Innovation in an educational institution can be both horizontal as well as vertical and deep. Horizontal innovations and changes imply expansion and diversification of activities. 'Deep approach' means qualitative changes or unlocking the culture of change (Weller, 1998); quality of the services (basic versus enhanced) provided by the institution. TQM looks at the process of change for depth and height. However, it does not exclude diversification or expansion wherever needed for qualitatively transforming the institution. Essentially, hence, TQM attempts change with a focus. The focus is on quality.

TQM foresees quality as an institutional culture; it becomes everybody's business to strive for excellence—*Yogaha Karmasu Kaushalam*—or skilfulness in whatever work one does. When a sweeper sweeps the floor, he does it to the best of his ability. The office staff manages the office with the highest competence and consideration for all those who need their service. Teachers teach to the best of their abilities and to the entire satisfaction of students and parents. The principal manages the institution to the satisfaction of staff, students, and parents. A good definition of TQM is 'quality at every step, by everybody and for everyone (client) related to education'.

Quality, as the culture of the institution, implies the concept of totality rather than partial application. Quality, in this context, cannot be just one item of the institution where other things lag. A school or a college with excellent academic results but no achievement in sports or cultural activities or prevalence of drug addiction among students cannot be considered a quality institution from the angle of TQM. TQM endeavours towards total qualitative development of the students in the four planes at which human beings live simultaneously: physical, emotional, intellectual, and spiritual. TQM must endeavour to upgrade and optimize living on all the planes. An institution that approaches to strike on all the planes to create a new vision of development is, in reality, practising TQM. For the institution, TQM means enhancing basic services to an acceptable level, then creating a niche.

There have been significant debates about piecemeal social engineering versus holistic massive changes. Kaizen brings in the strategic intervention concept and entry points for innovations. Every innovation activates certain forces that resist innovation. Opening several fronts at a time activates and maximizes the resisting forces, thus putting the innovation at risk. Kaizen is a strategic approach to choose an entry point to holistic organizational change. Undertaking small project-based interventions, one at a time, is a well-tested technique. Complicated and more comprehensive interventions can be built upon the success of the smaller efforts. The staff must taste success and develop confidence in innovations, and on themselves. The choice is for developing a culture of change over quick results. The kaizen principle enlarges its scope steadily and progressively to cover all aspects of the institution.

If we superimpose the management of change modalities, particularly the categories of adopters of innovations and stages of adoption of innovation, on the TQM approaches, it becomes evident that the principal ought to know his or her staff in terms of their disposition towards innovation, and the categories of adopters each one of them belongs to, so that appropriate strategies may be worked out to deal with them and derive the best advantage. On the other hand, while using kaizen principles of introducing small but definite innovations, the stages of adoption and internalization of innovation become relevant and important.

Road map

There are several alternative ways of developing the final plan or road map for implementing TQM in an educational institution. Crawford (1990) recommended eight stages in implementing TQM.

1. Vision: how the institution would like to be; what would constitute its greatness?
2. Define mission: compatible with vision
3. Set objectives: transformed into specific, attainable, measurable goals
4. Customers' requirements broken down into elements
5. Detailed process to satisfy customer needs
6. Specify materials, facilities, and standards to be met
7. Plan to bring together human, physical, and financial resources
8. Build in quality assurance mechanism

Crawford maintained that there have to be adequate efforts and investment in staff development. Frazier (1997) suggested a six-stage road map: prepare, assess, plan, deploy, sustain, and breakthrough. Navaratnam (1997) offered a six-stage quality journey plan comprising awareness and self-assessment; training and team building; quality planning; implementation process; comprehensive evaluation; and continuous improvement. Yudof and Busch-Vishniac (1996) insisted that the participants be given instructional material on TQM well in advance, and given specific assignments for developing position papers. This, the authors contend, will keep them focused. Further, TQM is a post-modern development, hence, dependent upon new information systems and technology for measuring progress towards quality journey. Chaffe and Tierney (1988) identified nine areas to provide a broad context within which to consider application of TQM.

1. Find internal contradictions
2. Develop a comparative awareness
3. Clarify the identity of the institution
4. Communicate
5. Act on multiple, changing forms
6. Treat every problem as if it has multiple solutions
7. Treat every solution as a fleeting solution
8. Look for consequences in unlikely places
9. Be aware of any solution that hurts people or undermines strong values

Chaffe and Tierney's nine stages are essentially process-oriented. Indeed, Shewart's (1931) classical Plan–Do–Check–Act cycle also offers a scientific basis for process development.

The three models proposed by Crawford, Frazier, and Navaratnam have many common grounds, e.g., Navaratnam's 'awareness and self-assessment' is similar to Frazier's 'prepare and assess'; 'quality planning' is 'plan', and what is 'implementation process' for Navaratnam is 'deploy' for Frazier. Yudof and Busch-Vishniac add the dimension of preparedness through advance reading and remaining focused through assignments on writing memorandums and papers. Chaffe and Tierney include some meaningful caution so that resistance is reduced. The lessons derived from these models and statements can be meaningfully integrated into developing a working model for implementing TQM in educational institutions.

TQM is a continuous search for new breakthroughs. Hence, the process of implementation fits better in a spiralling model, for that accommodates the spirit of continuity. Accordingly, the process comprises the following:

- Prepare the ground
- Define the baseline
- Set targets
- Plan for implementation
- Implement
- Revise baseline and take off

Prepare the ground

The first important step in implementing TQM is creating an environment conducive to the concept of quality. To begin with, the institution must be prepared to tolerate the concept; then move on to accept and receive it with enthusiasm. It is good to begin with some buzz sessions—expert presentations to staff on quality of education, indicators of quality, assessment of quality, and concept of TQM. A natural corollary will be informal discussions among staff in the corridors and staff room ranging from bitter criticism by laggards to enthusiastic appreciation by innovators and early adopters. Let that be, so that the word 'quality' may enter the social lexicon of the institution. In specific terms, the following are some of the concrete steps to prepare the ground:

- Talk informally to those receptive to new ideas
- Give them short papers on TQM, both theoretical and actual cases to read; avoid giving books
- Discuss at an intellectual level the strengths and weaknesses of the idea; do not defend TQM
- Create opinion leaders for TQM
- Be watchful if someone is emerging to try out a new idea of TQM; encourage him/her
- Once the subject of TQM has transcended to more than 50 per cent of the staff through informal chats, consider holding a staff seminar on TQM in education; it is safe and wiser to invite external expert to introduce TQM to the staff
- Use examples of adoption of TQM; show samples of institutional evaluation proforma to prove that it is non-threatening; let them try out themselves
- Allow the ideas to sink and get absorbed; repeat the exercise till you are convinced that the majority of the staff has understood the concept and is prepared to try it out

The second preparatory activity is staff capacity building and team building. The emphasis has to be on empowerment of people in the organization. TQM is a team game. It is not summative but productive. Individual excellence put together does not create organizational and systemic quality. Quality teams can be developed on the basis of projects and project teams. Teams can be smaller or bigger depending upon the need of the project. An important consideration, however, should be that the more, the better. Every effort must be made to involve everyone in the institution in the quality teams. Building teams is difficult, particularly surviving through the stage of storming discussed earlier, but it is necessary.

The third element of preparation is establishing the consistency of purpose. Since TQM is synonymous with CQI, it is important that the entire organization is prepared to accept it as an ongoing process and the constancy of purpose is visible and articulated.

Define the baseline

Before we begin our journey on CQI, it is important to define the baseline or the benchmark against which developments and improvements can be checked. Institutional self-assessment is necessary to develop the baseline so that one can examine whether, over a period, an institution is moving forward or remaining unchanged. Three clear steps need to be taken to assess the state of the art of the institution.

The first and foremost step in assessment is to choose an institutional evaluation instrument, from the many available. Almost all books on TQM provide instruments that have already been tried out for assessment of institutions. Each instrument has its own strengths and weaknesses. Some are very comprehensive, hence lengthy. Some are very short and crisp, hence miss out on details. The Mukhopadhyay's Institutional Profile Questionnaire (MIPQ; Appendix II) has been successfully used in literally hundreds of Indian educational institutions: degree colleges, colleges of teacher education, schools, etc. Given the uniqueness of each institution, it is a good practice to adapt these questionnaires, if needed.

The second aspect of assessment is to examine the amount and quality of data and facts available on record in the institution—the quality of data in terms of reliability, comprehensiveness, currency, etc. The purpose of assessment is to build a decision support system. Hence, upgradability and retrievability of data are also important considerations.

The third component is the SWOT analysis. In fact, SWOT subsumes data generated through institutional assessment. Yet, more than simple data is needed to create a descriptive profile, indicative of relative strengths and weaknesses. Besides facts, SWOT accommodates, feelings, perceptions, understanding of the organization, and inter-personal processes. For organizational development, none of these can be ignored.

Set targets

The organizational vision inspires and informs the targets. There are two different parameters of vision. One parameter is vision on a time frame, namely short term, medium term and long term. On the issue of long-term and short-term thinking, Peter Drucker (1974) wrote: 'Long-term thinking is learning the future by understanding consequences of what we do today. Long-term thinking requires willingness to forego short-term benefits that undermine future well being. Such thinking is congruent without knowing our mission and fixing on our customers with systemic improvement and continuing human resource development.' The second parameter is on a spatial term, namely micro, macro, and mega scenarios (Murgatroyd and Morgan, 1993). Vision has to be either collectively developed or collectively adopted and accepted. Should the principal be strong in visualizing, he or she can develop a vision and initiate intense and frank debate and discussion with the staff so that either the vision as it is, or in the modified version, is accepted psychologically by the staff. Once the vision has been clarified and accepted, it is necessary to reduce it into component missions, goals, and targets. We must also understand the psychological restrictions in visioning.

In one of my TQM workshops with the principals of a group of elite schools, a principal proudly mentioned that her school is the national champion in basketball. Her pride and satisfaction gave me the feeling that for her that was the end of the ambition. I asked her, 'Your students are tall, well-trained, competent.... Why are you not the international champions? What are the limitations?' She looked lost, completely clueless, and then answered, 'I never even thought of that.' She was satisfied with being the national champion, imagination and ambition being the limitations in this case. Indeed 'good is the greatest enemy of great' (Collins, 2001).

Planning for implementation

Planning for implementation is a multi-step process.

Step 1: An essay on the institution

Collect the teachers and other staff in a hall for 20–30 minutes during recess or on a Saturday afternoon. Ask each one of them to write an essay on the school in not more than 500 words. Do not give any outline; let them write whatever they wish to. To maintain anonymity, they need not sign the essays. If the number of teachers and staff is very large, you can sample about 20 teachers and staff representing different categories of teachers according to experience, subject specialization, gender, age, etc. Each essay is a documentation of the perception of a teacher or a staff about the school. You would be amused to see the enormous difference in their perceptions. Understanding these perceptual differences is extremely important. It will be good to carry out content analysis of these essays to understand differential perceptions of the staff about the school.

Another strategy is to present the essays in another session and allow the teachers to discuss each freely. It is a good idea to allow buzzing where teachers in twos, threes, and fours discuss among themselves their different perceptions about the school. These perceptions will indicate the beliefs of the staff. This exercise provides an opportunity to articulate the belief of each individual which otherwise is a secret. This also provides an opportunity to share and cross-check each other's beliefs and bring them into the open. Properly conducted, this exercise can bring in a relatively more common and more rational understanding and belief about the school.

Step 2: Identification of areas of improvement

It is quite common to find teachers and staff complaining and criticising their own institution on many counts. Once again, call them as a group at one place and ask them to develop a list of items/areas where improvements are necessary, all in about 10 minutes. It is good to specify a minimum number of improvements to be identified by each individual, say about 20 items to exhaust their diagnostic skills. As a follow-up to this listing, the areas of improvement identified by various members of the institution can be compiled and tabulated to find common as well as divergent areas of concern. Once the compilation and tabulation is done, it is necessary that the information be fed back to the group, allowing them to discuss it, both formally and informally, in buzz sessions. This will again bring convergence in their thinking regarding problem areas of improvement in the institution.

The most common area of improvement recommended in such an exercise will be infrastructure and facilities. The next in order will be improvement in others. Rarely, if ever, will improvement of self be identified. These are again based on beliefs such as (a) I am at my best; (b) whenever I do not perform, it is because of lack of facilities; and (c) my performance is not as much as I am capable of because others are not good enough. Even if the issue of self-development figures with one member of the group, bring that into sharp focus and pursue for consensus. Let me quote one of my experiences.

I was working on these exercises with a college of education with a small but very committed staff. Their essays indicated their tremendous sense of satisfaction and self-confidence. During discussion, some of them did not hesitate to claim that they are, indeed, the best in the country. Such was their belief. On the item of listing improvements, it was infrastructure and facilities all the way. Nothing else, except one teacher indicating the need for professional development. Taking out that statement, as if unnecessary since they are the best, I asked two apparently innocent questions.

1. How many papers did you write and get published during the last year?
2. What are the research projects you have completed or have in hand now?

When the answer from everyone was 'nil' to both, they started questioning their beliefs. They started asking counter-questions: On what themes can we undertake research? How should we develop proposals?

Step 3: Institutional assessment

The earlier two exercises are qualitative and perceptual. Also, they are not necessarily structured. The third exercise is institutional assessment; you can use the MIPQ. Institutional assessment generates both qualitative and quantitative data on which the profile of an institution as well as its growth pattern can be easily diagnosed. For example, in one exercise, we found that in one of the institutions, student enrolment had grown from 1,400 to over 2,200 during the last five years whereas the number of teachers remained constant at 136, the classrooms at 62, etc. There are several other such areas of trend data that can be used to assess the developments and change in the institution.

SWOT can be derived from the essays on the institution as well as from the data on institutional assessment. I prefer development of SWOT sheets. Please call the teachers and staff in a session of about 20–30 minutes and ask each one to write at least four or five items in each cell of the SWOT sheet. Once the staff members have filled up the sheets, the ideas under each head should be compiled and tabulated. The data should be fed back to the staff. This should be discussed at length so that the staff produces one agreed-upon SWOT list.

Step 4: Vision, mission, and goals

The next exercise is to build up a shared and acceptable common vision, a mission, and a set of goals. Drawing from the exercise of identified 20 improvements, staff members may be asked to write a brief note describing the school after 10 years, five years, and three years. A pointed question would be 'What should the school look like after five years?' You may consider providing a loose structure for recording the vision (Table 11.1).

Table 11.1   Format for vision statement

Vision	10 years	5 years	3 years	Comments
Teacher quality				
Student quality				
Programmes				
Performance				
Infrastructure				
Reputation				

Note: More items can be added.

What should happen to the school after five years? The notes should be subjected to content analysis to find common grounds as well as to find uncommon and divergent visions for the institution. This output should be fed back to the group encouraging the members to discuss further. The debate should be carefully steered to converge on an acceptable vision of the school after 10, five and three years.

During our visioning workshops, we found that most principals and teachers find it difficult to define and/or describe their institution five to 10 years on. They were candid that they are neither used to thinking about the future of their institution nor are they encouraged to imagine it.

In the next exercise, the participating staff should be asked to formulate the mission and goals for achieving the vision. There will be differences in the statements of missions and goals despite the accepted and shared vision. These mission and statements and goals should be collated, tabulated, and presented back to the respondents for discussion. Different dimensions of the vision can be assigned for different groups constituted out of all the respondents. The process of conversion of vision into mission and goals may be tedious and time consuming. You may have to spend couple of hours to come to an acceptable set of mission statements and goals.

Step 5: Prioritization
By now you have much data—different but interrelated—on the following:

- Beliefs
- Areas of improvement
- Strengths, weaknesses, opportunities, threats
- Vision
- A set of mission and goals

Similarly, there are some intangibles:

- Participation of people in organizational issues as a whole
- Certain new skills in diagnosing, projection, etc., in the staff
- A new set of beliefs that the staff can speak on the whole organization and that their views are important

All goals and improvements cannot be achieved at the same time. The improvements have to be prioritized; perhaps one or two items for implementation at a time. This can be achieved by asking the respondents to rank the goals in order of priority. It should be possible to find and calculate collective ranking of the goals. This can be presented back to the group for further discussion so that the arithmetic ranking can either be endorsed or changed on the basis of collective considerations.

In this context, you may face a dilemma between accepting a simple but limited target vis-à-vis an ambitious target with far-reaching consequences. The advantage of choosing a simple but limited target is its achievability that, in turn, provides the taste of success. The disadvantage is that it touches the fringe of the system. On the other hand, experimenting on difficult targets with far-reaching implications has the advantage of effecting systemic change. Because of the complexity, it also runs the risk of failure. In fact, kaizen encourages one to take a small step forward and keep expanding the process to include more and more areas. The strategic approach is to choose some simple targets that have limitless possibilities with far-reaching consequences. Let me quote an example.

In the case of the college of education mentioned earlier, the staff decided that nothing much can be done on infrastructure since it is part of a larger system and decision-making is not within the reach of the college. They decided to work on the apparently innocuous area of professional development. The targets were simple.

- Each one will read four books related to education in a year
- Each one will write two short papers for publication
- Each one will have a mini research project

Now, will the completion of these three targets enthuse the teachers to read more, write more and research more in subsequent years? Will that become a part of the institutional culture? Are classroom processes likely to be influenced by such professional developments? Is such impact on classroom processes likely to change student performance? It is obvious that professional development will trigger off a chain of positive reactions in the institution.

Step 6: Activity listing

In this exercise, the staff should be asked to identify and describe the activities that will lead to achievement of the selected goals. This can be developed in a workshop format where the group can be divided into small groups of five to six. Each group can be assigned one goal for translation into a list of activities. The outcome of each group exercise should be placed before all the members for further discussion and finalization of the document.

While listing the activities, the participants should specify the indicators of success so that activities and achievement of goals can be measured in real terms. These indicators should, as far as possible, be quantitative and measurable. Wherever these are qualitative, the group should spell out how that can be evaluated. For example, if a goal is stated as improving satisfaction on the job, which is apparently measurable, the group should be able to mention that a job satisfaction scale will be used at two different intervals of time to examine and assess shift in their satisfaction on the job.

Step 7: Resource assessment and allocation
Once the activities are finalized and the indicators of success identified, the next activity is the assessment of resources required to implement the activities. Four types of resources are important: financial, human, infrastructural, and temporal. Against each activity, the group should be able to identify the amount of additional finance that would be required, if at all. Similarly, what kind of infrastructure would be required? Who will be responsible for implementing the activity and in what time frame? These should be developed in the form of a PERT chart or table for ready reference (Table 11.2).

Along with assessment of the required resources, it would be important to locate such resources. In the second part of the exercise, namely allocation of resources, the principal and administration has to play a significant role because teachers may, or may not, be familiar with the kind of financial resources that are available in the institution.

Step 8: Evaluation and monitoring
At this stage, the group should carefully design and specify the mechanism of monitoring at every step and also the mechanism of evaluation so that success can be assessed through an acceptable modality. Please note that in Table 11.2, there are two columns, one each on indicators of success and person responsible for monitoring. The plan must indicate when and how the implementation of the innovative activity shall be monitored and evaluated. Also, it should indicate the persons or teams responsible for evaluation as well as the method of evaluation and monitoring. Mid-course corrections are the basic purpose of formative evaluation and monitoring. The plan must indicate the mechanism of mid-course corrections or replanning.

Step 9: Documentation
The whole set of exercises should lead to a document. The document should comprise output of each stage of the exercises. The first section can comprise all that describes the past and the present of the school. The second section will comprise the vision, mission and goals and their prioritization. The third section will comprise listing of activities, indicators of their success, financial requirement and allocation, fixing the authority and responsibility of selected staff for each activity, the time frame and location of implementation, and the mechanism of monitoring and evaluation.

Table 11.2 Master chart (format) for TQM implementation plan

Activity and sub-activities	Indicators of success	Duration and data completion	Person responsible for implementing	Person responsible for monitoring	Financial requirement and source	Infrastructure and physical facilities required and their location
Example: creating a collection of lectures in cassettes in the library X Y Z	20 lectures in a year deposited in the library	One year	Librarian	Ms Usha who volunteered to take this up and coordinate with other teachers	Rs 5,000 from student fund	Four cassette recorders and 50 audio cassettes to be located in the library

The subsequent stage would be actually carrying out the activities as planned. Participative monitoring was effectively used by Hansen and Jackson (1996) in their application of TQM to classroom instruction; one group was implementing the innovation and another peer group was in charge of monitoring and evaluation. In a subsequent activity, the groups can interchange their roles. As a result, the group members pick up the skills of both implementing and monitoring. TQM activities can and better be implemented in the form of projects; projects are time-bound and goal-oriented. They offer opportunities for greater objectivity in assessment.

Implement

Among the various stages of adoption of innovation, implementation is really the stage where innovation is actually adopted. In other words, implementation implies conversion of each of the planned items into action. It is an important and a good practice to meticulously maintain a diary of experiences in as much detail as possible as the plans are implemented. The records of such experiences provide data and information for review and decision-making for mid-course plan correction and modifications. Obviously, the stage of evaluation is also included within this stage, since evaluation is also part of planning.

On the basis of the experience gained through the adoption and evaluation, the process of adoption of innovation can be modified and continued. This continuation itself is the sustaining process when an innovation is internalized and becomes part and parcel of the organizational process and ethos. While a particular innovation is internalized into the system, it results in change in the process of working. As more and more innovations are internalized, institutions develop a new culture of change and self-renewal. This concept of sustainability (Frazier, 1997) is directly linked to the next stage—the onward journey.

Revise baseline and take off

On successful implementation of TQM strategies, the data on the targeted change areas should be collected and compared with baseline data. The difference indicate the shift in quality. Thus, baseline information with which the institution started is no more valid. A new baseline would have been created. With the new baseline, the journey begins again through the same spiralling process: setting new targets, creating new plans for implementation, and revising the baseline and continuation. This will make an organization continuously search for change and move forward.

TQM master

While TQM is all for participative management with a concern for all the perceners of the institution, it needs someone or a group to think continuously on quality issues and mobilize others, set the consultative processes, and so on. Rather than keeping all these new dimensions of management with the principal, one staff member can be identified, chosen, or nominated to act as TQM master for a specified time. He/she would act as quality manager. This management strategy will provide a focus and thrust to quality management in the institution.

Conclusion

It takes time to implement TQM and reach a level where quality becomes culture. It takes between three to five years. Crossing the stage of acceptance (psychological) is important. Projectization and project implementation is the first taste of TQM in the institution. Continuing this trend through continuous evaluation, monitoring, and pre-planning will lead to the level of change as a culture. Your investment in TQM is ready to pay-off once you have entered the stage of culture.

Unlike other approaches, TQM is a human-oriented, human-intensive technique. Infrastructure and technology may be additional aids in managing quality with TQM but TQM as a strategy does not get immobilized due to the absence of such facilities. Indian schools and colleges, the large basic–open category, despite the missing infrastructure and technology, are endowed with potentially rich human resources. By optimizing the human component, Indian educational institutions can go a long way. The challenge before the principal is to generate the culture of 'gung ho' creating the passion and sense of worth about teaching among the teachers, giving them independence and encouragement and, of course, mentoring leadership among colleagues.

Appendix I   Classroom Teaching Competence Scale (CTCS)

Instruction

Study the indicators given in the ground rules related to 0, 1, 2, 3, and 4 for each of the items prior to rating a lecture. Please check against any of the numbers against each item in each column. All items must be rated.

No.	Statement	0	1	2	3	4
1	Aims clear to teacher and students	0	1	2	3	4
2	Content appropriate to stated or unstated aims and level of students	0	1	2	3	4
3	Teaching techniques appropriate to the students	0	1	2	3	4
4	Introduction effective; caught students' attention and established rapport	0	1	2	3	4
5	Content broken into small bits to enable students to learn in steps	0	1	2	3	4
6	Learning of concepts and principles ensured through verbal or concrete examples	0	1	2	3	4
7	Sequencing is logical	0	1	2	3	4
8	Students actively participated in learning	0	1	2	3	4
9	Teacher questions at proper level	0	1	2	3	4
10	Students free to raise doubts and ask questions	0	1	2	3	4
11	Positive reinforcement evident	0	1	2	3	4
12	Communication effective	0	1	2	3	4
13	Chalkboard work effective	0	1	2	3	4
14	Student interest sustained	0	1	2	3	4
15	Assessment of student attainment in relation to aims appropriate	0	1	2	3	4
16	Link-up of main points at the end of the lesson proper	0	1	2	3	4
17	Planning of lesson evident	0	1	2	3	4
18	Confidence in content evident	0	1	2	3	4

Ground rules for classroom observation

I Aims clear to teacher and students

1. Aim not mentioned at all (Just mentioning the title of the topic is not statement of aim)
2. Aims mentioned but not made very clear (say, in behavioural terms)
3. Aims explicitly stated; explained in particular sequence to student

II Content appropriate to stated or unstated aims and level of students

1. Random selection of content; relevance with aims not established
2. Content with its own logic but not completely in correspondence with aims
3. Content with one-to-one correspondence with aims; teacher deliberately related content to aims

III Teaching techniques appropriate to the student

1. Technique adopted totally inappropriate
2. Technique adopted suitable but not properly executed
3. Technique adopted very well suited to the content; execution good and successful

IV Introduction effective; caught students' attention and established rapport

1. Commencement of content teaching abrupt; no introduction, not even a statement such as—we will discuss '_____' today
2. Attempt at an introduction with partial success; majority's attention not caught
3. Introduction made students eager to learn; almost all set to listen

V Content broken into small bits to enable students to learn in steps

1. Teacher simply delivered whatever he/she knew, as a total package
2. Content broken into small steps but no feedback taken
3. Content taught in small steps and feedback taken to ascertain learning

VI Learning of concepts and principles ensured through verbal or concrete examples

1. Understanding of concepts and principles taken for granted; examples/demonstrations not used
2. Examples used on most occasions but not always appropriately or examples used appropriately but on half the occasions
3. Appropriate examples/demonstrations used for concepts/principles; examples provided clarification

VII Sequencing logical

1. Content in bits and pieces, without any logic
2. Logic evident in many cases; equally, missing links as well
3. One bit appeared to be logical next step of previous one; logic evident in presentation

VIII Students actively participated in learning

1. Students had absolutely no work to do except listen, if they felt like doing so
2. At times, students had work: taking notes, answering questions, solving problems; half the time, students felt bored
3. Students kept alert; answer questions, participate in discussions, solve problems, sketch figures, also take notes
4. (2, emphasis on taking notes; 4, emphasis on answering, participation in discussion, solving problems, etc.)

IX Teacher questions at proper level

1. Students not asked questions ('You understand?' or 'You follow?' not treated as questions)
2. Some questions asked; only some were purposeful; only a few students involved in answering all questions
3. Questioning brought the lesson alive; numerous questions asked of majority of the students; teacher did not discourage students giving wrong or partially correct answers but used remedial measures where students could not answer

X Students free to raise doubts and ask questions

1. No question or doubt raised by any student; students discouraged from doing so
2. Some student questions brushed off or ignored while some others properly tackled
3. A number of questions asked by students; handled in a friendly and encouraging manner (either answered by the teacher or through another student)

XI Positive reinforcement evident

1. Lecture a one-way affair; no question of reinforcement (appreciation, praise, even rebuke) used
2. Either correct or incorrect responses reinforced or half the students' participation (response or question) reinforced
3. All responses reinforced, irrespective of correctness

XII Communication effective

1. Expression poor and incomprehensible; many distracting mannerisms
2. Students understand teacher partly; sometimes teacher checks whether students comprehend

3. Clear expression; frequent checking whether students understand or not, repetition if necessary, absence of distracting mannerisms

XIII Chalkboard work effective

1. Chalkboard not used when lesson needed it; if used to a limited extent, work slip-shod, handwriting not legible, no layout of chalkboard
2. Handwriting legible even by backbenchers, but sketch work poor or vice versa; chalkboard layout not satisfactory though legible
3. Handwriting legible by all; sketch work and layout good; chalkboard cleared while leaving class

XIV Student interest sustained

1. Students talk amongst themselves, dozed, created disturbances, yawned, looked outside, appeared to be getting bored for a considerable time; teacher ignored or connived; helpless situation
2. Students showed signs of getting bored but only half the time
3. Students were attentive, listening carefully, asking questions for minor doubts/clarifications, taking notes; teacher kept class alive using appropriate techniques to promote interest when it dipped

XV Assessment of student attainment in relation to aims appropriate

1. No efforts made to assess student attainment; infrequent efforts made have very little to do with stated/unstated aims
2. Assessment through oral questioning of few students at intermediate and final stages; students not sampled for assessment; evaluation of points other than key points
3. Assessment at intermediate stages and/or posing a few questions to students selected almost at random (purposeful means helping assessment of learning only)

XVI Link-up of main points at the end of the lesson proper

1. No summarizing; lecture concluded when time over
2. Some key points taught earlier mentioned at the end; neither link established nor record maintained on chalkboard
3. Main points recorded on the chalkboard or dictated to be noted down; summary collected by asking questions; link between consecutive points also clarified

XVII Planning of lesson evident

1. No time scheduling; no notes of any sort; either a eventless wait for the end of class or haste for completion towards the end; students make teacher go stray easily
2. Planned approach appears at times; sometimes does not

3. Kept time; planned and systematic approach evident; steady pace of progress; any attempt made at disturbance successfully tackled

XVIII Confidence in content evident

1. Teacher gets confused himself; creates confusion amongst students too
2. Confusion evident at times
3. No content errors committed; confidence exuded; points explained in different ways; prepared for any question; evidence of mastery over subject

Appendix II   Mukhopadhyay's Institutional Profile Questionnaire (MIPQ)

This questionnaire provides you with an opportunity to reflect on various aspects of your institution and creating a profile of your institution for you to see and examine. For your institute, statements given below may be

1) Very True OR
2) Largely True OR
3) Partly True OR
4) Not Sure OR
5) False

Please select your response against each statement and accordingly indicate the response. Please

1) respond to all items;
2) respond freely and frankly, lest the profile turn out to be not real; and
3) consider each item independently and respond in the sequence presented to you (instead of going back and forth).

Please do not write your name anywhere; this would facilitate in keeping your free and frank opinion confidential.

No.	Statements	VT	LT	PT	NS	F
1	Principal shows a lot of initiative	VT	LT	PT	NS	F
2	Teachers do prepare before teaching	VT	LT	PT	NS	F
3	It is an isolated institution	VT	LT	PT	NS	F
4	Students organize student activities skilfully	VT	LT	PT	NS	F
5	Co-curricular activities are considered necessary	VT	LT	PT	NS	F
6	Teachers review their teaching from time to time	VT	LT	PT	NS	F
7	Office of the institution is in lousy condition	VT	LT	PT	NS	F
8	There is good social relationship between principal and staff	VT	LT	PT	NS	F
9	There are almost no teaching aids available	VT	LT	PT	NS	F
10	Examinations are merely a routine, not used for improving teaching or learning	VT	LT	PT	NS	F

(Continued)

MIPQ *(Continued)*

No.	Statements	VT	LT	PT	NS	F
11	Most teachers do not enjoy their jobs	VI	LT	PT	NS	F
12	Principal is very dynamic	VT	LT	PT	NS	F
13	Most teachers teach just because they must earn their bread	VT	LT	PT	NS	F
14	Teachers and experts from other places visit this institution	VT	LT	PT	NS	F
15	Students are not much interested in studies	VT	LT	PT	NS	F
16	There is no significant place for co-curricular activities here	VT	LT	PT	NS	F
17	Teaching is mostly dictating notes or reading from texts	VT	LT	PT	NS	F
18	Officers do not indulge in underhand dealings	VT	LT	PT	NS	F
19	Each person/group is interested only in its own benefit	VT	LT	PT	NS	F
20	Material resources are quite good	VT	LT	PT	NS	F
21	Examinations use various test items like objective type, short-answer type, etc.	VT	LT	PT	NS	F
22	Most teachers enjoy their job	VT	LT	PT	NS	F
23	Principal does not enjoy the faculty's confidence	VT	LT	PT	NS	F
24	If they could, most teachers would avoid exam-related works	VT	LT	PT	NS	F
25	Institution does not contact outside agencies	VT	LT	PT	NS	F
26	Students are usually very good	VT	LT	PT	NS	F
27	Co-curricular activities involve all teachers	VT	LT	PT	NS	F
28	Most teachers manage their classes well	VT	LT	PT	NS	F
29	Office takes a lot of time to respond	VT	LT	PT	NS	F
30	Most teachers have intimate friends within the faculty	VT	LT	PT	NS	F
31	Library, laboratory, classes—every place is dirty	VT	LT	PT	NS	F
32	Examination papers are not in keeping with a well-developed assessment scheme	VT	LT	PT	NS	F
33	Staff always grumbles	VT	LT	PT	NS	F
34	Principal shows much concern for staff	VT	LT	PT	NS	F
35	Teachers are adequately trained	VT	LT	PT	NS	F
36	Former students often visit the institution	VT	LT	PT	NS	F
37	Many students stay away from classes	VT	LT	PT	NS	F
38	Only some students take part in co-curricular activities	VT	LT	PT	NS	F
39	Students are not properly assessed as to their learning by many teachers	VT	LT	PT	NS	F
40	Office is very helpful	VT	LT	PT	NS	F
41	Teachers are divided into warring groups	VT	LT	PT	NS	F
42	There is significant effort to build up material resources	VT	LT	PT	NS	F

(Continued)

MIPQ (Continued)

No.	Statements	VT	LT	PT	NS	F
43	Students get opportunities to discuss their results with teachers	VT	LT	PT	NS	F
44	Teachers are very happy	VT	LT	PT	NS	F
45	Principal does not take any interest in solving the problems of the staff	VT	LT	PT	NS	F
46	Most teachers have strong command over their subjects	VT	LT	PT	NS	F
47	Most teachers are not members of local clubs	VT	LT	PT	NS	F
48	Students take studies seriously	VT	LT	PT	NS	F
49	Co-curricular activities are organized throughout the year, to an annual plan	VT	LT	PT	NS	F
50	Teachers really care whether students understand their lessons or not	VT	LT	PT	NS	F
51	There is no common procedure in dealing with employees;—rules change with the person on top	VT	LT	PT	NS	F
52	Teachers work as teams	VT	LT	PT	NS	F
53	Laboratories are not adequately equipped	VT	LT	PT	NS	F
54	Essay-type tests most commonly used	VT	LT	PT	NS	F
55	Most teachers would leave the institution at the first opportunity	VT	LT	PT	NS	F
56	Principal avoids taking important decisions	VT	LT	PT	NS	F
57	Even if provisions were made, most teachers would not like to undergo training	VT	LT	PT	NS	F
58	Parents frequently visit and discuss their wards' performances with the teachers	VT	LT	PT	NS	F
59	Students are very weak in expression	VT	LT	PT	NS	F
60	Cultural activities are organized to patronize only a few pet students	VT	LT	PT	NS	F
61	Curriculum is not completed in class	VT	LT	PT	NS	F
62	Office manages admissions systematically	VT	LT	PT	NS	F
63	There are some warring cliques in the faculty	VT	LT	PT	NS	F
64	There has been considerable addition to material resources over the last few years	VT	LT	PT	NS	F
65	There are no partialities in awarding marks in examinations	VT	LT	PT	NS	F
66	Principal enjoys working in this institution	VT	LT	PT	NS	F
67	Principal has a development plan for every staff member	VT	LT	PT	NS	F
68	Teachers often complain about lack of facilities, increasing workload, etc.	VT	LT	PT	NS	F
69	There is no contact with other institutions	VT	LT	PT	NS	F

(Continued)

MIPQ *(Continued)*

No.	Statements	VT	LT	PT	NS	F
70	Students do not unnecessarily trouble teachers	VT	LT	PT	NS	F
71	Besides sports and games, there are many major student activities	VT	LT	PT	NS	F
72	Most teachers use audio-visual aids while teaching	VT	LT	PT	NS	F
73	Office makes a mess of the admission process	VT	LT	PT	NS	F
74	Administrative staff maintains good relations with teachers	VT	LT	PT	NS	F
75	Maps and charts are usually torn and moth-eaten	VT	LT	PT	NS	F
76	There is no scheme of continuous assessment	VT	LT	PT	NS	F
77	There are many complaints about management and facilities	VT	LT	PT	NS	F
78	Principal does not take any interest in co-curricular activities	VT	LT	PT	NS	F
79	Most teachers are well qualified	VT	LT	PT	NS	F
80	Institution maintains regular links with old students	VT	LT	PT	NS	F
81	Students look for opportunities to harass the principal	VT	LT	PT	NS	F
82	There is lack of balance in choice of co-curricular activities	VT	LT	PT	NS	F
83	Most teachers only give lectures, do not use any other method	VT	LT	PT	NS	F
84	Office records are properly maintained	VT	LT	PT	NS	F
85	Teachers do not visit each other at home	VT	LT	PT	NS	F
86	Library books are continuously updated	VT	LT	PT	NS	F
87	Much care is taken in paper setting and evaluating answer sheets	VT	LT	PT	NS	F
88	Hardly anyone complains	VT	LT	PT	NS	F
89	Principal has done many good things	VT	LT	PT	NS	F
90	Teachers criticize the principal behind his/her back	VT	LT	PT	NS	F
91	Principal is not a member of any local body	VT	LT	PT	NS	F
92	Students do not while away time	VT	LT	PT	NS	F
93	There is an institutional plan for organizing co-curricular activities	VT	LT	PT	NS	F
94	Most teachers develop teaching plans	VT	LT	PT	NS	F
95	Instead of service, office corners all facilities for itself	VT	LT	PT	NS	F
96	Teachers relate very well with students	VT	LT	PT	NS	F
97	Projectors are either not there or are out of order	VT	LT	PT	NS	F
98	It takes considerable time to announce the examination results	VT	LT	PT	NS	F

(Continued)

MIPQ *(Continued)*

No.	Statements	VT	LT	PT	NS	F
99	The principal is very unhappy in the present job	VT	LT	PT	NS	F
100	Principal finds it difficult to manage the staff meetings	VT	LT	PT	NS	F
101	Most teachers take active interest in the activities of the institute	VT	LT	PT	NS	F
102	Institute gets external people to speak to the students and faculty	VT	LT	PT	NS	F
103	Students do not attend classes regularly	VT	LT	PT	NS	F
104	Sports and cultural activities are usually very poorly organized	VT	LT	PT	NS	F
105	Most teachers do not teach well	VT	LT	PT	NS	F
106	Office records are easily traceable	VT	LT	PT	NS	F
107	Staff come and go, they do not socialize with each other	VT	LT	PT	NS	F
108	Library is very good	VT	LT	PT	NS	F
109	Examination results are used to give feedback for improvement in learning	VT	LT	PT	NS	F
110	Students are very proud of their institution	VT	LT	PT	NS	F

Scoring key

Instruction

1. Give a numerical score according to the following schedule.

   Very True (VT)   =   4
   Largely True (LT)   =   3
   Partly True (PT)   =   2
   Not Sure (NS)   =   1
   False   =   0

2. Please use one scoring sheet for each respondent. If there are 25 teachers responding to the MIPQ, there should be 25 such sheets.
3. The test items pertain to 11 sub-areas as indicated in the key below. Please transfer your score for every item in the blank space provided just below the item number. Add the scores of first five items that are positively keyed and enter in the last column. Add scores of the remaining five items that are negatively keyed and enter in the last column with the negative sign. To get your score on any item, like leadership, subtract score (b) from (a). The total score on each sub-area can be positive or negative. For collective score of a school, find the average of the scores from different response sheets on each sub-area. Do not add scores, thus arrived on 11 heads together; these scores on 11 areas are used to draw institutional profiles.

Sub-themes	Positively keyed items (a)					a	Negatively keyed items (b)					b	Total (a–b)
Principal as leader	1	12	34	67	89		23	45	56	78	100		
Scores													
Teacher quality	2	35	46	79	101		13	24	57	68	90		
Scores													
Linkages and interface	14	36	58	80	102		3	25	47	69	91		
Scores													
Students	4	26	48	70	92		15	37	59	81	103		
Scores													
Co-curricular activities	5	27	49	71	93		16	38	60	82	104		
Scores													
Teaching	6	28	50	72	94		17	39	61	83	105		
Scores													
Office management	18	40	62	84	106		7	29	51	73	95		
Scores													
Relationships	8	30	52	74	96		19	41	63	85	107		
Scores													
Material resources	20	42	64	86	108		9	31	53	75	97		
Scores													
Examination	21	43	65	87	109		10	32	54	76	98		
Scores													
Job satisfaction	22	44	66	88	110		11	33	55	77	99		
Scores													

Sample tabulation sheet

Teacher No. / Sub-themes	1	2	3	4	5	6	7	8	9	10	Average
Principal											
Teacher											
Linkage											
Students											
CCA											
Teaching											
Office											
Relation											
Resources											
Exam											
Satisfaction											

Appendix III   School Information Blank

1. Institution's results (performance index) in Board examination

    Class X   **Class XII**

    This year =   This year =
    Last year =   Last year =

    Increment/decrement =   Increment/decrement =
    No. of first classes =   No. of first classes =
    No. of distinctions =   No. of distinctions =

2. Total enrolment of the school: *Boys* _____ *Girls* _____
3. Class-wise enrolment: transition rates

Years → 1999 *Grades* ↓	*1995*	*1996*	*1997*	*1998*	
1.					
2.					
3.					
4.					
5.					
6.					
7.					
8.					
9.					
10.					
11.					
12.					

4. Resources and facilities

Years → Facilities ↓	1995	1996	1997	1998	1999
No. of classrooms					
No. of books in the library					
No. of periodicals subscribed to					
Total number of books issued					
Teaching aids available in the institution					
No. of charts					
Overhead projector					
Video cassette recorder/player					
Stereo system					
Computers					
Other aids					
No. of other rooms available in the school					
Hall					
Activity room					
Stores					
Staff room(s)					
Laboratories					
Art room					
Music room					
Library/reading room					
No. of toilets					
• For boys					
• For girls					
• For staff					
Drinking water taps					
No. of display boards					
No. of trees					
No. of flower pots					
No. of displayed pictures					
First aid facility					
Annual budget					
Development fund					
Staff sanctioned					
Staff in position					
Shortage of staff					

5. Outstanding achievements of the institution

Years → Activities ↓	1995	1996	1997	1998	1999
Public examination					
Sports					
Field events					
Track events					
Throw events					
Others					
Games					
Indoor					
Outdoor					
Cultural activities					
Dramatics					
Concert					
Painting					
Others					
Co-academic					
Debate					
Symposia					
Essay					
Competition					
Others					

Appendix IV   Principal's Questionnaire

Please read each statement carefully and indicate your agreement or disagreement on a five-point response pattern: Strongly Agree (SA), Agree (A), Not Sure (NS), Disagree (D), Strongly Disagree (SD).

No.	Statement	SA	A	NS	D	SD
1	I check with students what they want to achieve through studying here.	SA	A	NS	D	SD
2	I am quite satisfied with the quality of our education.	SA	A	NS	D	SD
3	Parents are involved in planning the future of the institution.	SA	A	NS	D	SD
4	I am a member of local community organizations.	SA	A	NS	D	SD
5	We organize lectures for parents.	SA	A	NS	D	SD
6	There is much scope for quality improvement.	SA	A	NS	D	SD
7	Teachers choose the responsibilities they want.	SA	A	NS	D	SD
8	Teachers are encouraged to experiment with teaching.	SA	A	NS	D	SD
9	Parents are involved in organizing annual days, sports and other programmes.	SA	A	NS	D	SD
10	Teachers participate in local community-based functions.	SA	A	NS	D	SD
11	I check with students about their expectations from co-curricular activities.	SA	A	NS	D	SD
12	Teachers discuss new developments in education and emerging career opportunities with parents, at length.	SA	A	NS	D	SD
13	Teachers collectively prepare their annual curricular plans.	SA	A	NS	D	SD
14	We encourage innovation in teaching.	SA	A	NS	D	SD
15	The Parent–Teacher Association reviews the quality of the school's academic programme.	SA	A	NS	D	SD
16	I participate in state-level meetings and programmes.	SA	A	NS	D	SD

(Continued)

Principal's questionnaire (*Continued*)

No.	Statement	SA	A	NS	D	SD
17	I check with parents about their expectations from the institution.	SA	A	NS	D	SD
18	We discuss with teachers and staff the expectations of parents and students.	SA	A	NS	D	SD
19	We have a clear plan of quality improvement.	SA	A	NS	D	SD
20	Teachers are allocated responsibilities on the basis of their choice and voluntary offers.	SA	A	NS	D	SD
21	Teachers undertake action research.	SA	A	NS	D	SD
22	We invite professionals from different walks of life to the institute.	SA	A	NS	D	SD
23	I ask parents about their expectations from their wards.	SA	A	NS	D	SD
24	Teachers are exposed to new developments in educational methodologies.	SA	A	NS	D	SD
25	Our priority is not only to pass the students, but to develop well-rounded personalities.	SA	A	NS	D	SD
26	Teachers are involved in school management.	SA	A	NS	D	SD
27	Teachers are free to innovate.	SA	A	NS	D	SD
28	Parents are involved in mobilizing resources for the school.	SA	A	NS	D	SD
29	We allow our facilities to be used by community organizations.	SA	A	NS	D	SD
30	I ask my staff about their expectations from the institute.	SA	A	NS	D	SD
31	Students are oriented on their rights and duties vis-à-vis the institute.	SA	A	NS	D	SD
32	We are making specific efforts to improve quality.	SA	A	NS	D	SD
33	Teachers and staff are involved in deciding the future development of the institute.	SA	A	NS	D	SD
34	The institute supports innovative activities.	SA	A	NS	D	SD
35	Parents are invited to address teachers and students.	SA	A	NS	D	SD

Scoring procedure for principal's questionnaire

The questionnaire has been developed around seven sub-areas: customer orientation, client education, satisfaction with quality, participation, innovation and independence, parental involvement, and linkage with outside agencies and community. Against each sub-area, the item's number has been indicated in the table below. Allocate a score of

    4   for SA,
    3   for A,
    2   for NS,
    1   for D, and
    0   for SD.

Calculate the score for each area separately.

Sub-areas	Items and scores									Total
Customer orientation	1		11		17		23		30	
Client education	5		12		18		24		31	
Satisfaction with quality	2		6		19		25		32	
Participation	7		13		20		26		33	
Innovation	8		14		21		27		34	
Parental involvement	3		9		15		28		35	
Linkage	4		10		16		22		29	

Appendix V   Students' Questionnaire

There are 10 statements about the school below. You may or may not agree with them. Please indicate your degree of agreement against each statement by checking against one of the five columns: Strongly Agree (SA), Agree (A), Not Sure (NS), Disagree (D), or Strongly Disagree (SD). Please respond to each item honestly and forthrightly. You do not need to write your name; your opinion will thus remain confidential.

No.	Statements	SA	A	NS	D	SD
1	My institution is preparing me for the future.					
2	I am proud of my institution.					
3	The teachers care a lot for us.					
4	The principal takes much interest in the institution.					
5	The teachers teach very well.					
6	The teachers are not partial in awarding marks to students.					
7	Our institution has good facilities.					
8	All students are encouraged to participate in co-curricular activities.					
9	The institution maintains strict discipline.					
10	The institution appreciates and recognizes good behaviour.					

Instructions for scoring

Score each item with a numerical score, as given below:

    4   for SA,
    3   for A,
    2   for NS,
    1   for D, and
    0   for SD.

Find the average of scores in each item for all student respondents. Record the average score against each item.

Appendix VI   Parents' Questionnaire

There are 10 statements about the institution below. You may or may not agree with them. Please indicate your degree of agreement against each statement by checking against one of the five columns: Strongly Agree (SA), Agree (A), Not Sure (NS), Disagree (D), or Strongly Disagree (SD). Please respond to each item honestly and forthrightly. You do not need to write your name; your opinion will thus remain confidential.

No.	Statements	SA	A	NS	D	SD
1	Parents are consulted on institution development.	SA	A	NS	D	SD
2	Teachers receive and treat parents well.	SA	A	NS	D	SD
3	The principal receives parents with respect and eagerness.	SA	A	NS	D	SD
4	Overall, parents are satisfied with the institution.	SA	A	NS	D	SD
5	The institution has good facilities.	SA	A	NS	D	SD
6	Co-curricular activities are treated as important in the institution.	SA	A	NS	D	SD
7	Parents are satisfied with discipline and management of cases of indiscipline.	SA	A	NS	D	SD
8	The institution is conscious of quality in education.	SA	A	NS	D	SD
9	The institution enjoys a good reputation among parents.	SA	A	NS	D	SD
10	The institution prepares children for future challenges.	SA	A	NS	D	SD

Instruction for scoring

Score each item with a numerical score as given below:

    4   for SA,
    3   for A,
    2   for NS,
    2   for D, and
    1   for SD.

Find the average of scores in each item for all parent respondents. Record the average score against each item.

Bibliography

Abu-Duhou, I., *School-based Management*, Paris: International Institute for Educational Planning, 1999.

Aggarwal, Y.P., *School Education*, New Delhi: Arya Book Depot, 1991.

Argyris, C., *Knowledge for Action: A Guide to Overcoming Barriers to Organizational Change*, San Francisco: Jossey-Bass, 1993.

Baddaracco, J.L. and R.R. Ellsworth, *Leadership and Quest for Integrity*, Boston: Harvard Business School Press, 1989.

Blanchard, K., *Whale Done!*, London: Nicholas Brealey, 2002.

Blanchard, K. and S. Bowles, *Gung Ho!*, New York: William Morrow & Co., 1998.

Bonser, C.F., 'Total Quality Education', *Public Administration Review*, 52 (5), 1992.

Botkin, J.W., M. Elmandjra and M. Malitza, *No Limits to Learning: Bridging the Human Gap, A Report of Club of Rome*, New York: Pergamon, 1979.

Boyer, L.E., '5 Priorities for Quality Schools', *Education Digest*, 62 (1), 1996.

British Standards Institution (BSI), *Quality Vocabulary Part 2: Quality Concepts and Related Definition*, London: BSI, 1991.

Burns, J., *Leadership*, New York: Harper and Row, 1978.

Cameron, K.S. and D.S. Whetten, *Organizational Effectiveness: A Comparison of Multiple Models*, New York: Academic Press, 1983.

Case, J., 'A Company of Business People', *INC. Magazine*, 15 (4), 1993.

Chaffe, E.E. and W.G. Tierney, *Collegiate Culture and Leadership Strategies*, New York: Macmillan, 1988.

Chakraborty, S.K., *Values and Ethics for Organizations: Theory and Practice*, New Delhi: Oxford University Press, 2002.

Cheng, Y.C. and W.M. Cheung, 'Multi-models of Education Quality and Multi-level of Self-management in Schools', *Educational Management and Administration*, 25 (4), 1997.

Cheng, Y.C. and W.M. Tam, 'Multi-models of Quality in Education', *Quality Assurance in Education*, 5 (1), 1997.

Chowdhary, N.R., 'Higher Education Delivery Systems—Trying the TQM Option', *University News*, 36 (38), September 1996.

Chowdhry, K., 'Institution Building: Two Approaches in Contrast', in R. Mathai, U. Pareek and T.V. Rao (eds), *Institution Building in Education and Research: From Stagnation to Self-renewal*, New Delhi: All India Management Association, 1977.

Clark, D., *Big Dog's Leadership Page*, http://www.nwlink.com/~donclark/leader/leader.html

Cole, B., 'Applying Total Quality Management Principles to Faculty Selection', *Higher Education*, 29 (1), 1995.

Coleman, J.S., E.Q. Campbell, C.J. Hobson, J. McParfland, A.M. Mood, F.D. Weinfeld and R.L. York, *Equality of Educational Opportunity*, Washington, D.C.: U.S. Department of Health, Education and Welfare, 1966.

Collins, J., *Good to Great*, New York: Harper, 2001.

Conley, S.C. and S.B. Bacharach, 'From School-site Management to Participatory School-site Management', *Phi Delta Kappan*, 71 (7), March 1990.

Cook, B.G. and M.I. Semmel, 'Are Recent Reforms Effective for All? The Implications of Tolerance Theory for School Reform', *Annual Meeting of the American Educational Research Association*, San Francisco: CA.

Costa, A.L and R.M. Liebmann (eds), *Envisioning Process as Content: Toward a Renaissance Curriculum*, California: Corwin, 1997.

Crawford, K., *Total Quality Management: Implementation, Assessment and Evaluation*, Washington D.C., 1990.

Crawford, L.E.D. and P. Shutler, 'Total Quality Management in Education: Problems and Issues for Classroom Teachers', *The International Journal of Educational Management*, 13 (2), 1999.

Crosby, P.B., *Quality is Free: Art of Making Quality Certain*, New York: McGraw Hill, 1979.

———, *Quality without Tears*, Singapore: McGraw Hill, 1984.

Dale, B. and C. Cooper, *Human Resources of Total Quality: An Executive Handbook*, New Delhi: Blackwell Asia Imprint, 1997.

Dale, B.G. and J.J. Plunkett, *Managing Quality*, Hertfordshire: Philip Allan, 1990.

Das, S.K., *The Education System of the Ancient Hindus*, Delhi: Gyan Publication House, 1986.

Dave, R.H., 'Towards Effective Teacher Education', in D.N. Khosla (ed.), *Competency-based and Commitment-oriented Teacher Education for Quality School Education Initiation Document* (Pre-service Education and In-service Education), New Delhi: National Council for Teacher Education, 1998.

Davies, B. and L. Ellison, 'Improving the Quality of Schools—Ask the Clients?', *School Organization*, 15 (1), 1995.

De Cosmo, R.D., J.S. Parker and M.A. Heverly, 'Total Quality Management goes to Community College', in L.A. Sherr and D.K. Tester (eds), 'Total Quality Management in Higher Education', *New Directions for Institutional Research*, 71, Autumn 1991.

DeBono, E., *Tactics: Art and Science of Success*, New Delhi: Harper Collins, 1985.

Deming, W.E., *Out of the Crisis*, Cambridge: Cambridge University Press, 1986.

Devi, U., 'A Study of Communication Process in Relation to Decision Making in the Offices of the Department of Education', unpublished doctoral dissertation, Mysore University, 1996.

Directorate of Education (DoE), *Self-assessment Tool for Improvement of Schools*, DoE, Government of Delhi, 1990.

Diwan, R., 'Transformational Leadership for Urban-based Schools: Reflections on Experiences in India', paper presented at the Cambridge Conference on Education, Cambridge, 2000.

———, *Women Leaders in Education*, New Delhi: National Institute of Educational Planning and Administration, 2004 (mimeo).

Drucker, P.F., *Management: Tasks, Practice, Responsibilities*, New York: Harper & Row, 1974.

Edwell, P., 'Total Quality and Academic Practice', *Change*, May–June 1993.

Evans, M., 'Using Story as a Method of Facilitating Staff Development in a Secondary School Department', in P. Lomax (ed.), *Quality Management in Education: Sustaining the Vision through Action Research*, London: Routledge, 1996.

Ezman M.J. and H.C. Blaise, *Institution Building Research: The Guiding Concepts*, University of Pittsburgh, 1966.

Feigenbaum, A.V., *Total Quality Control*, New York: McGraw Hill, 1983.

Fetler, M., 'Assessing Educational Performance: California's School Quality Indicator System', ERIC Microfische No.ED312300, 1989.

Fidler, B., *Strategic Planning for School Improvement*, London: Pitman, 1996.

Fields, J.C., *Total Quality for Schools: A Guide for Implementation*, Milwaukee: ASQC Quality Press, 1994.

Franke-Wikberg, S., 'Evaluating Education Quality on the Institutional Level', *Higher Education Management*, 2 (3), 1990.

Frase, L.E. and L. Sorensen, 'Teacher Motivation and Satisfaction: Impact on Participatory Management', *NASSP Bulletin*, 76 (540), January 1992.

Frazier, A., *Roadmap for Quality Transformation in Education*, Florida: St. Lucie Press, 1997.

Freeston, K.R., 'Getting Started with TQM', *Educational Leadership*, November 1992.

Gardner, H., *Frames of Mind: The Theory of Multiple Intelligence*, New York: Basic Books, 1983.

Gilmore, H.L., 'Product Conformance Cost', *Quality Progress*, 7 (5), 1974.

Glasman, N.S., *Making Better Decisions about School Problems*, California: Corwin, 1994.

Goleman, D., *Working with Emotional Intelligence*, New York: Bantam Books, 1998.

Goleman, D., R.E. Boyatzis and A. McKee, *The New Leaders: Transforming the Art of Leadership into the Science of Results*, London: Little Brown, 2002.

Hansen, W.L. and M. Jackson, 'Total Quality Improvement in the Classroom', *Quality in Higher Education*, 2 (3), 1996.

Harvey, L. and D. Green, 'Defining Quality', *Assessment and Evaluation in Higher Education: An International Journal*, 18 (1), 1993.

Haskin, K.A., 'Process of Learning: The Principal's Role in Participatory Management', paper presented at the Annual Meeting of the American Educational Research Association, San Francisco, 1995.

Havelock, R.G., *Planning for Innovation through Dissemination and Utilization of Knowledge*, Ann Arbor, Michigan: University of Michigan, 1973.

Henderikx, P., 'Management and Promotion of Quality in Distance Education', *Open Learning*, 7 (3), 1992.

Hersey, P. and K.H. Blanchard, *Management of Organizational Behaviour*, New Delhi: Prentice-Hall of India, 1992.

Hill, F.M. and W.A. Taylor, 'Total Quality Management in Higher Education', *International Journal of Educational Management*, 5 (5), 1991.

Holt, M., 'The Concept of Quality in Education', in C. Hoy, C. Bayne-Jardine, and M. Wood, *Improving Quality in Education*, London: Falmer Press, 2000.

Hooda, R.C., 'Effect of Mastery Learning Strategies (MLS) on Pupil Achievement', Department of Education, Devi Ahalya Viswa Vidyalaya, 1982 (mimeo).

Hormi, J.E. and C.E. Lingren, 'Educational Improvement Using Deming's Profound Knowledge', *New Era in Education*, 76 (1), 1995.

Hoy, C., C. Bayne-Jardine and M. Wood, *Improving Quality in Education*, London: Falmer Press, 2000.

International Encyclopedia of the Social Sciences, Vol. 13, New York: Free Press, 1979.

International Institute for Educational Planning (IIEP), 'Cost Analysis, Budget and Financing of Education: Practical Exercise', (training material for Annual Training Programme in Educational Planning and Administration), Paris: IIEP, 1990.

Ishikawa, K., *Guide to Quality Control*, Tokyo: Asian Productivity Organization, 1983.

———, *What is Total Quality Control*, New Jersey: Prentice-Hall, 1985.

James, M. and D. Jongeward, *Born to Win*, New York: Signet, 1978.

Swami Jitatmananda, *Holistic Science and Vedanta*, Bombay: Bharatiya Vidya Bhavan, 1991.

Johannsen, H. and G.T. Page, *International Dictionary of Management*, London: Kogan Page, 1986.

Johannsen, H. and A. Robertson, *Management Glossary*, London: Longman, 1968.

Juran, J., *Planning for Quality*, New York: Free Press, 1988.

———, *Leadership for Quality: An Executive Handbook*, New York: Free Press, 1989.

Juran, J.M. and F.M. Gryna, Jr. (eds), *Juran's Quality Control Handbook* (Fourth edition), New York: McGraw Hill, 1988.

Kaiser, A., 'Organisations', in A. Kuper and J. Kuper, *The Social Science Encyclopaedia*, London: Routledge, 1985.

Kalam, A.P.J. Abdul, *Ignited Minds: Unleashing the Power Within India*, New Delhi: Penguin Books, 2002.

Kaufman, R., *Mapping Educational Success*, California: Corwin, 1992.

Kaufman, R. and D. Zahn, *Quality Management Plus: The Continuous Improvement of Education*, California: Corwin, 1993.

Kepner, C.H., *The Rational Manager: A Systematic Approach to Problem Solving and Decision Making*, Bombay: Tata McGraw-Hill, 1965.

Kevin, B., 'Articulating International Curriculum. Part II: Continuity through Outcomes', *International Schools Journal*, 17 (1), 1997.

Knouse, S.B. (ed.), *Human Resources Management Perspectives on TQM: Concepts and Practices*, Wisconsin: ACQC Quality Press, 1996.

Kwan, Y.K.P., 'Application of Total Quality Management in Education: Retrospect and Prospect', *International Journal of Educational Management*, 10 (5), 1996.

Lal, H., *Total Quality Management: A Practical Approach*, New Delhi: New Age International Publishers, 1990.

Lalithamma, M.S., 'An Enquiry into Classroom Instruction', unpublished doctoral dissertation, Baroda: M.S. University, 1977.

Langford, D.P. and B.A. Cleary, *Orchestrating Learning with Quality*, New Delhi: Tata McGraw-Hill, 1996.

Latchem, C. and D. Hanna, *Leadership for 21st Century Learning: Global Perspectives from Educational Innovators*, London: Kogan Page, 2001.

Lessem, R., *Total Quality Learning: Building a Learning Organization*, Cambridge: Basil Blackwell, 1991.

Lewin, K., *Field Theory in Social Science*, New York: Harper and Row, 1951.

Lewis, R.G. and D.H. Smith, *Total Quality in Higher Education*, Florida: St. Lucie Press, 1994.

Lindsay, W.M and J.A. Petrick, *Total Quality and Organization Development*, Florida: St. Lucie Press, 1997.

Luft, J., *Group Processes: An Introduction to Group Dynamics*, Palo Alto: National Press Book, 1970.

Lynton, R.P. and J.M. Thomas, 'The Utility of Institution Building: Scrutiny for Strategies and Methodologies of Consultation', in D.P. Sinha (ed.), *Consultants and Consulting Stifles*, New Delhi: Vision Books, 1979.

Maassen, P.A.M., 'Quality Control in Dutch Higher Education: Internal versus External Evaluation', *European Journal of Education*, 22 (2), 1987.

Maheswari, A.N. and V.K. Raina, *Training of Primary Teachers through Teleconferencing: An Evaluative Study*, New Delhi: National Council for Educational Research and Training, 1997.

McLenighan H., 'Participatory Management of Co-curricular Activities', ERIC A. ED345340, 1990.

Mergerison, C.J. and D.J. McCann, *How to Lead a Winning Team*, Bradford: MCB Press, 1985.

Miller, J., A. Dower and S. Inniss, *Improving Quality in Further Education: A Guide for Teachers in Course Teams*, Ware: Herts Consultants at Work, 1992.

Mitra, C.R. and P. Mandke, *Knowledge Enterprise: Redefining Higher Education*, New Delhi: Sanskriti, 2003.

Moore, A.J., *Improving Schools: Quality Indicators Used When Selecting K-12 Teachers*, Kansas: Emporia State University, 1996.

Morehouse, D., *Essentials of TQM*, Aldershot: Gower, 1996.

Motwani, J. and A. Kumar, 'The Need for Implementing Total Quality Management in Education', *International Journal of Educational Management*, 11 (2-3), 1997.

Mukhopadhyay, M., *Barriers to Change in Secondary Education: Some Case Studies*, Udang: Education Books, 1981.

———, 'Distance Education: A SWOT Analysis', in M. Mukhopadhyay (ed.), *Educational Technology: Yearbook 1988*, New Delhi: All India Association for Educational Technology, 1989.

———, *Management of Change in Education: In Search of Indian Model*, New Delhi: National Institute of Educational Planning and Administration, 1989 (mimeo).

———, *Primary School Dropout Can Be Arrested: Udang Experiment*, Udang: IERSD, 1998.

———, 'Taxonomy of Educatedness', *University News*, 37 (26), June 1999.

———, 'Understanding Self', in M. Mukhopadhyay, *Management of Institutions*, New Delhi: National Institute of Educational Planning and Administration, 2000 (mimeo).

———, 'Management of Quality in Higher Education', *University News*, 38 (27), July 2000.

———, *Total Quality Management in Education*, New Delhi: National Institute of Educational Planning and Administration, 2001.

———, 'Educatedness for the Global Society', in M. Mukhopadhyay (ed.), *Education for a Global Society: Interfaith Dimensions*, New Delhi: Shipra, 2003.

———, *Leadership for Institution Building in Education*, Baroda: School of Environment, Resources and Development, 2004.

——— (ed.), *Value Development in Higher Education*, New Delhi: Viva Books, 2004.

Mukhopadhyay, M. *et al.*, 'Alternative Models of Teacher Training', Bhopal: Technical Teachers Training Institute, 1981, (study sponsored by the United Nations Development Programme).

Mukhopadhyay, M. and M. Narula, *Heading Schools: With What Competencies?*, New Delhi: National Institute of Educational Planning and Administration, 1992 (mimeo).

Mukhopadhyay, M. and M. Parhar, 'Instructional Design for Multi-channel Learning System', *British Journal of Educational Technology*, 32 (4), November 2001.

Mukhopadhyay, M. and N. Sinha, 'Utilization of Media in Education' (a commissioned study by Ministry of Human Resource Development), New Delhi: National Institute of Educational Planning and Administration, 1993.

Mukhopadhyaya, A.K., 'States of Consciousness: A Holistic Hypothesis', paper presented at NCERT seminar, New Delhi, February 1987.

Murgatroyd, S., 'A New Frame for Managing Schools: Total Quality Management (TQM)', *School Organization*, 12 (2), 1992.

Murgatroyd, S. and C. Morgan, *Total Quality Management and the School*, Buckingham: Open University, 1993.

National Open School (NOS), *Open Schooling: Perspectives*, New Delhi: NOS, 1995 (mimeo).

Navaratnam, K.K., 'Quality Management in Education Must Be a Never-ending Journey', in K. Watson, C. Modgil and S. Modgil (eds), *Educational Dilemmas: Debate and Diversity, Vol. VI: Quality in Education*, London: Cassell, 1997.

Navaratnam, K.K. and R. O'Connor, 'Quality Assurance in Vocational Education: Meeting the Needs of Nineties', *Vocational Aspect of Education*, 45 (2), 1993.

Neil, M.W., 'A Systems Approach to Course Planning at Open University', in A.J. Romiszowasky (ed.), *A Systems Approach to Education and Training*, London: Kogan Page, 1979.

Nisbette, R., *Geography of Thought*, London: Nicholas Brealey, 2003.

O'Brien, J.A., *Management Information Systems: Managing Information Technology in the Internetworked Enterprise*, Boston: Irwin/McGraw-Hill, 1999.

Oakland, J.S., 'Quality Assurance', in D. Lock and N. Farrow (eds), *The Gower Handbook of Management* (Second edition), Hauts: Gower Publishing, 1988.

———, *Total Quality Management*, Oxford: Heinemann, 1993.

Oakland, J.S. and L. Porter, *Cases in Total Quality Management*, Oxford: Butterworth Heinemann, 1994.

Page, G.T. and J.B. Thomas, *International Dictionary of Education*, London: Kogan Page, 1977.

Panjwani, S.S., 'A Profile of Polytechnic Teachers in India', Calcutta: Technical Teachers Training Institute, 1982 (mimeo).

Paramhansa Yogananda, *The Bhagavad Gita: God Talks with Arjuna*, California: Self-Realization Fellowship, 1995.

Parasuraman, A., V.A. Zeithaml and L.L. Berry, 'A Conceptual Model of Service Quality and its Implications for Future Research', *Journal of Marketing* 4 (4), 1985.

Pareek, U., *Beyond Management*, New Delhi: Oxford and IBH Publishing, 1981.

Pareek, U. and T.V. Rao (eds), *Handbook of Social and Psychological Instruments*, Ahmedabad: Sahitya Mudranalaya, 1974.

Parsons, T., *Social Systems*, New York: Free Press, 1964.

Paton, R.A. and J. McCalman, *Change Management: A Guide to Effective Implementation* (Second edition), London: Sage, 2000.

Pearn, M., C. Mulrooney and T. Payne, *Ending the Blame Culture*, Hampshire: Gower, 1998.

Pestonjee, D.M., *Third Handbook of Psychological and Social Instruments*, New Delhi: Concept Publishing, 1997.

Peters, T., *Thriving on Chaos*, London: Pan Books, 1987.

Peters, T. and N. Austin, *A Passion for Excellence*, Glasgow: Fontana, 1985.

Peters, T.J. and R.H. Waterman, Jr., *In Search of Excellence*, New York: Harper and Row, 1982.

Petrick, J.A and D.S. Furr, *Total Quality in Managing Human Resources*, New Delhi: Vanity Book International, 1996.

Porter, E.L., 'A Survey on Participative Management among Texas Community College Reference Librarians', ERIC A. ED325148, 1990.

Powar, K.B. and S.K. Panda, 'Accreditation as a Means of Quality Assurance in Higher Education', in K.B. Powar and S.K. Panda (eds), *Higher Education in India—In Search of Quality*, New Delhi: Association of Indian Universities, 1995.

PROBE—*Public Report on Basic Education in India*, New Delhi: Oxford University Press, 1999.

Radhakrishnan, S., *The Principal Upanisads*, New Delhi: Harper Collins, 1998.

Reid, W.A., 'Conception of Curriculum and Paradigms for Research: The Case of School Effectiveness Studies', *Journal of Curriculum and Supervision*, Spring 1997.

Robbins, H. and M. Finley, *Why Change Does Not Work*, London: Orion Publishing, 1997.

Rogers, E.M., *Diffusion of Innovation*, New York: Free Press, 1962.

Rogers, E.M. and F.F. Shoemaker, *Communication of Innovations: A Cross-cultural Approach*, New York: Free Press, 1971.

Romiszowaski, A.J., 'Systems Approach to Design and Development', in H. Torsten and T.M. Postlethwaite (eds), *The International Encyclopedia of Education*, Oxford: Pergamon, 1994.

Ross, J.E., *Total Quality Management: Text, Cases and Readings*, London: Kogan Page, 1993.

Ross, K.N. and L. Mahlck, *Planning the Quality of Education: The Collection and Use of Data for Improved Decision Making*, Paris: UNESCO, 1999.

Rossmiller, R.A. and E.L. Holcomb, 'The Effective Schools Process for Continuous School Improvement', paper presented at the Annual Meeting of American Educational Research Association, Atlanta, 1993.

Ruttler, M., *Fifteen Thousand Hours: Secondary School and their Effects on Children*, London: Open Books, 1979.

Sagor, R. and B.G. Barnett, *TQE Principal: A Transformed Leader*, California: Corwin Press, 1994.

Sallis, E., *Total Quality Management in Education*, London: Kogan Page, 1996.

Sansodhan, *A Matter of Quality: A Study of People's Perceptions and Expectations from Schooling in Rural and Urban Areas of Uttaranchal*, Mussoorie: Society for Integrated Development of Himalayas, 1999.

Saylor, J.H., *Total Quality Management Field Manual*, New York: McGraw-Hill, 1992.

Sceinder, L., 'Institution', in J. Gould and W.L. Kolb (eds), *A Dictionary of the Social Sciences*, London: Tavistock, 1964.

Schein, E.H., *Organizational Culture and Leadership*, San Francisco: Jossey-Bass, 1992.

Secretan, L., *Inspirational Leadership: Destiny, Calling and Cause*, Toronto: Macmillan Canada, 1999.

Seligman, P.M., *Learned Optimism: How to Change Your Mind and Your Life*, New York: Pocket Books, 1990.

Selznick, P., *Leadership in Administration*, Evanston: Row Paterson, 1957.

Semler, R., *Maverick*, London: Random House, 1993.

Senge, P.M., *The Fifth Discipline: The Art and Practice of the Learning Organizations*, New York: Doubleday, 1990.

Seymour, D., *On Q: Causing Quality in Higher Education*, New York: Macmillan, 1992.

—— (ed.), *Total Quality Management on Campus: Is it Worth Doing?* San Francisco: Jossey-Bass, 1994.

Sharma, M. (ed.), *Systems Approach to Education*, New Delhi: Himalaya Publishers, 1985.

Sheane, K.E., 'Participatory Management Emphasizing Quality: A Viable Alternative to American Corporations and Schools?' ERIC A. ED359665, 1993.

Shejwalkar, P.C., 'Total Quality Management in Higher Education', *University News*, 37 (38), 20 September 1999.

Sherr, L.A. and G.G. Lozier, 'Total Quality Management in Higher Education', in P.T. Terenzini and E.E. Chaffee (eds), *Total Quality Management in Higher Education*, San Francisco: Jossey-Bass, 1991.

Sherr, L.A. and D.J. Teeter, 'Total Quality Management in Higher Education', *New Directions for Institutional Research*, 71, 1991.

Shewhart, W.A., *Economic Control of Quality of Manufactured Product*, New York: Van Nostrand, 1931.

Sims, S.J. and R.R. Sims (eds), *Total Quality Management in Higher Education: Is it Working? Why or Why Not?*, Westport: Praeger, 1995.

Spanbauer, S.J., *A Quality System for Education*, Wisconsin: ASDQ Quality Press, 1992.

State Council for Educational Research and Training (SCERT), *A Study of Input–Output Relationship in the Context of Senior Secondary Schools in Delhi*, New Delhi: SCERT, 1993.

Teddlie, C. and D. Reynolds, *The International Handbook of School Effectiveness Research,* London: Falmer Press, 2000.

Teeter, D.J and G.G. Lozier (eds), *Pursuit of Quality in Higher Education: Case Studies in Total Quality Management.* San Francisco: Jossey-Bass, 1993.

Tovey, P., *Quality Assurance in Continuing Professional Education: An Analysis*, London: Routledge, 1994.

Tuckman, B.W. and M.A.C. Jensen, 'Stages of Small Group Development Revisited', *Groups and Organizational Studies*, 2, 1977.

Tuttle, T.C., 'Is Total Quality Worth the Effort? How Do We know?' *New Directions for Higher Education,* 86, 1994.

United Nations Educational, Scientific and Cultural Organization (UNESCO), *A Training Module on Institution Building and Institution of Management*, Bangkok: UNESCO, 1982.

———, *Learning: The Treasure Within*, Report to UNESCO of the International Commission on Education in 21st Century, Paris: UNESCO, 1996.

US General Accounting Office, *Companies Improve Performance Through Quality Efforts*, Washington D.C.: U.S. General Accounting Office, 1991.

Vanvught, F. and D. Westerheijden, *Quality Management and Quality Assurance in European Higher Education*, Enschede: Center for Higher Education Policy Studies, 1993.

Swami Vivekananda, *Raja Yoga: Royal Science of God Realization*, Calcutta: Advaita Ashram, 1999.

Wainer, H., 'Graphical Data Analysis', *Annual Review Psychology*, 32, 1981.

Wallis, R., 'Institutions', in A. Kuper and J. Kuper, *The Social Science Encyclopedia*, London: Routledge, 1985.

Weller, L.D., 'Return on Quality: A New Factor in Assessing Quality Efforts', *International Journal of Educational Management*, 10 (1), 1996.

———, 'Unlocking the Culture for Quality Schools: Reengineering', *International Journal of Educational Management,* 12 (6), 1998.

Westerman, S., 'How Total Quality Management Initiative Can Inspire Leadership', *New Directions for Higher Education,* 87, 1994.

Williams, P., 'Total Quality Management: Some Thoughts', *Higher Education,* 25 (3), 1993.

Winch, C., 'Quality and Education', *Journal of Philosophy of Education*, March 1996.

Woodall, J., D.K. Rebuck and F. Voehl, *Total Quality in Information System and Technology.* Florida: St. Lucie Press, 1997.

Woodcock, M., *Team Development Manual*, London: Gower Press, 1979.

Yadav, P.S., 'Effect of Mastery Learning Strategy on Pupils' Achievement in Mathematics, Their Self-concept and Attitudes Towards Mathematics', unpublished doctoral dissertation, Kurukshetra University, 1984.

Yudof, M.G. and I.J. Busch-Vishniac, 'Total Quality: Myth or Management in Universities?' *Change,* 28 (6), 1996.

Index

About the Author

M armar Mukhopadhyay is currently Director of the National Institute of Educational Planning and Administration, New Delhi. A specialist in management and instructional sciences, he has lectured on quality management in higher education at various international and national fora. Professor Mukhopadhyay has served as a consultant for a number of international and national organizations including UNESCO, the World Bank, and DFID. He has been Chairman of the National Open School, India (1993–96) and Vice-President (Asia) of the International Council of Distance Education, Norway (1995–99).

Among his numerous previous publications are *Leadership for Institution Building in Education, Value Development in Higher Education, Educational Technology: Knowledge Assessment, Indian Education: Development since Independence,* and *Governance of School Education in India.*